Parson Henry Renfro

Parson Henry Renfro

Free Thinking on the Texas Frontier

By

William Clark Griggs

UNIVERSITY OF TEXAS PRESS
AUSTIN

First edition, 1994

Requests for permission to reproduce material from this work should be sent to
Permissions, University of Texas Press, Box 7819, Austin, TX 78713-7819

ⓒ The paper used in this publication meets the minimum requirements of American
National Standard for Information Sciences—Permanence of Paper for Printed Library
Materials, ANSI Z39.48-1984.

Library of Congress Cataloging-in-Publication Data

Griggs, William Clark, 1932–
    Parson Henry Renfro : Free Thinking on the Texas Frontier /
by William Clark Griggs. — 1st ed.
        p.   cm.
    Includes bibliographical references and index.
    ISBN 0-292-72762-3
    1. Renfro, Henry.   2. Freethinkers—Texas—Biography.
3. Baptists—Texas—Clergy—Biograph.   4. Chaplains, Military—
Baptists—Biography.   5. Chaplains, Military—Confederate States of
America—Biography.   6. Pioneers—Texas—Biography.   I. Title.
BL2790.R46G75   1994
976.4'061'092—dc20
[B]   93-7349

Frontispiece: Henry Carty Renfro, about 1860. Renfro-Clark Papers.

For
Margaret Annette Renfro Clark
"Mu"
Who Kept Alive the Memory
of
The Parson

Contents

Preface

Countless persons throughout history have made a mark, for better or for worse, on our world. In most cases, the lives of the more prominent of these men and women have been documented with details of their achievements or failures historically recorded for the examination of those who follow them. Yet, there remain many persons of local, regional, or national importance whose accomplishments are obscure or even forgotten by the generations that follow them. The attainments of those men and women, although unknown, remain valid. Every bridge has its engineer, every building its architect, every book its author, and every drama its players. A resplendent tree in the wilderness, unseen and unknown for a century, retains its size and grandeur, as well as its knots and its distorted limbs, until the explorer discovers it once more. Similarly, historians may find the virtually unknown written records of the past. Previously unknown letters, documents, photographs, journals, and other accounts occasionally are located, allowing the events of long ago to be unlocked and enabling the historian to identify and understand the strengths, the weaknesses, the conflicts, and the accomplishments of those persons to whom the records relate.

Such is the case with Parson Henry Carty Renfro. The Parson left a significant record of his life as a student at Baylor University at Independence, Texas, as a Baptist preacher on the Texas frontier, as a

Confederate soldier and chaplain, and finally, as a Free-Thinker who was removed from his church after a charge of infidelity. His papers included a trove of speeches, sermons, letters, essays, and printed material which were virtually unknown to all but family, and, as a result, were unavailable for scholarly study or perusal for over one hundred years after his death.

My personal acquaintance with the Renfro-Clark Papers began when, as a very young man, I began to search through the mass of material that had been saved by my great-grandmother, Henry Renfro's daughter and most ardent admirer. Margaret Annette Renfro Baker Clark did not believe in throwing away anything that might conceivably be of value. In the washhouse behind the old Renfro home place in Burleson, Texas, she stacked boxes, bills, photographs, old clothes, furniture, trunks, and a myriad of other things that likely would have been disposed of by persons who endeavored to live more orderly lives. Most of all, however, she saved family correspondence. I suppose that every letter that she ever had in her possession was stored in a box, tied with a string, and carefully placed on a shelf. My interest, as a boy of seven or eight years, was the old stamps that graced the envelopes of all of this correspondence. Of course, most of the prized ones were already gone and secure in the stamp collections of my uncles Roy and Joe Clark. Still, with a diligent search, I occasionally found a treasure in an unopened box in a dark corner of the old structure.

What I did not realize in those days, the late 1930's and the early 1940's, was that the riches were not postage stamps but the information inside the envelopes. Fortunately, however, there were those in the family who recognized the value of the memorabilia that my great-grandmother had so carefully saved. Although all of my family recognized that the washhouse papers must have some value, my uncle, Noble Clark, and my mother, Thelma Clark Griggs, were among the most interested. Both occasionally examined the aged missives, some dated as early as the 1850's, and saw their historical importance. They put many aside, as did other family members, with the understanding that the fragile documents were tremendously important and that they would be of real value at some time in the future.

Even as a youth, my own interest was piqued by the letters, and I recall watching out for those which appeared to be of special interest.

On several occasions, I found fascinating pages written in flowing script that spoke of forgotten family members, places no longer on maps, or the tragedies of a long-ago war. These I carefully carried into the house to be saved. More often than not the letters found eager hands and were placed with other manuscripts that were "waiting" to be read and understood. As the decades went by, the papers were appreciated more and more by most members of the family. Copies were sometimes made and distributed, and my mother even made scrapbooks prepared with accompanying "translations" of the often hard-to-read script.

My own interest in the papers of the Renfro and Clark families increased progressively, particularly after I pursued the study of history and worked with the likes of Seymour V. Connor, Ernest Wallace, Alwyn Barr, and David Vigness in masters and doctoral programs at Texas Tech University. After years of research and writing on another book, *The Elusive Eden: Frank McMullan's Confederate Colony in Brazil*, which was published in 1987 by the University of Texas Press, my interest in the family papers redoubled. I determined to try to assemble the entire collection, conduct the research necessary to put together a coherent historical narrative, and write an interesting and informative book.

As I began this detailed project, I realized that there was one person around whom all of the letters, manuscripts, and other material revolved—Parson Henry C. Renfro, my great-great-grandfather—and that it was he who must be the central character in any narrative that I might write. It was his Civil War letters that I first compiled, then edited before mailing them to my six uncles and to my mother for comment. With this document was a plea to all that they forward to me any originals or copies of family papers which they might have in their possession so that my task could begin. The result was gratifying. As a result of my request, a large volume of original manuscripts was together in one place for the first time in decades. Without question, some papers remain hidden from view in forgotten drawers and boxes belonging to family members and others, waiting for the time that some future scholar will recognize their importance. Some important material was lost forever in the 1950's when, during a cleaning session, scores of letters and documents were burned. Despite the loss, the papers of the Renfro and Clark families constitute an imposing archive.

Even with an outstanding resource such as the Renfro-Clark Papers, however, a historian's work is dependent on a large number of other people in order to compile the entire story in a professional manner, and this book was no exception. The staff of *The Alvarado Bulletin,* a Johnson County newspaper still in publication after over one hundred years, provided the opportunity to secure new microfilm copies of their newspaper. This became one of the most prolific sources of information about Parson Renfro and his times in the Johnson County, Texas, area. Ellen K. Brown and Kent Keeth of the Texas Collection, the archives of Baylor University in Waco, Texas, were particularly helpful over a fifteen-year period. The professionals who operate archives of Southwestern Baptist Theological Seminary in Fort Worth also rendered valuable assistance. My son, John Griggs, spent many hours at the Barker Texas History Center at the University of Texas at Austin reviewing manuscript collections which we believed might shed additional light on the life and times of Parson Renfro.

The result of this research was the story of a man, his beliefs, and his family in the second half of nineteenth-century Texas. It is a historical narrative about an unusual individual as well as his family, his friends, and his enemies who lived in the Cross Timbers area south of Fort Worth when that region was a part of the frontier. This volume is not, nor is it intended to be, a comprehensive study of the Civil War, the Baptist Church in Texas, education on the Texas frontier, or Free Thought. It has no thesis to prove and offers no hidden meanings. Instead, it is an honest narrative that the author hopes will allow the reader to better understand, through first-person, original accounts, some of the crises and controversies which were faced by Parson Henry Renfro and those close to him. When possible, I have allowed the Parson to tell his own story through the use of direct quotations.

This biography of Parson Renfro reflects three interrelated themes beyond the strict chronological sequence of his life. The first involves the political, social, and cultural conflicts that engulfed the United States in the nineteenth century. These conflicts led to a civil war that radically changed the direction of the nation as a whole and the South in particular. The second theme includes some of the religious controversies between persons on the Texas frontier that were the result of honest differences of opinion in interpretation of the Bible within the orthodox church. The final theme of this book relates to the complex interrelationships caused by love, envy, death, and power and the resulting crises endured by Henry Renfro, his family, and other persons who lived on the edge of settlement in nineteenth-century Texas.

In completing this narrative, I have endeavored to avoid the traps which a historian is prone to trip in writing a book about a family member. Yet, I realize that this is difficult to do, and I apologize for any blatant partiality or unrealized failure to show the shortcomings as well as the virtues of the Parson.

William Clark Griggs
August 1992

Wedding photograph of Julius Baker and
Annette Renfro, taken on December 7, 1882.
Renfro-Clark Papers.

The Renfro home on Clark Street in Burleson, Texas, soon after its
completion in 1894. Left to right: James Clark, Annette Renfro Clark,
Mary Renfro, Jim Baker, Mary Pearl Baker. Renfro-Clark Papers.

Annette Renfro and her friend Eula Pickett. Renfro-Clark Papers.

Annette Renfro in 1904 at age forty. Renfro-Clark Papers.

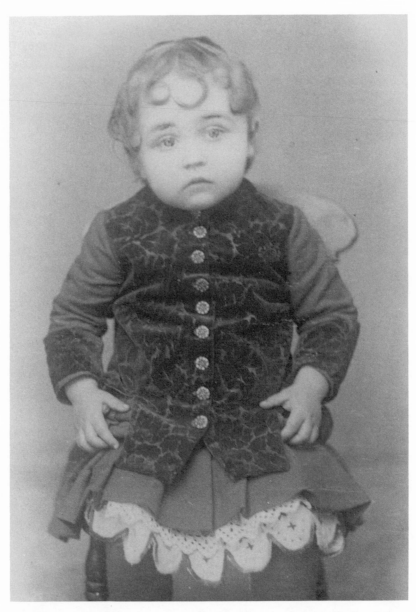

Mary Pearl Baker at age two, about the time she was abducted by her father. Renfro-Clark Papers.

Mary Pearl Baker and Jim Baker. Renfro-Clark Papers.

Annette Renfro at the age of
sixteen. Renfro-Clark Papers.

Mary Ray Renfro, c. 1884.
Renfro-Clark Papers.

James D. Shaw, Henry Renfro's friend and the publisher of the *Independent Pulpit*. Courtesy of the Texas Collection, Baylor University.

Wedding photograph of James Burleson Renfro and Kittie Miller, December 6, 1882. Renfro-Clark Papers.

Rufus C. Burleson, c. 1885. Taken at about the time of Henry Renfro's death. Courtesy of the Texas Collection, Baylor University.

James Burleson Renfro, "Burlie," at age eighteen. Renfro-Clark Papers.

Men's dormitory at Baylor University at Independence. Courtesy of the Texas Collection, Baylor University.

Chapter 1

Most Sanguine Expectations

Ⅰn the palmy days before the Civil War, Texas was a superb place to be. For those who loved adventure, searched for wealth, or yearned for land, it epitomized opportunity. For some persons, it was a safety valve—a place to rid oneself of past indiscretions or to escape encroaching civilization. For others, being a Texan offered a chance to find a new start—or a new love. For most who crossed the Sabine or Red river from the old to the new South, Texas was as much a concept as it was a place. Many of those families who elected to come to Texas already had experienced the thrill of breaking virgin sod, cutting timber which never before had felt an axe, or blazing a trail through forests which had never seen a road. The Renfro family was one of those, for its members already had lived in Tennessee and Georgia before they chose the Texas frontier as their new home. Their son, Henry Carty Renfro, also looked forward to going to Texas, for it was there that he would take the steps toward securing an education at a fledgling school at the town of Independence, Washington County, called Baylor University. Ultimately, he also would gain his credentials as a minister; in addition, he would have a wife and children of his own.

The stories told in letters and documents—the remnants of paper which record those memories—chronicle the first phase of Henry Renfro's story, a narrative which spans one-half the width of a continent—from Tennessee to Georgia to Texas—and the young man's quest for knowledge and the credentials of a Baptist preacher. The beginning of this account emphasizes Renfro's introduction to early Texas society, his contact and friendship with some of the most important persons in the Baptist Church, and the early recognition by those leaders of his leadership abilities.

The Renfro family came to Texas in 1851, and the saga of the man who would be known by one and all as "The Parson" would continue for thirty-four more years. By 1885, Henry Renfro's home was located about three and one-half miles southeast of Burleson, Texas, the town Renfro named after his old friend and Baylor University president Rufus C. Burleson. An inviting house surrounded by barns, corrals, and outbuildings, the structure was on the edge of the abrupt row of trees and vegetation, running north and south in Central Texas, known as the Cross Timbers. It was near the head of Crill Miller Creek on the east side of the tracks of the Missouri, Kansas, and Texas Railroad, northwest of the flourishing town of Alvarado. Although it had no gallery or veranda on the front like many "Texas-style" homes, it was an attractive box and strip frame house that boasted bright green shutters on every window, upper and lower. Surrounded by grassland, the house was on the east side of a north-south road. The bottom floor was split by an open air "dog trot" through which a cool breeze appeased the warm and humid Texas summers. Renfro built it himself about 1860, the year he began homesteading the 160-acre property and two years after he left Baylor University to serve as a minister of the Gospel on the Texas frontier.[1]

No one remembers for sure when Henry's widow, Mary, left the farm to move to town. It was probably about 1894, however, as the Victorian-style home still known as "Mama's house" by family and friends alike was constructed that year on the lane that later was called Clark Street in Burleson. Subsequently, the stately-looking old farm house on the head of Crill Miller Creek that harbored so many memories disappeared in searing flame and billowing smoke one clear summer night. The old Renfro farm home, like its controversial builder, left the world quickly. The old house was soon forgotten by all but family, but "the Parson" left a legacy that yet endures.[2]

Like most other Texans of the time, Henry Renfro was an emigrant to the Lone Star State. He was born on July 18, 1831, near Maryville,

Blount County, Tennessee, the fifth son of Absalom C. and Levicy Tipton Renfro. His parents were of pioneer stock and had migrated to the Tennessee frontier many years before from Montgomery County, Virginia, to Carter County, in eastern Tennessee. After the marriage of Absalom and Levicy in 1817, the two soon moved farther west, settling near the town of Maryville, Blount County. Levicy's grandfather, Colonel John Tipton, was a political opponent of John Sevier, the principal promoter of the aborted state of Franklin who later became the governor of Tennessee. Absalom's grandfather, Isaac Renfro, was a member of the famed Donelson Expedition, a group of adventurers that made a trail-blazing and dangerous river trip in 1786 from Fort Patrick Henry on the Holston River to French Salt Springs on the Cumberland. The Renfros were friends of Maryville's most distinguished citizen, Sam Houston, and family tradition notes that the man who was to become president of a republic toasted Absalom's health and friendship as the two men shared a drink the day before Houston left for Texas and Destiny. Although the conversation of the two men was not recorded for posterity, Henry Renfro's nephew, William S. "Uncle Billy" Renfro, was said to have been able to repeat "just what Sam said [to] Absalom," one hundred years after the event.[3]

The belief of pioneers such as Absalom Renfro that life was some-how better beyond the next hill was one that was common to most of the families on the far edge of civilized settlement in the nineteenth century. It came as no surprise, then, when the frontiersman an-nounced to the rest of the family that he was ready to leave Blount County and search once more for greener pastures. He had heard of the beautiful and sparsely settled Peavine Valley of Walker County in northwest Georgia, and he decided that it was the place he wanted his family to live. The area, locally known as "the ridges," was then a vast grazing area. According to one account, "One could see turkey, deer, and other wild animals as far as the topography of the country would permit." Streams, rivulets, and rills "covered the region," and their borders were ornamented in springtime with beautiful shrub-bery and "with flowers of different fragrance blending together and perfuming the atmosphere." In about 1836, Absalom and Levicy se-cured land near Rock Spring Post Office where they planned to settle down to raise their family of ten children—six boys and four girls.

Jefferson, the oldest of the children, had as friends the young Chero-kees who remained in Walker County, and his son, William, later recalled that his father taught him to "talk Indian."[4]

The Renfros were not long in becoming members of Peavine Church, a small Baptist chapel nestled among green hills on the south side of the picturesque road that wound through the green hills and trees east of Rock Spring. Henry felt a closeness to the church and, even as a youth, dreamed of becoming a minister. He studied the Bible at every opportunity and, at the age of fifteen, declared himself ready to join the fellowship. In August 1846, at a water hole on a nearby creek, Henry Renfro was baptized by Elder G. W. Selvige, Peavine's pastor.[5]

Within five years after Henry's formal association with the Baptist Church, the Peavine Valley was no longer the sparsely settled pastureland that it had been only a few years before. Settlers arrived almost daily, and, as a result, Absalom Renfro decided that the time had come, once more, to move to a less populated region. Therefore, the Renfros turned farming duties over to their son Jefferson and his wife Lucinda, then weighed the advantages of other, less populated climes. An invitation from Absalom's brother, Henry, to visit the family in Carter County, Tennessee, was timely, as there was no urgency in making a choice of a new home. "We are all anxious," wrote Henry, "that you should come and see us this spring or summer [of 1851]; likewise any of your family that could accompany you." Absalom and Levicy, who had been married thirty-three years before in Carter County, happily accepted his brother's invitation as many on both sides of their family still lived there. Although the distance from Walker County, Georgia, to Carter County, Tennessee, was relatively short, poor or nonexistent roads made the trip very arduous.[6]

Although everyone in the family would have enjoyed the visit to Carter County after being invited by Absalom's brother, several remained in Walker County to care for crops and to honor commitments already made. As previously noted, Jefferson and his wife Lucinda remained in the Peavine Valley to tend the Renfro farm, as did brothers Tipton and Isaac. Sister Margaret and her husband Benjamin Harris had a young family and consequently could not afford the luxury of leaving their home for a long period of time. Summerfield, Absalom and Levicy's youngest child at only six years of age, accompanied his mother and father, as did sisters Levicy, Melinda, and Evaline. Twenty-year-old Henry and his brother James relished the excitement of a long visit with the Tipton and Renfro relatives, and they also went to Tennessee.[7]

The old Renfro farm near the Watauga River in Carter County was far from being the unsettled frontier to which Absalom wanted to move, but life there was good and the family enjoyed the congeniality of relatives and old friends. Many of the children met cousins for the first time, and it is likely that they were awed by the number of persons in their family.[8]

The stay in Tennessee was pleasant to all, but no thought was given to the possibility of making Carter County a permanent home, as it offered neither challenges nor opportunities that were not present in Georgia. Within a month, the family returned to the Peavine Valley, and Absalom continued to consider locations where he and his family might wish to settle. He soon narrowed his list to two choices. One of the possibilities was Kentucky, where other members of the Renfro family had settled many years before; the other was Texas. Absalom determined to visit the former first and was accompanied by his father, Joseph Renfro. Even in old age, Absalom's father was eager to see new horizons.[9]

Although no record remains concerning the trek to Kentucky, Absalom ultimately decided against settling there. Instead, he resolved to join the large number of people who were moving to Texas. The new state was attracting thousands of Southerners, and letters from those already there to the families left behind were full of praise and enthusiasm for the republic-turned-state, where good land could be secured almost for the asking and where virgin soil virtually assured good crops. Soon after Absalom's return from Kentucky, the Renfro family loaded their wagons and began the long overland trip. In this move, which Absalom promised would be the family's last, they were joined by brothers James and Isaac, both of whom were excited about prospects in the Lone Star State. Margaret and Benjamin Harris, with their children Amanda, James, Ellen Caroline, and Lucinda, also decided to follow her parents, brothers, and sisters on the long trip to Texas from the Old South. In June 1851 the contingent, almost a wagon train in itself, crossed the Red River into Cass County, on the state's eastern border. Every family secured land shortly after their arrival, with Absalom receiving a grant for 320 acres. He soon built a house and began cultivation of a farm he called Hickory Hill.[10]

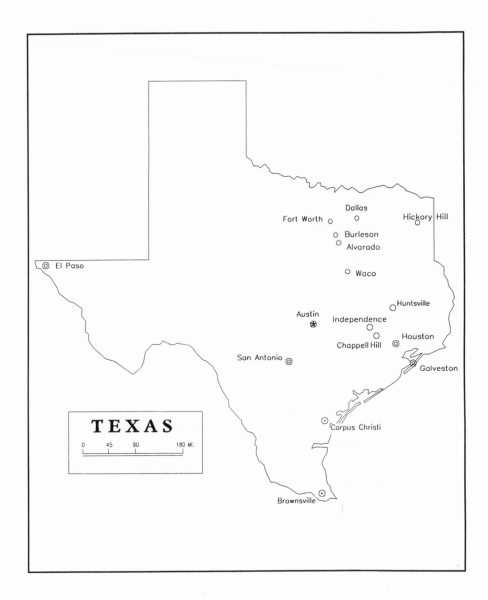

Figure 1. Overview of Texas Cities during the Life of Henry Renfro.

Twenty-year-old Henry Renfro was delighted with the change of scene and became a Texan with the vengeance of one converted. The tall and serious young man also was pleased with the number of young people in Cass County, and one pretty young lady, a Miss Gerl, quickly attracted his attention. It was not long before local gossips were abuzz with hints of an impending marriage. The rumors were premature, however, as a wedding was not in Henry's plans at that time. He was infatuated with the young lady, but his desire to become a Baptist minister, a decision made at the time of his baptism five years earlier, caused him to forego any thoughts of settling down. To Miss Gerl's disappointment, Henry began making plans to attend college.[11]

In the small Washington County, Texas, town of Independence, a new institution of higher learning called Baylor University was founded in 1845 by the Baptist Church and chartered by the state. Only a short time after its establishment, the four-year school already had earned a good academic reputation. For Henry Renfro, the school appeared to be the answer to his needs. Compared with other Baptist institutions of higher learning in Tennessee, Georgia, and other parts of the South, Baylor was relatively close to his new home in Cass County. It offered the coursework that the young man desired, and the faculty was considered to be excellent. Henry determined to visit Baylor and decide for himself on its merits. In late summer 1851, he left the Hickory Hill farm on horseback, alone, following the trails and half-roads to Independence. After conferring with faculty and other students about the prospects there, Henry was pleased with the university's prospects, and with a loan from the school to pay his tuition, he enrolled on September 1, 1851, with fifty-two other students.[12]

An excellent scholar, Henry relished the academic climate of Baylor. He was soon absorbed in his educational process, and he relished the full range of coursework that was available. In a note to his brother Jefferson in the spring of 1852, Henry made an effort to communicate through his writing style and the content of his letter that he had become an educated "man of the world." Responding to his brother in July, Jefferson noted that he had received Henry's "very interesting and neatly executed epistle," and that it exceeded his "most sanguine expectations" of his brother's advancements. Continuing, Jefferson exclaimed that nothing afforded him more pleasure than "to witness in every succeeding letter the manifest improvement in style, in the richness of language, in sublimity of thought, and the art of blending together the things that belong to different subjects." Jefferson noted that Henry's letter was an "exact facsimile of my beloved Brother, which I fail not to introduce to every friend that may come."[13]

Jefferson also was pleased with Henry's continued interest in the ministry but warned his younger brother to be wary of the temptation to question established Baptist beliefs. Jefferson noted that their brother Tipton had veered from Baptist doctrine and that he had been stamped as "a revisionist, emphatically so." Jefferson then asked rhetorically, "What say you, the Faculty, Students, and Citizens of Baylor to this thing[?]" He cautioned Henry to keep his priorities in order and to be sure and begin his education properly, particularly insofar as doctrine was concerned:

> My dear Brother, as you are preparing to discharge the functions of the highest office on earth, (I mean the office of a minister of Christ.) I hope you will not consider it officiousness in me; nor impute it to a desire to dictate for you, if I give you a few plane thoughts relative to that matter; which I submit in love, and in the hope that they may meet your approbation, and be of advantage to you in years to come. I will begin by saying that I know nothing of your peculiar views of the Bible, which is true. I will not assert, that it is an easy matter for a man to begin [w]rong (In theology as well as anything else.) And once [w]rong, it is a hard matter to get right. If the evil stopped with the man himself, it would not so much matter. But a public man in error, is not long getting others in error.

Jefferson then continued with a long commentary on men he considered to have been "obnoxious to the claims of orthodoxy." Despite the warnings, however, neither of the men could imagine Henry as having other than strong Baptist beliefs.[14]

Jefferson missed his brother and the rest of the Renfro family, and in his letter to Henry, he discussed moving to Texas himself. His ties to Georgia were extremely strong, however, and he procrastinated every time he considered leaving. "I am unprepared to say," he wrote, "whether I shall emigrate to Texas this year as I have a host of friends here, all of whom will protest against my going west. I think

I shall, why should I not." Jefferson then changed the subject of his letter to Walker County, obviously more interested in happenings there than what was going on in Texas. "Our camp meeting commences Friday before the first sabbath in August at Peavine. The advance are putting up their tints [tents] to camp. Brother, you can't imagine the change that Walker Co. has undergone since you left. Many new houses would meet your eye, turn which left or right. Industry and enterprise is the order of the day." Without question, Jefferson dearly loved the transformation caused by encroaching civilization in Georgia that the rest of the Renfro family chose to leave behind.[15]

Although Texas was on the frontier, continuing change was as inevitable there as in settled areas, and Baylor University was no exception. At the June 14, 1851, meeting of the governing council, Henry L. Graves, the university's president, tendered his resignation. Although a request was made that he reconsider, all of the trustees knew that Graves's decision was final. As soon as a vote of thanks was given, Trustee Abner S. Lipscomb nominated for the presidency young Rufus C. Burleson, a rising star in the Baptist Church in Texas.[16]

Although only twenty-seven years old, Burleson already had proven himself a first-class minister and an able scholar. A native of Alabama and an 1847 graduate of Western Baptist Theological Seminary in Kentucky, Burleson had volunteered to be a missionary in Texas. Although he expected to be assigned to a mission congregation near Gonzales, the death of Reverend William M. Tryon, the minister of the First Baptist Church in Houston, prompted church officials to send Burleson to the Bayou City instead.[17]

Burleson's performance in Houston, considered by church leaders to be outstanding, and his active participation and interest in the affairs of Baylor gained notice among the Baptists of Texas. The deciding factor in his election as Baylor's president, however, was the enormous prestige of Abner Lipscomb, the trustee who supported the young man for the position. In addition to being a member of the Texas Supreme Court, Lipscomb was also a former member of the Alabama Supreme Court and the governing board of Alabama University. As Lipscomb's nominee, Burleson was elected without dissent or opposition. At a candlelight meeting June 17 at the Independence Baptist Church, the Board of Trustees and local leaders met with members of the Baptist State Convention, by coincidence meeting in Independence at the same time, to begin raising funds to operate the university under Burleson's leadership. The pledges that night of $5,355 exceeded everyone's wildest dreams, and for the first time, Baylor had substantial backing from the entire Baptist community of Texas.[18]

Because of the pressing need for an administrator for the university, Burleson began his duties immediately. The problems that he faced, however, must have been discouraging. Rumors about the possible departure of Dr. Graves from the presidency of Baylor had prompted some of the faculty to leave even before the former leader's resignation. Many of the educators believed that the school would be disbanded, and they saw no cure for the sad condition of the university's buildings or equipment. One writer noted that "the buildings were inadequate and unsuitable; there was no prospect of obtaining scientific and philosophical apparatus; and not even the nucleus of a library." There was no doubt but that the new president of Baylor, not much older than some of his students, had work to do.[19]

Recognizing the need to get off to a good start, Burleson quickly began an information campaign among the state's Baptists to assure them of the continuation of the university and to inform them of his lofty goals. Utilizing printed circulars as well as several articulate young spokesmen who covered the state on horseback, Burleson wasted no time in letting it be known that the new school was to be of the highest caliber. For the first time in the university's brief history, Burleson instituted a curriculum leading to a degree, and he proclaimed that the education one might receive at Baylor would be second to none.[20]

Despite Burleson's obvious talents, his age and lack of administrative experience caused questions among some Baptists about his ability to lead the school. The new president recognized this problem, and to dispel any further criticism, he wrote to several educators "of known ability and acknowledged success" asking for their advice in building a great university. In response to their replies, Burleson established an eight-part policy on the governance and coursework of the institution, then he began a search for new faculty members who would help him make his formula a success. If Burleson encountered problems he could not solve, it would not be because of his tender years.[21]

Henry Renfro was in the first new class to enroll at Baylor after the selection of the new president, and he enthusiastically began his college coursework as Rufus Burleson started his career as an educator. At nearly twenty-one years of age and more mature than many entering students, Henry immediately recognized Burleson's dynamism and resolved to support the new leader any way that he could. Other students and faculty members were also caught up in Burleson's fervor, and most determined to do whatever was necessary to support his efforts on behalf of Baylor. Many wrote letters to friends at home as well as to former students of the university urging them to visit or return to the school and to enroll. It was said that never before had there "been such enthusiasm in study, [and] such love and harmony in social intercourse," and that "Baylor University under the Presidency of Dr. Burleson, would become a grand success and some day the glory of the Lone Star State." Henry Renfro was an eager participant in the frenzied campaign. He personally liked the new president, and his involvement in the promotion of the university was the beginning of a friendship between the two men that was to last for a lifetime.[22]

The Board of Trustees also enthusiastically supported the broad educational initiatives of Burleson, and during their November 1851 meeting, a committee was appointed to study the organization of a department of theology at the university. Although the committee reported that such a department would be "inexpedient," they did ask that formal coursework begin to encourage Baylor students to study for the ministry. It recommended, therefore, that "the President arrange such young men in a Theological class and give them whatever instruction he may be able." In addition, the Committee requested that George Washington Baines, the pastor of Independence Baptist Church, "deliver to said class lectures on Pastoral Theology." Henry Renfro was delighted at the decision, and he enrolled in the program as soon as it was offered.[23]

As Baylor University grew and prospered, Renfro continued to pursue his studies, studying religion and theology as well as other coursework that he believed would advance his goals. He became an adept public speaker and, in 1853, a charter member of the Erisophian Society, a twenty-member debating club. Despite President Burleson's objections to "secret societies," Henry joined the Tryon Chapter of Phi Gamma Delta at Baylor. More important to his chosen career than clubs or fraternities, however, was the opportunity he was given as a student to participate in area revivals. Although the theory taught in the classroom was essential to being a good minister, the practical experience gained in area churches provided an understanding that was to be invaluable to the would-be minister. By mid-1855, Henry Renfro was recognized by faculty and area ministers alike as an up-and-coming young theologian. He seemed to have all of the ingredients of a first-rate Baptist preacher, and it was soon realized that Henry had the ability to be extremely successful both in and out of the classroom.[24]

Consequently, in August 1855, Henry was chosen to join Dr. Burleson, R. E. B. Baylor, Hosea Garrett, and William Wright in a revival at Providence Church in the nearby Washington County community of Chappell Hill. Reporting to *The Texas Baptist*, Garrett said that the meeting was a success, and that "we have received by experience 17, by letter 3, by restoration 2, in all, 22 [converts]." It is significant that as a student Renfro was chosen to work with such distinguished men, persons that history would recognize as among the most prominent nineteenth-century leaders of the Baptist Church in Texas.[25]

The news of their Henry's accomplishments was a source of great pride to his parents. Absalom, Henry's father, always had been active in the church, and the realization that his son was already on his way to success was exciting news. Although there had been other ministers in the Renfro family, Henry was the first to receive formal training for the profession. Henry's sister, Margaret, was especially proud of her brother. She looked forward to his cheery letters, as they provided rays of happiness in a sometimes dreary life punctuated by family illness and death.[26]

Margaret's daughter Amanda had been sick for many months, and the little girl's condition became serious after the move to East Texas. Margaret and her husband had hoped that the change from the Georgia climate would provide the elixir for recovery, but the illness became progressively worse. Soon, Benjamin Harris, Margaret's husband, also developed symptoms of disease, and in an effort to find a cure, the family decided to move again, this time farther west. Margaret's cousins by marriage, Elisha and Susan Ray, already lived at the Marystown community near the north central Texas town of Alvarado, in Johnson County, so Benjamin and Margaret decided to move there also. Their hopes that a change in climate would help

Amanda were unfounded, however, as the little girl died on June 18, 1856.[27]

When the news of Amanda's death reached Henry Renfro, he was distraught that he had not been able to attend his niece's funeral. Although he had known that she was sick, he had no way of knowing that her condition was critical. Henry left Independence as soon as was possible after receiving the bad news, and he arrived at the Harris home after several days of hard travel. Soon, his parents, brothers, and sisters also reached Alvarado after making the long trip from Cass County. The family was together again but under tragic circumstances. Unfortunately, Henry was unable to remain as long as he would have liked; he had to return to Baylor or risk losing work already completed in the 1856 school year. As he began the long return trip to Washington County, however, he promised Margaret that he would return in August for a longer stay, partially to comfort his sister but also to fulfill a promise.

One of the persons that Henry had met at his sister's home was a Baptist minister from Erath County, William Robinson, described in one account as "a circuit rider who made semi-annual trips across the country, preaching and selling bibles." Robinson, known locally as "Choctaw Bill," had presided over little Amanda's funeral, and on his visits to the Harris home, he became well acquainted with Henry Renfro. The two shared common interests, and they soon became good friends. Upon learning that Renfro would return to Johnson County in August, Robinson asked him to participate in a long-anticipated revival to be held in the pastorless Cross Timbers Bethesda Baptist Church, the first and only Baptist congregation in the county. Henry readily pledged to do so, and soon after his return, a two-week religious meeting began. Upon its successful conclusion in August 1856, Renfro penned a long letter to George Washington Baines, his former professor at Independence who was the editor of *The Texas Baptist*, published in Anderson, Grimes County. Henry noted that "in answer to prayer, eight immortal souls were made to rejoice and to testify that God has power on earth to forgive sins." Describing the dedication of those in attendance, Renfro said that he had never "heard christians and sinners pray more fervently, nor have I ever seen such a manifestation of the spirit of God as was displayed the night our eight mourning friends were brought to a knowledge of the truth as it is in Jesus."[28]

Renfro's description of Johnson County in the same letter was of note. "Well, Brother Baines, this church is situated in the Cross Timbers, where water is very scarce. The wells, however, afforded enough for ourselves and horses to drink, and we went some five miles, to Village Creek, to baptize, because there was much water there." Henry also described the spiritual destitution in the region. "There is not an ordained minister in this county. Brother Robinson comes sixty miles to preach at this church. Is not the harvest great! Are not the laborers few?"[29]

Noting the proximity of Johnson County to Texas's western frontier, Henry also took the opportunity in his letter to Baines to make an appeal for more sympathy for the native Americans. "I understand that there is a set of 'lewd fellows of the baser sort' who are actually degrading some of the Indian tribes on our frontier. My heart bleeds for the poor children of the forest, who are fast sinking behind the western hills. Shall the last remnant of this unhappy race go down to the grave without an effort being made to point them to the lamb of God?" Renfro then expressed a plea for missionaries. "Is there no follower of Jesus who will go and bear the standard of the cross among the benighted Indians, and tell them that 'the times of this ignorance God winked at, but now commandeth all men every where to repent.'" Ending his letter with a philosophical statement, the young aspirant to the ministry expressed a moving hope for the future: "I love every spot in Texas, and long to see the period when every community will be blessed with a church and a preacher—a school and a teacher. When in every village throughout our wide land may be seen the tall temples of our devotion, gleaming and glittering in the sunbeams of heaven."[30]

Henry Renfro's hopes for a more utopian Texas, however, were sometimes tempered with harsh reality. Unfortunately, Amanda's death was not the last calamity for Henry's sister Margaret. Soon after the end of the Bethesda revival, on October 1, 1856, Benjamin, Margaret's husband, also died. Upon receiving the dismal news, Henry left Baylor and returned to Johnson County again, vowing to stay as long as was necessary to be sure that Margaret was physically, spiritually, and financially able to continue on her own.[31]

Henry Renfro also determined to continue the missionary work that he had begun during the Johnson County revival. He delivered sermon after sermon to any and all who would attend the meetings,

desiring to fill what he considered to be an impelling need for preaching in the frontier community. His positive influence was felt, and it
was not long before the members of Bethesda Baptist Church, prod-
ded by Renfro and circuit rider Bill Robinson, declared themselves
ready for a full-time minister, an event which was not long in coming.
The completion of the revival signaled the need for Henry to return
once again to Cass County and Hickory Hill. His parents remained at
Margaret's home in Alvarado, and they determined to remain with
their grieving daughter and her children as long as necessary. It became Henry's responsibility to care for the family farm.[32]

Soon after Henry arrived in East Texas, rumors about the young
Baylor student began once again. The speculation about the romance
between Henry and Miss Gerl was rife; after all, the pretty young lady
was still unmarried, and many said that she had been "holding a
torch" for Henry during the time he had been at the university. Of
course, there was some basis to the stories, as Renfro still "courted"
the young lady on his infrequent trips to Cass County. Yet, Henry's
resolve to gain an education and go into the ministry remained para-
mount, and the relationship between the two did not change.[33]

Another rumor, however, was harder for Henry to explain. Mur-
murs were heard that Renfro, although attending a Baptist school,
had somehow departed from the precepts of that church and embraced Presbyterianism. Henry was nonplussed by the story and believed it so ludicrous that it needed to be denied and corrected as
soon as possible. In October 1856 he wrote once again to his former
professor "Brother Baines" at *The Texas Baptist* to set the story straight
once and for all. "No," Renfro wrote fervently, "I am no Presbyte-
rian—I am no Pedo-Baptist. 'Tis true I was reared in the lap of Methodism, heard more preaching on apostasy than on the final persever-
ance of saints—saw more infants sprinkled than believers baptized.
. . . When I acknowledge anything but the immersion of the believer
as Spiritual baptism, let my right hand forget her cunning, and let my
tongue cleave to the roof of my mouth. Tell it not in Gath." Renfro
then stated that this explanation should correct any false stories circulating about him, particularly in eastern Texas, as he had "a good
many friends" there who would "like to have an explanation of this
matter."[34]

Although Henry's residence was officially in Cass County, he made
such a dynamic impression during the revivals in Johnson County

that the members of the Bethesda Baptist Church considered the yet unordained young man to be their *ad hoc* minister. He had been enormously popular during the revivals and subsequent preaching, and, after all, his sister lived near Alvarado in the vicinity of the church. Renfro's father and mother also lived there on a semipermanent basis, and Absalom already was taking an active part in local affairs. Therefore, when the Bethesda Church members and the West Fork Association began selection of delegates to the statewide Baptist convention to be held in Huntsville in October 1857, Henry was elected as one of the Johnson County representatives. Henry viewed his selection as a great compliment, and he readily agreed to go. He left Cass County as soon as possible to discuss his responsibilities with members of Bethesda Church, to make personal preparations, and to meet the second appointee who was to attend the statewide meeting.[35]

Henry and the other delegate, Reverend John C. Hunton, "a good travelling companion and a noble-hearted man," who as a missionary often preached at the Bethesda Church, left Johnson County a full month before the beginning of the convention. Henry had suggested the early start, as he knew the delays and obstacles a person could encounter on unfamiliar and indistinct roads. Too, he wished to arrive in Huntsville in time to meet with old friends and acquaint himself with the convention agenda. Henry's caution was justified when, in Cherokee County, his horse died, and it appeared that he might miss the meeting entirely. "You can imagine," he wrote to his sister Margaret, "how sad I felt, left in the wild and wide world, a foot." Hope was renewed for the young man, however, when different groups along the way asked him to preach. When the plate was passed after the sermons, the proceeds were given to the unlucky student. In the letter to his sister, he stated that "he had preached, or at least tried to preach, more since I left Johnson than I did while I was in it." Henry reported that he reached Huntsville "one month from the day we left," and he now owned a horse worth $125 and "as much money as I had when I left home. All things have worked together for good." Henry also sent his sister three dollars, "two for yourself—a half for sweet James Henry, and the other half for little Henry C. Renfro [son of James and Elizabeth Renfro]. My dear sister I wish I could send you more. I will when I can."[36]

The old friendship between the Renfro family and Sam Houston was still intact when Henry arrived in Huntsville, and Henry received an invitation to stay at the famous man's home. On November 2, 1857, he wrote to Margaret with the matter-of-fact remark that he was "now in Huntsville, lodging with Gen. Sam Houston during the sitting of the convention." He also noted that Baylor's president and his wife were there and that "Brother and sister Burleson met and greeted me very kindly." Closing his letter to his sister, Henry asked her to "tell Father and James to take care of my concerns in Johnson." He then requested that she give his love to all, "the girls in particular." Obviously, Johnson County offered new attractions to the young man. Henry promised to write to his sister again upon his return to Independence and Baylor.[37]

Problems were quietly brewing at Baylor University and the Independence Baptist Church even before the 1857 convention in Huntsville, and by November, they were becoming increasingly evident to the faculty and to church members. A controversy had begun between Rufus Burleson and Horace Clark, head of the Female Department of the university, about which of the two men had the ultimate authority over the women's division. The break became so serious, in fact, that it divided the academic community and split the congregation into factions, threatening the very existence of the Independence Baptist Church.[38]

One of Burleson's preconditions before assuming the presidency of Baylor was that the male and female divisions of the university be separated. The Board of Trustees had agreed to the request and subsequently appointed Dr. Clark as principal of the Female Department. Burleson retained full authority over the men as well as the presidency of the university. As time went by, however, Clark became convinced that the board had given him complete authority over any activities relating to women, despite the fact that Burleson remained Baylor's chief executive. Both men's claims had some validity, and as the controversy continued, the gulf between the two educators and their supporters became wider and wider.[39]

At the Independence Church, the problem was as threatening as it was at the university. Dr. Burleson had resigned the pastorate in 1856, and the lack of spiritual leadership magnified the disagreements between the two factions. While the feud was still in progress, Burleson could not consider returning to the pulpit, and others who might have done so declined until the problems between Clark and Burleson were resolved. Burleson realized that the fortunes of the university were, in many ways, tied to those of the Independence Baptist Church. Consequently, he believed that the vacancy in the pastorate needed to be filled quickly by someone who was capable, who had not been personally involved in the Burleson-Clark controversy, and who would be accepted by the rank and file membership of the church. Without question, it was a difficult order to fill.

In a review of potential candidates for the position, Burleson narrowed his selection to Baylor student Henry Renfro, a young man whose noteworthy accomplishments were common knowledge among faculty, students, and the members of Independence Church. Henry was described by Burleson as a "model student in every department," and he noted that the young man "excelled in oratory." Not only had Renfro spearheaded a major revival in Bethesda Church in Johnson County, but also he had been elected to represent that church and the West Fork Association at the state meeting in Huntsville. It was generally recognized that the young man had proved his mettle when called to preach alongside such respected and experienced ministers as Hosea Garrett, R. E. B. Baylor, and Rufus Burleson himself. Henry Renfro could serve Independence Baptist Church well, Burleson reasoned, and the university president believed that the young man would be acceptable to both factions in the Burleson-Clark controversy. Renfro was called to Burleson's home, briefed on the proposal, and asked whether he would accept the post if offered. Awed by the responsibility offered to him, Henry nevertheless was excited about the call and agreed to serve, subject to his ordination, approval, and election by members of the congregation. Dr. Burleson discussed the idea with his brother Richard, then a member of the Baylor faculty, and with others who held influential roles in the Independence Church. All agreed that Henry Renfro, at that time a mature twenty-six years of age, had the ability and the judgment to assume the difficult position.[40]

Events moved rapidly. Renfro's ordination was set for the fourth Sunday in the month, November 22, 1857, only a few days after his call and election to the church post. All preparations were completed, but extremely foul weather forced a postponement for another week. The sun rose on a clear sky the next Sunday, however, and the ceremony proceeded on schedule. Dr. Burleson preached the ordination sermon entitled, "The Rise, Spread, and Destiny of the Church." His delivery, according to one account, was "in the usual felicitous style, pointed force, and stirring pathos of this well-known and estimable man of God."[41]

Next came the examination of Candidate Renfro, a requirement in all Baptist ordinations. This phase was carried out by Richard Burleson, and it was "so clear and simple as to be intelligible to all." The correspondent for *The Texas Baptist* noted that the questions to Renfro "embraced all the doctrines of the church relative to the scheme of human redemption, and proved highly satisfactory." The charge was delivered by minister Hosea Garrett of Chappell Hill. It was reported to be "of that solemn, grave, and appropriate kind to be expected from a veteran of the cross to a young and relatively inexperienced co-laborer."[42]

Following the ceremony, Henry, now an ordained minister, led a revival at the Independence Church. Although he had been sick prior to the ordination, probably from nervous exhaustion, he exceeded all expectations. His ordination address was said to have been "marked with that christian zeal and ardor which have already won for him the love and confidence of all who know him, and inspired the highest expectations of his usefulness in the noble calling to which he has devoted his life." The correspondent for *The Texas Baptist* called the sermon "unusually impressive" and recalled that Renfro's anxious inquiry of "what shall I do to be saved" was "depicted upon many a countenance." At the close of the service, several persons "presented themselves for the prayers of the church."[43]

Henry Renfro's first revival after his ordination did not end on the first evening but continued for eleven long days. During this time, Henry preached for several consecutive nights until he was exhausted and unable to proceed. Rufus and Richard Burleson continued the services, and because of the high drama of and interest in the revival, morning services were added as a supplement, beginning at 10 A.M. daily. When a final count was complete, it was announced that seventeen persons were added to the rolls of the church "by experience." Two more came by letter, and two others were received into the church "under its watch-care." Of the new members of the church, it is of interest that nine were Renfro's fellow students at Baylor.[44]

By any yardstick, the revival was a complete success. Renfro had justified the faith put in him by Dr. Burleson, and there was no question but that he could serve well as a spiritual leader. Sincere congratulations were offered to Henry on his new position and for the extremely successful revival at the Independence Baptist Church. As a memento of the occasion, Georgia Burleson, Rufus Burleson's wife, presented her husband's student and friend with a leatherbound notebook, a gift that the young man valued all of his life. On December 19, he was elected as pastor of Independence Church, the first and only time a student of Baylor ever received that honor.[45]

It is of interest that although several members of the male department of Baylor were among those who became new members of the Independence Baptist Church during the December revival, none of the female students under the authority of Dr. Clark were allowed to attend the services. Henry Renfro, now the Reverend Renfro, was appalled at Clark's decision to bar Baylor women from the event. Although his friendship with Burleson was common knowledge, Renfro had been careful not to take sides in the controversy between the two leaders. Consequently, he saw Clark's actions as an insinuation that he sided with Burleson in the problems of authority at the university. Dr. Burleson was also extremely displeased at Clark's seeming derision of Renfro, as were other church and university leaders. Consequently, the issue of the nonattendance of women in church was placed on the agenda for the December 17 meeting of the Baylor Board of Trustees. The minutes of the board show that Clark received no support in the matter: "We therefore deem it necessary for the best interests of the pupils and the promotion of the great ends for which our institution was established that both the President of B. U. and the Principal of the Female Department shall as ministers, cooperate in a cordial, Christian, and prudent manner with the pastor of the Independence Church in all Revival Meetings he may hold, and encourage the attendance of all pupils, unless it shall be against the known will of their parents or the expressed desire of the pupils."

In a larger sense, however, Rufus Burleson lost much more than he gained by the actions of the Board of Trustees on December 17. Addressing the question of whose authority—that of Burleson or that of Clark—was greater insofar as the Female Department was concerned, the trustees determined that there should be a permanent division. "The time has arrived," their statement read, "when the two departments of Baylor University should be separated." Whatever authority Burleson might have had over Dr. Clark and the Female Department ceased with the passage of the resolution.[46]

The decision of the trustees did not quell the Burleson-Clark controversy, however. The enmity between the two men grew rather than diminished after the board decision, and the problems intensified at Independence Church. Despite his efforts to remain neutral in the fight, Henry Renfro increasingly was seen as a "Burleson man" by those who backed Clark; as a result there was little or no support for him from that faction. Believing that the satisfactory continuance of the church was more important than his tenure as pastor, Henry Renfro resigned as the spiritual head of the institution on February 20, 1858, only two months after assuming the position. Henry resolved to leave Baylor and return to Cass County and Hickory Hill to follow a plow until the bitter acrimony was resolved.[47]

But Henry Renfro's resignation and departure from Independence did not in any way slow the debates between Rufus Burleson and Horace Clark and their supporters, and the fires of jealousy and anger continued to smolder. In May 1860, the resignation of law professor Royal T. Wheeler and his subsequent move to Brenham to begin a new lecture series in competition with Baylor caused the verbal conflagrations to rekindle. During discussions on the issue at Independence Baptist Church, arguments began anew between Burleson and Clark, and the debates once again began to dominate the atmosphere of the church and the university. Charges and countercharges were made by both men, and formal presentations were made to the Board of Trustees in June 1860. Subsequent efforts to settle the situation seemed to indicate that the feud might be over, and the meeting of the trustees ended in "singing, extending hands of fellowship, and 'shedding tears of joy.'"[48]

Yet, the supposed settlement was not unanimous. Proxy Trustee Abner E. Lipscomb, the nephew of Judge Abner Lipscomb, defended his sole vote against the seeming end to the controversy with a statement that he did not believe that the settlement was "based on Gospel principles." He demanded that Clark and Independence Baptist Church pastor Michael Ross make further efforts to resolve the problem. When Lipscomb failed to secure the support of the trustees, he took his argument to the conference of the Independence Baptist Church which was held on July 14, 1860. After several days of discussion, the conference determined Lipscomb to be in error and asked him to drop his charges. When Lipscomb refused to do so, the conference voted to withdraw fellowship from the strong-willed leader. In October, Lipscomb published a twenty-four page pamphlet entitled *Defense of Abner E. Lipscomb* and addressed it to the Baptists of Texas. It seemed that the fights and recriminations would never end.[49]

Still, cooler heads tried to prevail, and on March 20, 1861, efforts were once again instituted by the Baylor University trustees to solve the problem that was threatening the very existence of the educational institution. Horace Clark was interviewed by the board, and he gave assurances that he had intended no offense to Burleson, but that if he had, he withdrew them. Burleson accepted the apology, and once again it appeared that the conflict might be ended. However, there were some persons who could not "leave well enough alone," and the dissatisfaction of some members of Independence Baptist Church with the settlement prompted a new conference to review the matter. Church officials "invited sister churches at Washington, Brenham, Chappell Hill, Bethlehem, Mt. Zion, and Gay Hill, each to send two of their most prudent brethren to sit as a council upon the case." Held in July 1860, the conference found that accusations against Clark and his allies as outlined in *Defense of Abner E. Lipscomb* were, on the whole, unfounded. It determined, too, that Lipscomb could be reinstated into fellowship if he issued a withdrawal of his charges "by [inserting] a card in the *Texas Baptist*." Lipscomb, who by that time desired reinstatement, did as was requested and was re-accepted into the church.[50]

Rufus Burleson was in attendance at the council meeting, however, and he was infuriated by the outcome of the decision regarding Lipscomb. According to one account, Burleson "walked deliberately to the rostrum, thrust his finger into the face of the moderator Ross, and said: 'You have been guilty of unfairness, and have used the power of your official position to adopt this motion, and nothing but your gray hairs protect you from the punishment you so justly deserve.'" Although Ross adjourned the meeting without comment, Sam Houston, who also was in attendance, told Burleson that he would not "take your hand until convinced that you have sincerely repented." The wedge between the two old friends was not long-standing, however, as Houston once again offered Burleson his friendship after Burleson repented during a subsequent gathering at Independence Church. After being called on to pray for the success of the meeting, Burleson, "attired in his black frock coat and trousers, silk plush vest, standing collar and white stock cravat, prostrated himself in the aisle 'and poured out his soul to God for a blessing on all he had offended.'" Once again, a truce seemed to have been declared.[51]

With the furor over the proposed secession of Texas from the Union, however, Burleson and Clark once again took opposite sides, with Clark stating that there should be "a re-construction of government on a basis that will guarantee the security of our rights, or separation." Burleson, on the other hand, supported the position of his friend Sam Houston. Houston's plan, declared the Baylor president, "was to secure men 'in all the great centers of influence . . . to proclaim their unalterable devotion to the South and opposition to the abolition fanaticism, but to declare that our wisest and safest plan is to make our fight in the Union.'" A student debate was declared won by secessionists, and Burleson wrote that "Mayor Task Clay cut down our liberty pole and the Stars and Stripes lay tattered and torn in the dust."[52]

In February 1861, Rufus Burleson finally found a solution to the controversy when he was offered the presidency of Waco Classical School (later Waco University) by J. W. Speight, the president of the Board of Trustees of the institution. Speight, a former pupil of Burleson when both lived in Mississippi, evidently had been considering Burleson as a possible head of the central Texas Baptist school for several months. Since Burleson believed that conditions at Baylor would continue to deteriorate, he accepted the invitation and moved to Waco along with several key Baylor faculty members. He remained extremely bitter, however, concerning the Clark debates and their aftermath. In 1869, he wrote a successor at Baylor, William Carey Crane, that "the board of Trustees and State Convention were the pliant tools of . . . Horace Clark and they left me to struggle on and sink or swim as best I could." Burleson claimed that "secret conventions were made to expel me from the institution. My private correspondence was inspected and ordered to be burned. I was summoned repeatedly before the board and catechized and finally impeached . . . until self respect, peace and usefulness demanded my removal to Waco."[53]

Regardless of the truth of Burleson's allegations, there is no question but that there was at that time a history of conflict within the Baptist Church. As early as 1845, the Southern Baptists withdrew from the conventions which included Northern churches. This conflict and subsequent removal was, according to one contemporary definition, "partly from the wish to avoid agitation and partly from the desire [of the South] to engage their members more fully in the missionary enterprise by concentrated action." In 1848, Baptist historian David Benedict recognized that this bickering between church members was self-destructive. Although Benedict's remarks were directed primarily at the "anti-mission" elements within the Baptist Church, they struck home in relation to all internal church conflict. "The fact is," wrote Benedict, "that personal altercations, rivalships, and jealousies, and local contests for influence and control have done much to set brethren at variance with each other. . . . New men and new measures have run faster than the old travelers were accustomed to go, and they have been disturbed at being left behind."[54]

Discussing the conflicts which seemed to be inevitable in the church, historian Donald Mathews noted that when people have misgivings about a position, they naturally turn to leaders who best can express their misgivings. "If people begin to feel restless about the propriety and trustworthiness of traditional [church] leadership, they will respond positively to persons who can articulate their uneasiness. And if those same persons can give them a sense of doing something to improve the situation and elevate their own sense of worth, a new leadership emerges." This, in essence, was the crux of the Burleson-Clark conflict. For some persons, Rufus Burleson did not fulfill an exemplary leadership role, and they turned to Horace Clark. In this case, however, Burleson managed to maintain his leadership within the church with his movement to Waco University.[55]

Historian Howard Miller noted that the feud continued until Baylor University and Waco University were combined into one institution. "It is clear," wrote Miller, "that most of the bitter divisions between two apparently irreconcilable groups of Baptists can be reduced to a dispute between the supporters of the two schools. They were united in Waco in 1886, and the resulting Baylor University was thereafter as effective an instrument of denominational unification as its two predecessors had been sources of contention."[56]

While the Burleson-Clark affair was essentially a Texas debate, it is unlikely that it would have occurred had there not been a willingness within the Baptist Church on a national and regional level to allow and condone political maneuvering and power brokering by its leaders. All Texas Baptists were affected to some extent, and Henry

Renfro was no exception. Although he had no way of knowing it when he left Independence for Cass County in early 1858, the continuation of politics and the use of power by persons within the Baptist Church would continue to exert influence on Henry Renfro for the rest of his life.

Chapter 2

The Time to Come to Texas

For many persons from Tennessee, a compatible land which shared heroes such as David Crockett and Sam Houston, going to Texas was almost like going home. Such was the feeling of kinship between the states in the mid-nineteenth century. Elisha Ray, a young but solid farmer from Concordia, Tennessee, had already made the decision to cross the Red River and settle in middle Texas by 1851, so it likely surprised no one when his sister, Mary, decided to join him. Like most travelers to the new land, Elisha and Mary were searching—he for land and wealth, she for home and family. For you see, Mary had not yet found the man of her dreams. The Southern myth that a lady could have it all if she had relative wealth, uncommon looks, and sufficient piety and wit had not yet been fulfilled for the young woman from Tennessee.[1]

Mary Ray was to search for and find her dreams in Texas in the person of Henry Renfro, a young preacher born in Tennessee and raised in Georgia, who also was beginning a search for his future. Neither Mary nor Henry Renfro realized at first the changes that were happening in their lives, and their letters provide a rarely found view of nineteenth-century Texas decorum, frontier courtship, and family values on the frontier of Texas. In addition, Mary's notes and letters to and from family and friends in Concordia gave an unaccustomed glimpse of the perceptions concerning emigration to Texas in 1856.[2]

As her mother and father were both dead, Mary Ray had no real reason to remain where she had lived almost all of her life. Her mother, Ann Ray, died in September 1835, only hours after the birth of Mary's little brother, John Joseph. Nine years later, when Mary was thirteen years old, her father, Michael Ray, also passed away, leaving her a young orphan girl dependent on her two oldest brothers, William George and Elisha Boykin Ray, neither of whom was much older than she. Fortunately, however, their father had been a good farmer and businessman, and he left the six children a considerable fortune consisting of land, livestock, and other property including eighteen slaves, three of whom became a part of Mary's inheritance.[3]

After the marriages of brothers Elisha and William, Mary moved to Mississippi to live temporarily with an aunt and uncle. She clearly missed her own family, however, and she was upset that none of them took the time or trouble to write to her regularly. Corresponding with Elisha's wife, Sue, Mary presented a dismal picture of the lack of attention she had received from her brothers and sisters. "I have never received a letter from . . . Elisha. I am fearful that his letter has been misplaced and I will not get it." Older brother William George, Mary complained, was in a "state of taciturnity. . . . I suppose," Mary concluded, "that he devotes so much of his time and attention to his wife and children, that he has not time to bestow one thought on me. Marrying has converted him into a perfect old man." Speaking of her sister Charity Ann (who was called Chellie), who still lived at the old home in Concordia, Mary noted that she had "not heard from home but twice this year, though I am expecting a letter every day. Do not atribute [attribute] sister Chellie's silence to forgetfulness, for she scarcely ever writes to me. It seems that she does not like to write."[4]

Elisha Ray and his wife Susan, like many other Tennesseans, had moved to Texas in about 1851, and they were well pleased with their new situation. They settled in Johnson County on a trial basis, and they were sufficiently happy with their new home on the frontier that they decided to make the change a permanent one. Elisha spoke positively about the new state, and he wrote to one friend with the advice that "now is the time to move to Texas—land has rose [sic] a hundred percent." He was inquisitive, however, about the conditions farther west on the upper Brazos River, and determined to inspect that land before he made a permanent decision about where he would finally locate. Elisha wrote of the planned exploration to his brother William George (who also was considering a move to Texas) just before Christmas 1853, and he and a "Cousin David" left soon after for the unsettled and relatively unknown country to the west.[5]

Months passed, and William George received no correspondence from his brother about the success or failure of the trip. He was becoming disheartened about the possibilities of his settling in Texas, and in February, William George wrote his brother a scolding letter. "I can hardly excuse you for not letting me hear from you, when you returned from Brazos. . . . I am affraid [afraid] you nor Cousin David either is satisfied! If not tell us so. Jes says if you don't settle yourself and get satisfied he will look [for] him[self] a home near Searcy, Ark. And I will look [for] me one in the Devil's Elbow." Continuing, William George admonished Elisha to "Let me hear from you oftener, write sunday if no other time. You can write at night also." Evidently, William George soon received the word that Elisha was indeed happy in Johnson County, and his plans to go there were reactivated.[6]

In addition to the letters received in Tennessee from Elisha, letters from Texas also came from Mary's cousin, Elizabeth "Bet" Bockmon. Bet married a young man named Isaac Renfro at the ripe old age of thirteen, and the two lived on a 179-acre farm which Isaac obtained as a Texas land grant. It was Bet who enthusiastically encouraged Mary to leave Concordia, Tennessee, in 1853 and come to the frontier. "If you want a man that's smart, come to Texas," wrote Elizabeth. "There is lawyers, Preachers, Doctors, and gigarareitys of all kinds. If that's what you are waiting for, I think it's time you was ready to have it."[7]

Continuing her letter to Mary about romantic prospects, Elizabeth discussed the reasons for her own marriage, humorously warning her cousin Mary that "if you ever intend to [marry] you must not do like I did, let him come until he eats all of your chickens. I had nearly got out of the notion, but I had to marry to get shut of him." At the time Mary received Bet's letter, however, she already was considering several options as to what she wished to do with her life and where she wished to live.[8]

Certainly, Mary was enthusiastic about the joys of wedded bliss, but still, she believed that there were circumstances where remaining single was preferable to wedlock. Answering a query from her sister-in-law Susan Ray in 1852, Mary said that she still gloried "in the cold embrace of celibacy. It is not much of a glory, either," Mary continued, "but, however, I am still single, and destitute of one to love at this time." Anxious to assure Susan that her situation had not always been so bleak, Mary noted that she had several suitors whom she easily could have married. "But I have loved fondly, fervently, devotedly, but it has always been my misfortune to love unworthy objects who were not calculated to make me happy. I have succeeded in banishing these images from my memory."[9]

Mary continued her letter with an admission that she was going with a gentleman who, unfortunately, was unimpressive. "I have a suitor at this time who is a most unexceptional young man, and who is well calculated to make me happy, could I but love him. I would sooner suffer martyrdom, than go with him to the altar, and there stand in the presence of God and man, with a falsehood on my lips. If I were to marry him," Mary continued, "I should have to promise to love him, and that I can never do. When I marry I shall have to know (or at least believe) that he whom I love, loves me devotedly in return; and he must be worthy of me in every respect." Mary then brushed aside her thoughts of marriage. "But away with these silly notions, I sometimes think I will not cultivate them any more." Realizing that perhaps she had said more than necessary, Mary asked that Susan not tell anyone of her thoughts. "Please do not repeat this nonsense I have communicated to you," Mary implored, "I am sure someone would laugh at it."[10]

Her brother and sister-in-law's satisfaction with their new home, combined with the happiness of her cousin, Elizabeth "Bet" Renfro, in Cass County, redoubled Mary's thoughts of settling in Texas also. When her older sister, Mat [Martha], and her brother William George and his wife Bettie finally decided to go west, Mary made the decision to accompany them. When the time came in January 1855, she assembled everything that was dear to her—including the three slaves Sopha, Rote, and Tank—and prepared for the family journey.[11]

After he learned of Mary's plans, her brother Elisha wrote a discouraging letter to her about the upcoming move. Not realizing that Mary was eagerly looking forward to the adventure, Elisha in his letter expressed a dismal note. "How I would [like] to be there when you all start. I recon [reckon] I would see some monstrous tears fall from your eyes." Elisha told Mary that he could "not help but feel sorry for you when I think of you leaving your native state. I know you will hate it so bad." On a practical note, however, Elisha asked Mary to bring garden seeds with her. "Tell Sis [Martha] to bring some lunch bean seed, turnip seed butter beans & . . . some peach and plum seed." He also requested "my Holly [Holy] War book from Pa, and some others [books] if she can." As for his children, Elisha asked Mary to bring his daughter "Ana Bet" an apple. "I have not seen one," Elisha said, "since I left [Tennessee]. Tell Martha to bring Bucy an orange, that she has never seen one." He then concluded his message to Mary with the request that she "bring about a peck of minis peach seed with you." [12]

In a postscript to his brother William George, Elisha was apologetic about the lack of the amenities of civilization. "I hope that you will not be disappointed when you come and find no orchards. I am sorry for Martha, she loves fruit as well." Continuing his requests that the family purchase items not available on the Texas frontier, Elisha told William George that he "would be glad if you would buy me one of those little dollar clocks in Memphis if you can find room for it." Elisha then concluded his letter from Texas with the news that he had killed "a few turkeys and 2 deer lately." [13]

Mary's cousin Sarah "Sallie" Jackson and her family accompanied the caravan as far as Memphis, but there they sadly left and returned to Concordia. In a letter to Mary written on March 27, Sallie said that she and her family had arrived at their home on Sunday, the day after leaving the family. "I was very lonesome after we came back home," wrote Sallie, "and missed you all very much. I have looked up the road a many a time and thought of you all but could not see non [none] of you coming as I have done [in the past]." On a pessimistic note, Sallie noted that her cousin did not express an opinion about Texas. "Mary, you didn't write whether you was satisfied or not. I don't expect you are. Tell Mat to write to me. You must write soon for I would like to hear from you any time." [14]

For most of those who stayed behind, the enthusiasm for Texas remained. Mary's sister Chellie wrote on April 18, 1855, that she expected "Uncle Anderson will go to Texas when Jo comes. Aunt Mat, and Jack is keen to go, he says if he can sell he will go." Mary's cousin Sallie Jackson wrote from Concordia in March that a Mr. Kives "talks some times of moving out there some time next fall," and by September, Mary learned that "Mr. Reaves talks of starting to Texas the 15th of October. He says he expects to go where you all are." Chellie was not yet sure about Texas, however, and she did not know when she might go west. "Not soon, I recon [reckon]."[15]

Some of those who did go to Texas from Tennessee were not completely satisfied, and one man returned to Concordia telling sad tales of the terrible problems Elisha and Susan Ray had faced since their emigration to the west. Writing to Mary, Charity Ann asked her sister to tell Elisha that "old John M has give him a turable [terrible] name since he landed [returned] here. I saw him and his lady at the baptist church, but I did not speak to them. I intended to enquire about you all until I heard the report. he says Sue has throne [thrown] herself a way and is as yellow as a mexican and brother E [Elisha] is doing no good at al." Presenting the other side of the story, Chellie reported to Mary that the information she had received about John M was that "he was run out [of Texas] for stealing hogs." John M and his family, Chellie concluded, "are here visiting those thay would not look at before thay left here." No doubt it was hard to return without admitting defeat, but John M made his excuses by saying that those who remained in Texas were making a mistake.[16]

Some emigrants from Tennessee to Texas stayed in the new state only long enough to finalize plans to go farther west. Although the lure of gold in California was not as strong as it had been after the strike at Sutter's Mill in 1849, the fever for settlement in California remained extremely strong. Mary Ray wrote in 1856 that "there is a company of a good many persons starts for California this morning, some from this neighborhood, and some from Ellis County." But the Ray family had found a home in Johnson County, and they had no desire to move again.[17]

Mary's sister Martha remained unmarried in 1856, but it was not long before she had a serious suitor. A widower named Upten came "down from the Brazos" to see "Mat," but, according to Mary, her sister got rid of him on the second visit. The rumor was circulating that the two were planning to be wed; in fact, Chellie Ann, writing from Searcy, Arkansas, had heard the news of the planned event. In an effort to correct the misunderstanding, Mary wrote to her sister about the facts of the situation. "You said in Bet's letter that you had understood that Mat was going to marry, well if she is, I dont know it. She denies it to me." Evidently, Martha thought she could do better than becoming the wife of a widower from the Brazos River country.[18]

By late July 1856, many were putting up tents around Bethesda Church in anticipation of the camp meeting that was to begin the last part of the month. Both Mary and Martha Ray were particularly interested because of news that Isaac Renfro's brother Henry, a university student at Baylor, would be the principal speaker at the big revival, preaching alongside "Choctaw Bill" Robinson, the itinerant preacher from Erath County that Henry met after the death of his little niece, Amanda. Isaac's wife, cousin "Bet" Renfro, had no doubt written them from Cass County with the news and, in Elizabeth's typical style, had probably emphasized the fact that Henry was single, good-looking, and smart—a rare combination. Both Mary and Martha looked forward to meeting the young man and hearing him preach.[19]

The event was eagerly anticipated by almost everyone who lived in the Johnson County Cross Timbers region. As early as April, Mary Robinson Ray wrote her sister Charity Ann that everyone was making plans for the event. Although it was still three months before the revival would begin, Mary explained, their brother Elisha's wife, Susan, and her cousin Ann were already getting ready for the occasion. Mary, who only recently had moved to Texas, was extremely enthusiastic about the event, as camp meetings were one of the few social activities available for a young, unmarried woman on the Texas frontier. People streamed to the church from miles around, especially young men and young ladies who had little opportunity to get acquainted except on special occasions.[20]

Mary Ray planned to attend for spiritual reasons, of course, but there is no question but that she was interested in the human aspects of the several days–long event. Although Mary was embarrassed to admit it, she was very interested in marriage, and the availability of eligible bachelors with interests common to hers was limited. The problem was compounded for Mary because, at twenty-five years of age, she already was considered by many to be an "old maid." It was not unusual for young ladies to be married at sixteen, and some were already enjoying wedded bliss much younger than that.[21]

Mary Ray and Henry Renfro did get acquainted during the period of the revival, but evidently the budding minister showed no immediate romantic interest in the new arrival to the Cross Timbers. Henry Renfro still had an education on his mind, and he had little time for an infatuation. Too, Henry and Mary each were "going" with someone else at the time of the revival. Henry continued to visit Miss Gerl in Cass County, and Mary had begun to date a man named Jessie Douglas in Johnson County. Consequently, the first meeting between Henry and Mary did not result in anything other than friendship.[22]

After getting acquainted with Henry at the August revival, however, Mary decided that the young Baylor student was promising, and she determined to look her best the next time they met. As a result, she visited Tandy and Gilmore's general mercantile store in Alvarado and purchased eighteen yards of calico and four and three-quarters yards of gingham. In addition, Mary bought several yards of plain cotton fabric and a hank of spun thread. It was clear that the young woman planned to do some serious sewing. Mary's appearance, even on the Texas frontier, was important.[23]

On his return trips to Johnson County, Henry and Mary always found an opportunity to visit, even if only for a few minutes after church, and the friendship between the two grew stronger as the months went by. The courtship, if it might be called one, was therefore long and drawn out, and it was to be nearly three years before the feelings between the two became serious.[24]

After Henry left the pastorate of the Independence Baptist Church in Washington County in February 1858, he spent more and more time in Johnson County. Now an ordained minister, he had no plans to return to school, and although he had not yet made a decision to leave Cass County permanently, he visited with his sister Margaret near Alvarado on a regular basis. Too, Henry's parents, Absalom and Levicy, continued their stay with their daughter. There were fewer reasons for Henry to return to Hickory Hill. As a consequence, he saw less and less of Miss Gerl and more and more of Mary Ray.[25]

Nevertheless, Henry felt obligated to spend a considerable amount of time in Cass County minding the Renfro farm and on occasion, preaching at area churches. In April 1858, he wrote to his sister Margaret, commenting on his life there. "I have ploughed hard all day this day," Henry said, "and am very tired to night, but I must answer your kind letter which I received last Saturday." He expressed relief that Margaret's family and his parents remained in good health, especially since the last word he had received was that his mother was sick. "I was on my way to Daingerfield when I received your letter," he continued. "I had done more than a half a day's work, then went to D___ that evening, preached there Saturday night and Sunday and returned to William Bockmon's that evening." Then Henry described his experiences of the day. "On my way from Daingerfield I was caught in the hardest rain I ever saw since my eyes first opened on the world. I got wet from head to foot. That night Sister Malinda put my clothes on the back of a chair to dry them, when I awoke next morning they were in flames. The vest, pants and drawers burned." Relatively unconcerned, however, Henry closed the subject commenting "But I have more and better ones. *So much for Jonah.*" [26]

Mary was becoming accustomed to her new life in Texas, as were the three Negroes Sopha, Rote, and Tank, and Mary did her best to care for them properly. Since many of the eighteen original slaves that were left in the will of Michael Ray to his children intermarried with each other, the blacks who came to Texas with Mary had family links with the Ray family Negroes in Tennessee. They endeavored to keep in touch with their kin as did the whites, and often letters from Mary's relatives in Tennessee had notes of interest. In an April 1855 letter, Mary's sister Chellie inquired about the blacks. "What have you done with Rote," she said, "and [let me know] if Sofe is like the same gal. . . . Write me how the darkeys are pleased [with Texas]." In December 1855, Mary's cousin Sallie Jackson asked that Mary "Tell Sopha that her Aunt Savery has a fine boy born 12th of last Oct. She has named him Jacob." In a heart-rending letter composed a few months later, however, Chellie wrote her sister that Mr. Coody, her husband, "has got clear of the family negos [negroes] at last. he let Joe have Ked for nine hundred, and Jesse Cothran have Julie for four. And then give Jess one thousand and fifty for Ann, that mulattoe girl of his, and give eight for a boy. Big Clark was here yesterday, she dont like her name much." The sale of the Ray family slaves in Tennessee did not influence a similar action in Texas, however. Yet, other troubles were evident within the family. [27]

William George Ray, Mary's brother, although appearing to be in good health, unexpectedly died on October 18, 1858. Since the death of her father, Mary had depended on Elisha and William George for almost everything. He had been her brother, her friend, and her confidant, and his loss created a chasm in her life that she thought she would never fill. When William George's wife Bettie decided to return to Tennessee, the loss was even greater. Little Annie Ray and the other children, Billy, Arthur, and Georgia, would be missed almost as if they were Mary's own children. Without her newfound relationship with Henry Renfro, Mary's life might have been dismal, indeed. [28]

By September 1857, Henry's mother and father finally had decided to make Johnson County their permanent home. Space was at a premium in their daughter Margaret's house, however, and it soon became evident that another home was going to have to be constructed in order to make possible her parents' continued residence there. In early 1858, Margaret wrote to her brother, then still in Cass County, that their father Absalom wanted him to come to Alvarado and build a new house. In reply, Henry said that he would be delighted to do so, for her, just as soon as he could. "If you want a house, as soon as I lay by my crop I will come and build you one." Henry was perturbed with his father's proclivity to move, however, and since one of the principal reasons for a new residence was to provide more room for his parents, Henry expressed one reservation. *"I want Father to be sure that he is settled for life before I do this."* To emphasize to Margaret that his feelings concerning his father's continual movement had nothing to do with her desires, however, Henry told her that he was "at your service, Sister M—whatever you want if it is in my power to command you shall have it." [29]

There is little question, however, that Henry needed little prodding to return to Johnson County whenever the occasion presented itself, whether for building a house or for preaching. A visit there gave him the opportunity to visit with Mary Ray, whom he affectionately called "Mollie." It was a pleasure that he relished more and more as time went by. Mary, no doubt, felt the same way, but opposition to their relationship surfaced. Some believed that the budding romance between Henry Renfro and Mary Ray was a mismatch, and they did everything that they could to break it up. One "Miss Et," herself enamored with Henry, evidently attempted to create discord by making derogatory remarks about Mary, but the effort was to no avail. In a letter to Mary, Henry said that the efforts by "Miss Et" were "entirely vain. . . . It makes me think more of the oppressed and less of the oppressor." Henry continued by saying that "Et" and one "Doctor H" would "make sad havoc of all that I hold dear, on one subject, at least. Let them talk on. Let things go as they may I am your friend now and will remain so forever." [30]

Others, friends of the Gerl family in Cass County, decided to try to influence Henry to abandon Mary Ray in favor of his former sweetheart. Although Henry had not yet made a permanent break with Miss Gerl, he knew by January 1859, when he and Mary went "to and from the prayer meeting together," that the old romance was over. Discussing the occasion, Henry wrote Mary that he knew at that time that he would be unwilling to "turn away from you for any woman upon this globe."[31]

On June 14, 1859, after a three-year courtship with the young lady from the Cross Timbers, Henry decided to break with Miss Gerl permanently, and he finally asked Mary Ray to be his bride. Soon after, he wrote a short note to her in which he reaffirmed his feelings. "My friends in East Texas are making an effort to get me to go there and marry Miss Gerl. But my heart is *thine*. While this heart beats in my bosom it shall beat in unison with *thine*. I will never forget the vows I made on the 14th of June. Remember this. I live for *thee* and for happiness. Those art *my own dear, my own sweet Mollie*."[32]

In a confidential letter to sister Chellie on June 19, an excited Mary Ray revealed her feelings for the young Baptist minister. "I went out to church yesterday to hear a Methodist circuit rider preach, he is a tolerable fair preacher, for a young hand in the cause." Mary then described to her sister another minister she considered much better. "I will give you a slight description of one that surpass[es] him by far, he is more beautiful more intellectual and more captivating [than] the person I have just described. [He] is a young Baptist preacher by the name of Henry Renfro, for instance, my affianced." No doubt this is the first announcement she made to anyone of her engagement to the Baptist evangelist.[33]

In a reply written in September, Chellie expressed absolutely no enthusiasm for her sister's plans for a wedding. "I received your kind letter a few days ago and was glad to hear from you all once more, but sorry to hear, that you was going to get married. I was in hopes that we would spend the remainder of our few days together." Then she expressed her wish that Mary and her new husband might move to Arkansas. "Mary, if you do marry, I want you and Mr. Renfro to start here immediately after you are married. I think it would suit Mr. Renfro, verry [very] well to come here. We have but one Baptist preacher in the whole place, and he is not much. The church gives him three hundred dollars this year to preach twice a month. I want you to be sure and come, and bring Mat with you." Perhaps it never occurred to Chellie that the two might have plans of their own.[34]

But there was still much to do before a public announcement of the engagement between Henry Renfro and Mary Ray could be made.

First and foremost, Henry had to return to Cass County and, once and for all, break off his long-standing relationship with Miss Gerl. Henry dreaded doing it, but to have ignored her would have been an unpardonable social blunder. Henry had to go back, and he had to leave as soon as possible. Writing to Mollie of his decision, Henry noted that "the time for me to visit East Tex. is near at hand. As the people in this settlement know nothing of our arrangements, they will doubtless tell you that I have made my departure never to return to Johnson Co. an unmarried man." Then, Henry wrote Mary of his love and loyalty to her:

> But I hope that you will not doubt for one moment my promised return, with a design to accomplish *that* which has been to me of all others the most absorbing thought of my life, especially for the last six months. I shall leave you, *dearest Mollie,* with a heavy heart. I shall reluctantly bid you adieu, and travel with a gloomy spirit until I reach my friends in East Texas. But will I forget you there? No, no, even there surrounded by relations and friends, with Miss Gerl's Rosey Cheeks and Sparkling Eyes before me; my mind will turn away from surrounding scenes and friends, to *Her* who is the object of my present love and devotion, and who is to become the *Companion* of my bosom and the *Partner* of my future happiness.

Continuing, Henry recounted the problems that he and Mary had faced in their courtship. "The people generally in this settlement and surrounding country have been exerting the utmost influence in their power to blast your hopes of happiness or at least to defeat you in one project. *You understand what this is.* And I understand why so many would defeat you if they could. Because you refused to enter into an alliance with their much esteemed friend, Mr. Jessie Douglas." [35]

Nearing the end of his letter, Henry then recounted some of the reasons for his loyalty to her. "As I see you," said Henry, "without a father to advise, without a mother to console, persecuted by an ungrateful people; the warmest pulsations of my heart are aroused and the highest sympathies of my nature flow out for you." Emotionally, the young evangelist continued. *"Orphan Girl; Persecuted one,* here is a heart to beat in unison with *thine."* In closing, Henry bid his Mary goodby: "Adieu, *Miss Mollie* . . . , until I return to claim you for my Bride."[36]

When Henry did not receive an immediate reply, he wrote once again to Mary asking for a response. "I have written freely to you and expressed the feelings of my heart," said the young minister. "What honor now it would be for you to respond to this letter. It would not violate female propriety or decorum, while it would be a great pleasure conferred on me." In reference to his trip to Cass County, Henry said that he needed additional support from Mary. "When I leave for East Texas, I want something in the way of kind words to carry about my heart to shield it from that Sweet . . . (once Sweet), [Miss Gerl]."[37]

Mary Ray was intensely pleased with Henry's messages to her, particularly the first one, and six days later, on August 10, she wrote a reply to "one of the most interesting . . . letters I have ever received. Although I have near and dear relatives, also good friends to write to me, but never have I received a letter I esteemed so much." Apologizing for her lack of knowledge concerning romance, Mary continued with a statement that "I have no experience in writing what is called a love letter, therefore you may no [know] I am not a very expert hand in such matters." In regard to Henry's reference to Jessie Douglas, Mary noted that she at one time "took him to be quite a gentleman, but he acted otherwise. I once loved him but it is not so with me now. I wish him a happy life, and when he departs this life, I hope he may be prepared to meet his God."[38]

Concerning Henry's planned trip to East Texas, Mary professed the lack of any worries about her fiancé. "I have the utmost confidence in your fidelity. Therefore, [I] will give myself no uneasiness about your return, should you live." She closed with a one-verse poem:

In this bosom beats a heart
   From sin and folly free
In a moment of blissful hope
   I gave this heart to *thee*.[39]

The first day after Henry finally left for Cass County, he sent six peaches to Mollie and enclosed a short note. He urged her to eat the fruit "in remembrance of the donor," then told her of his boredom. "Last Monday was a dull and lifeless day with me. My travelling companion could not interest me. His best talk was but the foam of folly to me. No one could make amends for the absent *one* I loved. . . . This morning I take up my solitary watch to the East. *How lonely I feel,* but I must go. Once more, Goodbye."[40]

True to his promise, Henry returned from Cass County an unmarried man. Almost immediately, Henry and Mary publicly announced their engagement, and Henry soon began the search for vacant land in Johnson County that he could secure under the homestead laws and where he could begin construction of a house in which he and Mollie might live after their marriage. After a diligent search of available properties, Henry found what he believed to be the best farmland available. It was near Alvarado—three and one-half miles northwest, and the "lay" of the land was excellent for farming. Although the 160-acre property had never been broken by a plow, the soil appeared to be excellent, and Henry had no doubt but that it would be productive. He began at once to set in motion the procedures necessary to secure the land and begin construction on a house.[41]

Knowing that two of his brothers also had plans to secure Johnson County real estate, Henry suggested to Isaac and James the possibility of their securing adjacent properties. The two men were eager to do so, and the brothers followed Henry's lead in beginning the steps to secure vacant Johnson County land. Isaac's farm was directly east of Henry's, and James's tract adjoined Isaac's on the south.[42]

As he was pleased with the significant progress of the transactions with the State of Texas in securing a homestead, the groom-to-be turned his attention to a means of supporting his new bride. Although he was a minister, he had no church. As a result, he looked forward to the Waco meeting of the Baptist State Convention to be held in October 1859, where he could survey the potential openings for ministers and possibly secure a position near his Johnson County home. Since he had not attended the 1858 state meeting at Independence Baptist Church, this was the first convention for Henry since the Huntsville meeting two years earlier that he attended while still a Baylor student. Although he had many friends statewide, he could not help being concerned at his prospects for a job.

However, the rapid expansion of the evangelism program of the Baptist Church in Texas afforded an answer. In order to address a need to spread the Gospel throughout the state, the Convention appointed a committee of three persons "to consider the subject of colportage within the bounds of the Convention, and report to the next session of this body a plan of operations in their directions." Appointed to chair the new committee was Horace Clark of Independence, the head of the Female Department of Baylor. Committee members were George W. Baines, the editor of *The Texas Baptist* and one of Henry's professors at Baylor, and J. W. D. Creath, a trustee of Baylor when Rufus Burleson was selected as president of the university. Based on recommendations from the committee on colportage, the Board of Directors of the Convention appointed several missionaries to work in the field. Included was Henry C. Renfro, who was assigned "Fort Worth, Bienville, and Buchanan, at a salary of $300." The young minister could not have asked for a better assignment than the one that he received.[43]

The appointment of Henry as a missionary, combined with excellent progress on the acquisition of land for their new home, enabled Henry and Mary to set the date for their wedding much sooner than they had originally planned. They decided to pronounce their vows before Christmas 1859, much to the chagrin of those who would have preferred that each wed someone else. Despite the naysayers, the Renfro and Ray families met at the home of Mary's brother Elisha Ray on November 24, 1859, and the bachelor and the spinster were married.[44]

Less than four months later, on March 15, 1860, Henry and Mary's property, "situated in the Cross Timbers about N.E. 13 miles from the town of Buckhannen [Buchanan]," was surveyed by one W. Douglass, C. S. [certified surveyor]. Henry and Mary began the mandatory three-year occupancy period necessary to gain full title to the land. Life was good for Henry and his wife, and both were delighted when, on September 9, 1860, a son was born. They named him James Burleson Renfro; James for Henry's brother, and Burleson for Rufus C. Burleson, the man whom Henry admired more than anyone he had ever known. They would call the little boy "Burlie."[45]

Chapter 3

The Mournful Peals
of the Muffled Drum

Little more than forty years after the formation of the United States of America, the alliances so tediously formed between the states during the formation of the nation began to unravel. The triple motivations of power, politics, and wealth had begun to drive a wedge between North and South, and the question of the extension of slavery into new territories in the West became the emotional question about which the opposing sides in the debate centered their arguments. The problem first became serious when Missouri asked to be admitted to the Union. After the usual bills for enabling a territory's entrance had been introduced in Congress, an amendment to the bill was offered which barred the introduction of slaves into the new state. In addition, the amendment provided for the freedom of slave children already there upon their twenty-fifth birthday. The proposed change, introduced by Congressman James Talmadge of New York, set off the first major constitutional debate on slavery. In the meantime, Maine also applied for admission as a state, and the stage was set for compromise. It was proposed that Maine be allowed to enter as a free state and that Missouri could come into the Union as a slave state. In addition, territory in the Louisiana Purchase north of 36° 30' would in the future be free, while all south of that line would be slave. Known as the Missouri Compromise, the bill became law on March 2, 1820.[1]

The annexation of Texas and the Treaty of Guadalupe Hidalgo which ended the Mexican War in 1848 put a severe strain on national unity and caused questions concerning the Missouri Compromise. New territories acquired as a result of the treaty were not in the Louisiana Purchase and therefore were not subject to the provisions of the act. Many Southerners felt that the 36° 30' line should be extended all the way to the Pacific, therefore including New Mexico, Arizona, and California in slave territory. Others, including John C. Calhoun, argued that Southerners should be allowed to take slaves into any territory because of their constitutional rights to property. Many Northerners, on the other hand, felt strongly that none of the new public lands should be slave. The feelings of the two groups grew so strong that the very existence of the Union was threatened. To effect a new compromise and prevent secession of Southern states, Stephen A. Douglas of Illinois and Henry Clay of Kentucky introduced a measure which could at least temporarily solve the problem. They proposed that California be allowed to enter as a free state and that Utah and New Mexico be allowed to enter as territories, to decide for themselves whether they would be slave or free when their constitutions were written prior to becoming states. To complete the proposal, a more stringent fugitive slave law was written, and the slave trade was abolished in the District of Columbia. After considerable debate in Congress, the Missouri Compromise was partially replaced with the Compromise of 1850.[2]

Four years later the fragile compromise was repealed and replaced with the Kansas-Nebraska Act, legislation which allowed for popular sovereignty in territories above the 36° 30' line. This bill regarding entry into the Union ignited the ire of many Northerners who regarded the concept of popular sovereignty as a betrayal of trust. A coalition of persons with varying political viewpoints but united in opposition to the Kansas-Nebraska Bill went so far as to call for a new political organization. On July 6, 1854, at a state convention in Jackson, Michigan, the group adopted the Republican Party as its name. The new organization declared slavery to be a moral, social, and political evil and condemned the repeal of the Missouri Compromise as "an open and undisguised breach of faith."[3]

The Kansas-Nebraska Act remained intact, however, regardless of the sentiments of those in the new party, and settlement in the two territories increased on the general assumption that Nebraska, because of its geographical position, would be free and that Kansas would be slave. In conformance with this belief, the first Kansas settlers came from areas such as Missouri, Tennessee, and Kentucky. Most were pro-slavery and some even brought their slaves with them. Sensing that "popular sovereignty" would be interpreted as the ability to vote on whether a territory would be slave or free, some New Englanders even formed an emigrant aid society to assist potential settlers whose sentiments were anti-slavery and whose votes might overbalance the huge numbers of pro-slavery emigrants who were already there. The vote for the election of legislators in March 1855 produced a flare of emotion between the two groups that could not be subdued. Worried about the possibility that imported anti-slavery forces might win, over five hundred Missourians invaded Kansas on election day, guaranteeing the election of a pro-slavery legislature.[4]

The threat of violence was so great that President Pierce issued a proclamation on February 11 condemning both sides in the controversy and warning all armed groups to disperse. Also, he called for citizens of states outside of Kansas to "abstain from unauthorized intermeddling in the local affairs of the territory." The efforts would be to no avail, however, as raiding by both pro-slavery and anti-slavery factions erupted on a regular basis.[5]

Another matter which was to have profound influence on the question of slavery was the Dred Scott case, a lawsuit which was acted upon by the United States Supreme Court in its December term of 1856. Dred Scott, a slave, claimed that travels with his owner in Illinois and the Wisconsin Territory, where slavery was outlawed because of the Northwest Ordinance, made him a free man. Scott filed suit to prove his case, and it ended in the nation's highest tribunal. The issue which was of most far-reaching importance, however, was not whether Dred Scott was free but whether Congress had the power to outlaw slavery in the territories. In a landmark decision, the Supreme Court ruled that Scott, as a Negro, was not a citizen and therefore could not sue in Federal court. Furthermore, the ruling declared that the Missouri Compromise was illegal because in it Congress deprived slave owners of liberty and property without due process of law, a violation of the Fifth Amendment. While most Southerners praised the decision, the majority of Northerners were appalled by the outcome of the Dred Scott case. Many believed that it was a Southern plot to extend slavery to every part of the nation.[6]

Although there were divergent viewpoints regarding questions such as slavery in the territories and the Dred Scott decision, the majority of Texans supported the Southern view that it was the constitutional right of all Americans to own slaves, and they enthusiastically supported the verdict of the Supreme Court. Furthermore, they believed that if this right were denied, the slave-holding states had the right to leave the Union of States just as they had joined it. This disunion, then, would "not be revolution, but a mere dissolution of partnership, and ought to involve no more trouble than making an equitable division of common properties and common liabilities." With the election of Abraham Lincoln in 1860 to the presidency, the lines of division became even more pronounced, and secessionists throughout the South gained more and more power.[7]

Henry Renfro, the recently ordained and newly wed Baptist preacher in Johnson County, Texas, supported the Southern viewpoint as did most of his friends and neighbors. Born in Tennessee, raised in Georgia, and a Texan by choice, his thoughts concerning slavery were similar to those of most young Southerners. Although Henry's father and mother had never owned slaves, the family believed in the right to do so. As his wife Mary Ray had inherited three slaves from her father, Henry also became a slaveholder upon his marriage. Like many from the South, Henry believed that the threat of abolition of slavery and the possibility of imposition of the Northern will upon the South were twin issues that must be opposed. The confrontation that he and others believed to be almost inevitable would be, in his eyes, an economic and political conflict as much as one for or against the ownership of human chattel.[8]

Since they had just begun married life and a family, however, Henry and Mary Renfro tried very hard to avoid thinking about the imminent possibility of war. In the early 1860's, their concerns were the building of their home place as well as the corrals, fences, and outbuildings that were essential to successful farming and stock-raising. They economized whenever possible, and with their savings they purchased cattle, pigs, horses, and sheep, cautiously but enthusiastically beginning the process of accumulating wealth from the rich but raw Texas land on which they had settled. As an ordained minister charged with serving several area congregations, Henry Renfro also spent many nights and all of his Sundays in the pulpit, preaching the message of the Bible to the congregations of the three churches that needed his support.[9]

But the wishes of Henry and Mary that there would be no controversy were to no avail as the unresolved problems between North and South intensified. The highly charged emotional climate in Dixie made it more and more difficult for any Southerner to set himself apart from the developing controversy. On December 20, 1860, South Carolina, in a step widely believed in the South to be legal, seceded from the Union, and by January 1861, five additional states had voted to leave the United States. In Texas, a delegation of county delegates to a state convention in Austin on February 1 voted 166 to 8 in favor of secession. A statewide referendum on February 23 confirmed the convention action when 76 percent of the persons who went to the polls voted to break their ties to the Union. One month later, on March 23, 1861, the convention ratified the Constitution of the Confederate States of America. Despite pleading from Governor Sam Houston, Texas committed itself to a forlorn hope—a collision course with violence tied to State's Rights, slavery, and the emotion that connected them as one.[10]

The bombardment of Federal forces who refused to leave Fort Sumter, South Carolina, in April 1861 by South Carolina troops set in motion a chain of events that was to last over four years and see the death of over one-half million Americans. By July, the first large battle of the war took place on Bull Run near Manassas, Virginia, and although Southern forces were victorious, the Union loss galvanized Northern resolve and prompted the call by Lincoln for seventy-five thousand volunteers. Enthusiasm south of the Mason-Dixon Line also skyrocketed as men from all over the South from Virginia to Texas joined the Confederate armies, many of them believing that the conflict would be only a skirmish, after which the Yankees would give up the fight.[11]

As the North-South confrontation became more volatile, all of the Renfro brothers, like most young men on the frontier of Texas, were caught up in the furor by early 1862. Henry, Isaac, and even young Summerfield decided that they also must become active participants in the Southern effort. "Summer," the youngest of the three at eighteen years of age, was the first to go, leaving on April 5, 1862, after answering Colonel Allison Nelson's call for volunteers for the 10th

Texas Volunteer Infantry. Upon his little brother's departure, Henry Renfro poetically expressed his feelings about the war and the enemy that Southerners were to face:

> He's gone to contend with that fiendish band
>> That threaten to subdue our southern land
> May he conquer the foe that shall him meet
>> Nor bleed nor die to accomplish the feat
> He's gone to fight for the best spot on earth,
>> The rich southern soil that gave him birth
> On the march, in the camp, on the battlefield
>> O, God be his strength, his sun and his shield
> Willing to go, but reluctant to start,
>> From loved ones at home he dreaded to part
> When goodbye was o'er, the parting tear shed
>> Summerfield marched to the field of the dead.
> I've prayed for the brother in days that are past
>> I'll pray for the brother while life in me last
> When our time is o'er, our life is revered
>> We may meet again in the courts of heaven [12]

Mary tried to understand the compelling forces that caused Henry to want to be a part of the war. Any objections from her would have been fruitless, and therefore she voiced none when Henry told her that he was going to follow Summerfield into the Confederate Army. After a sad parting on May 5, 1862, Henry rode to Fort Worth, where he enlisted the next day as a private in Company C of Major William H. Griffin's 21st Texas Infantry Battalion. Henry left Mary in charge of the couple's business interests, including the operation of the stock farm, and before the end of the month he was on duty in Houston training to be a part of the state's coastal defense. Like his brother Henry, Isaac Renfro also left behind his wife "Bet" and joined Griffin's Texas Infantry as did the brother-in-law of the two men, Isaac A. Jackson. [13]

Because he was an ordained minister, Henry was told at the time of his enlistment that he would be considered almost immediately for appointment as the regimental chaplain. His friend and former Baylor president Rufus Burleson recently had enlisted under similar conditions as the chaplain of Joseph W. Speight's First Texas Infantry Regiment, and Renfro had no question but that he would receive a similar position. For unknown reasons, however, Major Griffin chose not to grant the request, and Henry Renfro remained in the ranks as a private soldier. As he reminded his superior officers of the promise, however, the issue became one of rank and authority rather than one of an unfulfilled promise, and Renfro became more and more estranged—not only from Griffin, but also from his company commander, Captain Samuel Evans. Evans evidently thought Renfro was trying to evade regular duty by becoming a chaplain, and consequently, he made life difficult for Henry in every way that he could. It was not long before Henry was detached from his company and sent to Eagle Grove on the north side of Galveston Island to stand guard duty on a remote dock which offered no protection from rain and winds.[14]

After days of what he considered to be abuse and mistreatment from officers of Griffin's Regiment, Henry Renfro decided that he must change his situation, whatever the consequences. He was sure that his status as an enlisted man under Captain Evans would not improve and that, in all likelihood, it would become worse. Consequently, Henry decided that the situation warranted desperate measures. He did not desire to leave the service; he had voluntarily enlisted, and he believed strongly in the cause for which the South was fighting. But he was also convinced that he had been misled and that his talents were being wasted—even misused. He felt that he must leave Evans's company and Griffin's Regiment, and he knew of one way to do so which, although unusual, was assumed to be legal and honorable. Only weeks before, a private in Speight's First Texas Infantry was unhappy with his situation so he left the regiment and joined another company in another unit. When the commanding officer of the Trans-Mississippi District of the Department of Texas was asked to rule on the matter, he said that the offender could remain with his new command. The word of the affair had made its rounds among enlisted men in the various Texas regiments, and the disposition of the case gave credence to the conclusion that leaving one military organization to join another was an honorable way to deal with an unpleasant situation.[15]

Sixteen days after his enlistment, Private Henry C. Renfro decided to test the ruling. On May 22, 1862, he left Houston bound for Camp Speight, Brazos County, to join the First Texas Infantry Battalion.

There, he was warmly greeted by his old friend and professor from Baylor, Rufus Burleson, who personally introduced the fellow minister to Colonel Speight. Henry told his story to Speight and Burleson, sparing no detail, and asked to be inducted into Speight's Regiment. He acknowledged that he had voluntarily taken the oath to serve in the Confederate Army but noted that officially he had never been mustered into Griffin's Regiment or any other. Believing that he was within his rights to do so, Colonel Speight personally gave the oath of allegiance to Henry Renfro, mustering him into Company B of the regiment. Finally, the young minister thought, he could serve his country and be happy in doing so.[16]

Major Griffin, however, had a much different view of the matter. He considered the disappearance of Private Renfro to be desertion, and he resolved to take the steps necessary to bring him back to Houston. After questioning other enlisted men in his command, Griffin learned of Renfro's plans to go to Speight's Regiment and, after a conference with the acting commander of Company C, Lieutenant W. H. Coltharp, he decided on a course of action. On orders from Griffin, Coltharp detailed Sergeant J. T. Hardin and two privates to Camp Speight to arrest Renfro and return him to the command.[17]

When Hardin and his detail reached Camp Speight, the sergeant was escorted directly to Colonel Speight to make his report. After listening to Hardin's explanation of Major Griffin's request for Renfro's return, Speight politely declined to honor it, then wrote a letter for Hardin to hand-carry back to Houston. Private Renfro, said Speight, "whom you have ordered arrested, is in my camps. He represented to me, that he had taken the oath to serve the Confederate states usually administered, but had never been mustered into any company or Regiment. That he desired of his own choice to attach himself to this command." Continuing, Speight said that because of the circumstances of the case, he had himself sworn Renfro into Company B of his regiment. Citing his reasons for doing so, Speight said that he was "under the impression that Genl [P. O.] Hebert [Commander of the Department of Texas] had decided that such a course of proceeding was right; and I had it in my mind at the time, the case of Private Fuget, who, under the same circumstances, left a company of this regiment and was mustered into the Service in another Regiment." In a conciliatory note, however, Speight left the matter open for discussion. "I have declined to deliver Mr. Renfrew [sic] up to your detail, but, at the same time, I desire to act advisedly in the premises and will therefore forward a statement of facts to Genl Hebert for his decision. I trust this will be satisfactory to you, assuring you, in the mean time, that should the General decide that you are entitled to him, I will send him to you with great pleasure." [18]

After Sergeant Hardin reported empty-handed to Major Griffin, the battalion commander resolved to do whatever he could to win Renfro's return. Consequently, he immediately wrote a personal request to Captain George R. Nelson, Aide-de-Camp and Acting Assistant Adjutant General of General Hebert, asking for the return of Henry Renfro to his regiment. He noted that Renfro had been sworn into Speight's Regiment "by Colonel Speight himself," and that the Colonel "refused to deliver him to the detail." He then asked Commanding General Hebert "to send Private Renfrow [sic] back to Capt Evans' Company." Evans, Griffin continued, had paid Renfro $25.00 of his own money as a part of the enlistment bounty and "has the receipt for same." The bounty, Griffin implied, constituted the intention of Renfro to enlist directly into Evans's company; therefore, the parallel to the case of Private Fuget was invalid. Evidently General Hebert concurred with Griffin, as Henry Renfro was forced to return to Houston within days. [19]

On Tuesday, June 17, Mary Renfro received the first news from Henry that he had been required to return to Houston. Writing a letter to him the following morning, Mary told her husband that she was "truly sorry and troubled to think one whom I love and desire the happiness of so much as I do yours, have [has] to stay in such a disagreeable place as Houston, and among such men as there is [are] at that place. Oh! it grieves me to know this is the case with you." Continuing, Mary wished that Henry could have "got [sic] to stay with bro Burleson in Speight's Reg[iment]." Worried that her husband might try again to leave, she implored him to be cautious. "Mr. Renfro, do not venture too much in trying to get away from that abominable city. Oh! that I could release you, I would have you away in a few hours." [20]

Mary then gave her husband an account of everything that was happening at home. "We are well and hearty, and have been ever since you left home, our little Burlie grows fast, and is one of the most interesting children that I have ever seen. He is geting [getting] to be [a] very rude and mischievous boy," Mary continued, "he still sucks yet. . . . If it were not for my Burlie, what would I do, he is the greatest company, [and] satisfaction that I have since you left home." Speaking of the farming operations, Mary noted that the crops and livestock seemed to be in generally excellent condition. "Our corn looks fine[;] with one more season we will make a splendid corn crop, I think. Bro. Elisha says the hungarian is very good, the oats tolerable good. Sofe pens the pony's [ponies] once a week, she attends the stock very well so far, two young colts came since you left. . . . The sheep are not but very little trouble yet. I do not think any of them have strayed off. . . . Sofe has been helping James with his wheat. Worked four days last week and will work until twelve today which will make in all six and one-half days."[21]

Closing her letter, Mary returned to Henry's plight in Houston. "Mr. Renfro, I will ask and beg of you again not to undertake to leave that despicable place unless you know there is no danger by you leaving. Do not rush into danger. This is the advice of your wife with tears in her eyes. I hope there will be a way fixed for you to get away without running any risk atal [at all], and that soon. . . . I will close with these words. My pray[er] is that you may out live your troubles . . . [;] I hope you may have the privilege of coming home to your family to stay all the time." Mary then asked Henry's sister, Margaret Harris, to add a footnote. "Bro Henry," she said, "do not yield to despair. The blackest sky today may wear a sunny face tomorrow. I do hope that peace will soon return to this once happy land."[22]

Six days later, Margaret once again wrote to her brother Henry. She had received a letter from him as well as correspondence from two brothers and one brother-in-law, all in Confederate service, and she was eager to inform Henry of what she had heard. "After reading your interesting and welcome letter to me, and one from William and Paulina [Bockmon], Brother Isaac, and one from Brother Summer all at the same time, my feeling is such that I would rather weep than write." William Bockmon and his family were well, she wrote, and "Summer is now in camps [within] four miles of Little Rock." Thinking of his brothers and hoping to see them soon, Summerfield told Margaret of a rumor he had heard that Henry and Isaac had joined Ewine's company of Colonel Allison Nelson's 10th Texas Volunteer Infantry Regiment. A search for his brothers in the regiment yielded no results, however, and Summer wrote to his sister, "Alas, I looked in vain."[23]

Summerfield Renfro was like many young Southerners—adamant that what he believed was right and confident that the Southern cause, almost in itself, provided the momentum necessary to defeat the Union. Writing to his sister Margaret from Arkansas, Summer said that he soon expected the 10th Texas to engage the Northern troops. "I do not care when we have to meet them," he said. "We are all anxious to meet the enemy—we are ready for them any day." Conscious of the uncertainty of war, however, Summerfield ended his note to Margaret with a request for their spiritual support. "I ask you all to pray for me that I may be shielded in the day of battles and return at last to my home."[24]

In a letter to her brother Henry, his sister described her feelings upon receiving Summerfield's letter. "I can not pen these words without tears flowing from my eyes," said Margaret. "Bro Henry, I have often wanted to see you, but I don't think I ever wanted to see you worse than I do now. Oh, will the time ever come [once] more [for] me to see my dear brothers again in this life. I would rejoice to see you all again."[25]

Recalling Henry's recent problems, Margaret said that it was her "daily prayer that you may get away from that place of trouble, but I want you to leave there in peace and harmony. We are afraid to send you a horse—afraid you will make the bad worse. We want you to be safe when you leave again and not be in danger of anything your unkind officers can do with you. Look before you leap. I do not think you will have long to stay there. I hope not at least." Henry realized that he must reconcile himself to the unpleasant situation, however, as it appeared that there was to be no transfer or promotion to chaplain, at least not in Griffin's Regiment. Yet, the attempt to change regiments did accomplish something for Henry, as he wrote on July 5 that he was no longer being subjected to the ordeal that was instrumental in his leaving Griffin's Regiment. Henry told Mary "not to uneasy yourself any more than you can help. I do not have to undergo the hardships now that I did two weeks ago. Guard duty is considerably lighter than it was. And there are houses for us to shelter in when it rains on the wharves and we do not have to take the rain and cold wind as we did at Eagle Grove."[26]

By November, a ray of hope came to Henry Renfro in a letter from Rufus Burleson with the information that he planned to leave the chaplaincy and that he wanted Henry to replace him. Although

Henry was excited about the possibility, he recognized the disappointments he already had suffered, and he refused to let his hopes soar. He did, however, make an effort to learn if the appointment as chaplain was possible if offered. In a letter to Mary written on November 11, 1862, he told his wife that "Bro Burleson sent me word by Lieu [Lieutenant] Iglehard that he had or was going to resign his position as chaplain of Col Speight's Regt, and that he wanted me to take his place. I talked to some of the most talented officers in this Batt [battery] and they say that there is nothing to prevent me from going provided I can be promoted to the chaplaincy of that Regt. Bro Burleson requested me to write to him about it which I did immediately. I hope the matter can be effected." [27]

It appears that Henry Renfro continued to fulfill the duties of a minister of the Gospel regardless of whether or not he was officially referred to as a chaplain. The men in his unit knew that he was a Baptist minister, and they regarded him as such. Writing to Mary, Henry told his wife of a request for his help from a dying man. "One of the soldiers of our Batt[ery] sent for me last night to read and pray for him. I did so and left him apparently resigned to his fate. I expect he is dead this morning." The word from Dr. Burleson about the opening in Speight's Regiment gave him hope of a formal ministry, however, and Renfro's spirits were much improved even at the possibility of the change. [28]

But hopes are easily dashed, and discussion of a transfer was all but forgotten by Christmas 1862, when Henry wrote a poignant letter to his wife with the awful news that he was going into battle. "I have one half an hour to prepare for a force march to Galveston, and the first of that I will give to you and my *Sweet Burlie.* The Federals, it is said, landed a great force on Galveston a few days ago, and we are ordered there immediately. God only knows what is to be the result. I expect to discharge the duties of a soldier as well as I can, and should I fall I will fall at my post. If these are my last words to you, I want you to be sure and have *our Sweet Burlie well educated.* Neglect everything other than that. . . . I leave you and my *darling* boy in the hands of a merciful God. No pen can paint, no tongue can tell the keen sensation of the word *farewell.* May God guide and direct you in all things. Goodbye Mollie, Burlie, and all." [29]

The Southern strategy did not call for an immediate attack on Northern positions in Galveston, however, and by December 31,

Henry wrote again from his unit's camp at Eagle Grove, the terminus of the railroad bridge from the mainland on the north side of Galveston Island. "My Dear Mollie," he said, "Tomorrow is the day the Confederate forces have to attempt to retake Galveston. I expect to bear my part in the struggle." The letter continued:

> For the love I have for you, for my Boy and my relations and country I expect to fight and die if it is the will of God. There are many things for which I desire to live, the greatest of all is to guard the interest and welfare of you and our *Sweet Burlie*. To see his training. I have desired above all to give him a good education. I give him to you, my dear Mollie, and ask you to allow no other person to occupy a higher seat in the affections of your heart as he does, for I know that you love him with all the strength and fervor of your maternal heart. I want you to keep all my letters and poetry about *Burlie* till he gets old enough to read; and should I fall in battle, I want my pen knife sent to you for a *keep sake of me*. The *pin* I gave you when we were married I want you to keep and give to Burlie when he gets old enough to wear it. I have always desired to give all my name sakes a good present. You must at least give James Henry a good present for me when he gets old enough to appreciate it. How I would love to see you and our *darling* Burlie this evening. But I cannot. *Fare thee well* and if forever *still forever fare thee well*. Can I, can I say farewell.[30]

The demands of conflict gave no time for Henry to mail the poignant letter that he wrote from Eagle Grove on New Year's Eve 1862. Major General John Bankhead Magruder, who had replaced General Hebert as head of the Department of Texas, moved quickly to gain an advantage against the Union forces. Placing cotton bales on their decks as protection from Northern bullets, Magruder decided to send two river steamers carrying artillery fieldpieces against the Federal naval force. Before daylight on January 1, Renfro and others from Griffin's Regiment boarded the schooner *Neptune*, offshore from Eagle Grove, with orders to fire the two twenty-four pound cannons on the ship. Supported by the ship *Bayou City*, the *Neptune* charged the Federal ship *Harriet Lane* at dawn. Fire from the Confederate naval guns surprised the Northern sailors, who expected fire from shore batteries but not from other ships. The *Harriet Lane's* crew recovered quickly, however, and a shell from the Yankee pivot gun shattered the hull of the *Neptune*, causing the ship to sink in shallow water.

Fortunately, neither crewmen nor soldiers from Griffin's Regiment were lost. The *Harriet Lane* was captured after being rammed by the *Bayou City*. With the loss, the other ships, with the exception of the Northern flagship, the *Westfield*, left the scene of action for the high seas as an alternative to surrender. The *Westfield's* captain, Commander W. B. Renshaw, set a fuse to the ship's magazine rather than give her up. He was killed in the explosion.[31]

On land, the tide of battle changed after the capture of the *Harriet Lane* and the abandonment of the fight by other Union naval forces. Without the protection of the ships offshore, the Forty-Second Massachusetts Infantry, with 264 officers and men, was captured by Magruder's men. The battle for Galveston was over, and the Confederates had carried the day. Union forces suffered 150 casualties. Twenty-six Southerners were killed, and 117 were wounded. Finally, Henry Renfro was able to mail his letters. Before doing so, however, he added a postscript to the foreboding correspondence in which he had all but predicted his own death. "Dear Mollie," he said, "these were my words to you before the battle in Galveston, while my heart bled at every thought of home. But oh, how thankful I am. God has preserved me amid all dangers."[32]

The end of the January 1 battle did not, however, end the presence of Federal ships in Galveston Bay. On January 13, Henry Renfro reported to his wife that "2 to 6 vessels are in sight all the time and we do not know what a day may bring forth at Galveston. Indeed, we are all the time looking for an attack, but it may not come this month. We are making all the arrangements possible for the early or late approach of the enemy." He reported that within the past week the enemy had bombarded Galveston once more, but "there was nothing killed but a goat, and they shot 105 bombshells into the city and Fort Point close by." Prudently, however, the Confederate forces stayed on a high alert because of the possibility of another invasion.[33]

Indeed, Henry Renfro believed that the capture of the island by the Southerners was a mistake. "It seems to me," he said, "that it was bad policy to retake Galveston with such advantage . . . the enemy had over us and with the knowledge that it would be so expensive and hazardous to hold it." He then described a scare that he and the others in Griffin's Regiment had had on the night of January 12. "About three o'clock we were aroused from our slumbers by the ringing of bells and the beating of drums and [we] thought that a fight was upon us, but we soon found that it was a house on fire and we went and put out the fire and returned to bed."[34]

After the victory of the Confederates over the Union forces on January 1, many soldiers in Galveston began to believe that the end of the war was in sight, although Henry himself was not so gullible. In a letter to Mary, Henry described the sentiment:

There are a great many who say that the war will end in spring or summer next. We have good news in general from all parts of the country. According to reports we have been more successful for the last month than we have been since the war first began. But I am so incredulous that I cant draw as much comfort from the newspapers as some others; however, I think the prospect for peace is brighter now than it has been before, though it may be that this is but the evening of the abominable war and the dark night is yet to come. My own opinion is that this is the *midnight of the war*. And I hope that the old *war clock* will run fast till she soon runs down; and that peace and love will again dawn upon the world.[35]

Peace was indeed a scarce commodity in the South in 1863, and the continuation of the conflict and prolonged separation strengthened the love between Henry and Mary Renfro. The letters between the soldier and his wife were the one constant that helped both of them survive the lonely days and nights of the war. "How I delight in reading letters from you," wrote Henry, "and how tremulous with anxiety I feel till I come to the last word in your letters or at least till I read of the health of you and Burlie and all." Yet mail did not take the place of the personal contact for which they yearned. "Mail facilities seem inadequate to express and make known the occurrences that are daily transpiring and the thousand thoughts that agitate the minds and hearts of the husband and wife, parents and children, bros and sisters so far separated. How many things I could tell you if [I] was with you which I cant express on paper. How long is the present state of calamities to exist, and the innocent suffer instead of the guilty."[36]

Still, all correspondence received was eagerly anticipated, and when Henry Renfro received a letter from Mary during the night of January 12, he wrote to her that he "eagerly . . . arose from slumber, seized your letter and ran to the light to read the lines your hands had penned for me alone to read." However, his wife's letters did not always bring cheering news, and in this case, she told her husband that her separation from him had begun to tell on her. She wrote that she "had the *blues* in the deepest degree" because of her husband's absence and that she found it hard to get over them. In Henry's answer, he acknowledged that he had similar problems. "O, Mollie," Henry replied sympathetically, "has your heart felt the pain and agony that mine has felt? Then you are troubled indeed. And as for me I look for nothing else but trouble and sorrow until this war is over at last. But it grieves me," he continued, "to hear that those at home are in like trouble with myself. I know that if I could brush away care and sorrow from your heart they should not be your companions a day longer."[37]

In closing his letter to Mary, Henry entreated Mary not to worry and suggested a spiritual solution to her problems. "Let me ask you again," Henry wrote, "not to trouble yourself about me and refer you again to the promises of the gospel as the healer of all of earths sorrows. In the 1 epistle of Peter 5 Chap and 7 verse we are exhorted to cast all our care upon God, who careth for us. There is one consolation, tho the enemy kill the body, they cannot kill the Soul. They cannot follow the Spirit to Heaven, invade the happy realms of the glory world, nor disturb the songs that warble from immortal tongues. But let me ask you to pray fervently for me that I may be preserved in the day of battle and shielded from harm."[38]

In addition to her loneliness, Mary was clearly feeling the stress of operating the farm by herself, and although Henry was sympathetic to the problem, he offered no real solutions. "All I can say to you about the stock and the farm," he wrote, "is for you to do the best you can with them." Henry placed great confidence in his wife's abilities, however, and he even asked her to continue his earlier negotiations for the purchase of an adjacent farm known locally as "The Russell Place," offering as payment livestock that would be difficult to keep while he was gone. Although the farm was owned by Hezekiah Russell, one "Brother New" was the person with whom she had to negotiate. Evidently, New tried to convince Mary that Henry had offered money in addition to animals for the property, and he refused to close the deal on the terms which had originally been discussed. Making a real effort to complete the transaction, however, Mary offered to pay New ten dollars cash as well as the livestock for the property. She was somewhat worried about what Henry would say, but he was pleased with her efforts. "You did right in paying old man

New the ten dollars. I hope he is satisfied now, and will not misrepresent me any more about our trade. He will move away from that settlement I suppose." Although the transaction appeared to have been completed, problems later developed which prevented Mary from finalizing the purchase. It would be nearly ten years before the Renfros could finally buy Hezekiah Russell's farm.[39]

Still, Mary's handling of the property proved to be competent despite the fact that it was the first time in her life that she had been thrust into a management role. Too, she had the option of calling on Henry's brother, James, for help when needed. Although James had his own priorities and was not always as interested in helping Mary with her problems as Henry might have liked, he nevertheless was of great assistance. In Henry's letters, he consistently suggested to Mary that she ask James for help with some of the more difficult problems that arose. When two colts strayed from the farm onto the unfenced range, for example, Henry suggested to his wife that she contact his brother. "If roan and fanny are not yet found try your best to get James or Mr. Watson to go after them immediately. I do hope," said Henry, "that James will not refuse to do this. I am willing to pay any body well for finding them."[40]

But help from James was not to continue indefinitely, however, as the young man was convinced that he also should join the Confederate Army. If he did not, he reasoned, he would surely be drafted and thus would have no say in where he would be sent or what he would do. James asked Mary to inquire of Henry Renfro as to what unit he should join should he enlist. Perhaps thinking of his own errors in selecting an excellent regiment, Henry was noncommittal. "Tell James to do as he thinks best," said Henry, "about where he will go when he goes into the service." Henry was more emphatic about the possibility of his brother being drafted, however, and he warned James to look at it closely. "I have read the exceptions from the last Conscript Law," Henry wrote, "which are objectionable indeed; it is a mean law. James must not talk too free about it. A man who has 500 head of cattle, 250 head of horses, 500 head of sheep, or 20 negroes is exempt from the law, which shows the law is doggish and I fear will result in mischief to the South."[41]

As for himself, Henry was becoming reconciled to the army, to Galveston, and to his position as a private soldier. In a letter to Mary written in January 1863, Henry described his situation.

I am still blessed with most excellent health and [it is] well for me that I am for I have to stand guard every other night. I stand upon the wharf—there are ten of these which are situated thus. From 3 to 4 hundred yards in the bay and about the same distance from each other, with bridges 18 feet wide leading from the land to them. And no person is allowed to pass without a written pass from headquarters. We stand 2 hours and rest 4 making 8 hours for every man in 24. How lonely I feel and especially at night when all but the guard is sleeping except the star spangled heavens above and the roaring billows of the gulf. That is an hour for memory and for tears and the poor soldier is left in darkness and solitude to reflect on the horrows [horrors] of this war and of the *loved ones at home.*[42]

The consistent disappointment at not being appointed as a chaplain had dulled Henry's enthusiasm; yet, he continued to receive encouragement from Rufus Burleson. On January 26, soon after the recapture of Galveston, Henry wrote to Mary with the news. "I received a letter from bro. Burleson yesterday," he penned, "at the close of which he said he was *determined* to have me in a pleasant and useful position before he quit [the chaplaincy]. He is looking for Col Speight and says he will arrange the matter as soon as he reaches [him]." Henry did not comment to Mary about his own opinion concerning his chances.[43]

Henry did his best to keep in good spirits, however, and on Sunday morning, February 1, 1863, he wrote a long and positive letter to his mother and father. "After a long silence," he began, "I have concluded to address you a few lines this Sabbath morning. Thanks to our Heavenly Father I am in possession of as good health as I have ever enjoyed since my first recollection. Though I am not surrounded by as favorable circumstances as I could desire, yet the circumstances by which I am now surrounded are more favorable than they were one month ago this morning. Then I was surrounded by ball shot and shell which seemed to threaten the annihilation of our army at this place; but now all is quiet." Henry told his parents, however, that he was not sure as to how long the city would continue to be safe from attack. "But we do not know how long it will be before we will be called upon to meet the enemy again. Four or five vessels are in sight all the time and when they will attempt to land their forces and take the city is not known to us."[44]

Henry commented that he did not think that another attack on Galveston was imminent but that he believed that those conditions could quickly change. "We think . . . they will not bring a force sufficient to take Galveston, while Vicksburg is in our hands; but if the Federals ever get in possession of Vicksburg we may look out at this place for a fleet and forces sufficient to overwhelm us. Though, we are all the time liable to a bombardment from their place of anchorage which is some 4 or 5 miles distant. They were shelling the city . . . last Friday and I had to close my letter to Mollie abruptly to fall into line to be ready in case they attempted to effect a landing." [45]

The lingering worries about the possibilities of a Federal invasion of Galveston were always in Henry's thoughts, and these concerns were bolstered by other reminders of the futility of war which added to the dreariness of his and his fellow soldiers' lives. On the last day of January, Henry and others in his company participated in a cheerless funeral which added to their unceasing yearnings for home and family. "Yesterday evening," Henry wrote, "we formed a funeral procession and marched to the graveyard to bury a citizen of this place. He was an officer and was killed at the battle of Corinth. . . . The scene was solemn. We slowly moved along, the 'Brass Band' in front. The first piece they gave us was an old familiar tune I had often heard at Independence, called 'The Old Folks at Home.'" Henry then described the emotions that he experienced:

> What a tide of feeling rushed upon my heart, as the mournful peals of the muffled drum fell upon my ears as it beat our measured, funeral march to the grave. How I was carried back to the days of my boyhood and how I contrasted the pleasures of those days with the calamities and distresses of the present crisis, I will not attempt to describe. Then I was an innocent, happy boy, surrounded by home and friends, now I was engaged in an ungodly war enduring all the hardships of a camp life and liable at any moment to be exposed to all the dangers of the battlefield, and the music reminded me that I was "far from the old Folks at Home." [46]

Henry's yearning for home and family was made worse by the news that much of the 10th Texas Infantry Regiment had been captured in the battle of Camp Hindman, Arkansas. Writing to his mother and father, Henry said that they had "doubtless heard of the capture of our forces at the Military Post in Arkansas. Among the Texas Regt that were captured was that of Col Nelson's or Mills' in which is my dear bro. Summerfield. And I recken he was among the captured. O how I would love to be with that dear, darling bro. whether as a *captive* or *as a conqueror*. I hope he will be paroled if he has been taken, and will get to come home. Mother must not grieve about him for probably that will be the means by w[h]ich he can get to come home." In a letter to Mary, however, Henry noted that he had mailed two letters to Summerfield, "but my poor brother will not get his, I fear. I see that the prisoners captured in Ark. have been taken to Cairo in the state of Ohio [Illinois]."[47]

Aside from thoughts of his family and the fate of his brother, Henry thought almost continually about what he would be doing on the farm if he were not a soldier. Writing to Mary, Henry revealed his preoccupation with home. "I dreamed last night that my corn was planted in good style. It should not be covered deep and if it is it must be harrowed off or brushed off in some way." In another letter, Henry went into more detail about some of the things he believed needed to be done. "Tell James Henry he must take good care of the sheep if he wants one of them. Have the sheep put in the Woods pasture of nights and not in the horses lot among the hogs[;] and if there is any barley for the ewes with the young lambs they should be turned on it till the lambs are old enough to keep out of the way of the hogs. Be very careful about feeding away too much corn—none at all only to Buck [Renfro's horse] unless it is something that will die without it. You have not told me about the meat you killed[;] whether you have enough or not."[48]

A few days later, Henry continued his item-by-item listing of things that needed to be done. "Mollie I forgot in my answer to your last letter . . . that I want you to get some body to put a bell on the gray mare that lost the bell that was on her. You will have to get a bell some where and a good coller [collar] and get some body to put it on for you. I want Soph to plant corn early and have the oats sowed early also. You could probably get Cheps Negro man to help her about planting the corn and sowing the oats. And if James [Renfro] and Elisha [Ray] will attend to my two year old horse colts before they leave for camps it will confer a great favor on me." Without question, it must have been difficult for Henry to be away when he believed so many things needed his personal attention.[49]

With all of his worries about the chores that needed to be done on the farm, however, Henry thought less and less about the problems of being in the army. "I am getting to be tolerably well reconciled to my fate," he wrote Mary, "and am as well satisfied as could be expected. Sometimes I sing and sometimes my head is bowed down and my harp is hung upon the willow. *Home, Sweet Home* is the only thought that moves my heart when I am alone but when I am in company I pass away the time as pleasantly as possible." In an attempt to relieve any worries that Mary had about his being in the military service, Henry told her not to "uneasy yourself about me any more than you can help."[50]

Continuing his optimistic appraisal of his situation, Henry noted that he was "as well satisfied as it is possible for me to be under the circumstances. Indeed as well as I could be any place this far from home and in the army. I and those who volunteered at the time I did received the rest of our bounty last Monday. Also the whole Batt [Battery] received two months pay and I have got the rest of the money that was due me for my horse which makes me 85 dollars, which I would send to you if I knew you would get it, but I hear complaints that money has been stolen between here and Houston, and I am afraid to send it by mail." Wishing to please his wife, however, Henry found a dress pattern in a Galveston store he believed to be her size. "Write in your next if you would like to have it and if I can get it off I will get it for you." Concluding his positive letter, Henry said that he was pleased to hear that "your sweet Burlie had not forgotten to say Pa. How I want to see the little white headed creature and kiss his sweet lips."[51]

But the moods of persons far from home are especially subject to change, and Henry Renfro's were no exception. On February 15, he told Mary that he "must say something to you this gloomy sabbath evening. Where are you now? And are you as well as I am this evening? And do you feel as sad and gloomy as I do? Surely little Burlie does not but probably, my dear wife does. O how sick the heart can get when one desires the presence, association, and friendship of those he loves, and yet knows that fate has decreed that it shall be otherwise. It is too much happiness for a wretch like me to meet his kind and tender wife to mingle our tears of joy together and talk over the many events that have transpired since we parted or to take up my lovely boy, press him to my bosom and kiss his sweet lips once more." Five days later, on February 20, 1863, Henry composed a long poem named "Home, Mollie and Burlie" that ended with this verse:

Let me go to my home, I'm tired of strife
  The horrors of war and the ills of life
 What a world of bliss, what a world of joy
  At home with Mollie and Burlie Boy. [52]

Despite Henry's assertions that he had made up his mind to be content with his lot in Galveston, he still nursed a hope that he could become a chaplain. He felt strongly about his calling as a minister, and he believed that he was wasting his time and talents by remaining a private in the army. Despite the promises of Rufus Burleson to help Renfro to receive an appointment to Speight's Regiment as his replacement, no correspondence was forthcoming from anyone but Burleson. Although he had no doubt that the former Baylor president was doing what he could to help, Henry determined that his appointment was no one's priority, save his, and that it was unlikely that anything would happen unless he made it so. Consequently, Henry decided to make one more try, and on March 1, 1863, he addressed a letter to the Adjutant General of the 2nd Regiment, Arizona Brigade, commanded by Colonel George Wythe Baylor, a kinsman of R. E. B. Baylor, one of the founders of Baylor University and the person for whom the institution was named. "I have the honor," said Henry, "of applying to the comdg. Genl for the position of Chaplain in the 2nd Regt. Arizona Brigade. I am a minister by profession, but am at present living as a private in Capt Evans Company, Griffin's Battalion." [53]

Less than two weeks later, Henry wrote his wife Mary about his new effort to gain a chaplaincy, noting that he was

> concerned about my application to . . . Baylor's Regt. Yet I am not over anxious to go to Arizona, but I would have to go to Vicksburg if [I] was to get into Speight's Regt, as I hear it is there. Though I may not get into either and it may be better for me as my health has been so very good since I have been on the Island that it may be better for me to remain here. I will try to be content with my lot wherever it may be cast; and I shall not make any more efforts to change my situation. I am getting tolerably expert on handling an Endfield [Enfield] rifle and probably it would be better for me to stay in this company. [54]

Regardless of where he was to be permanently stationed—in Speight's Regiment, in Baylor's Regiment, or in Galveston—Henry joined others in hoping that the war would soon end. "There is great talk about peace of late," he wrote Mary, "Every body seems to be hopeful. Those who seem to be posted think that peace will be made in 8 months." Henry sincerely hoped so, if not for relief for his own situation, for that of his brothers. Henry learned that his brother James also had become a soldier. Altogether, four, and perhaps five, of the Renfro brothers were serving the Southern armies. Henry was particularly worried about Summerfield, but he tried to reassure Mary and his parents about the young man's situation as a prisoner of war.

It distresses me to hear how you all seemed to be troubled about bro. Summerfield; and especially my old Mother. I feel for her because I know something of parental affection. But Mother gives herself a great deal of unnecessary trouble about her children. If bro. Summerfield is a prisoner in the enemies' country he will be treated as a prisoner of war and not a traitor. . . . I see in the Galveston News that the Arkansas Post Prisoners were taken to Alton Illinois and would not be exchanged soon. Well, they will not have to fight nor perform any military duty—which will be a great relief. I have just come off guard and know how hard it is to perform this part of the duties of a soldier.[55]

For the first time, Henry was beginning to sound as if he was really adapting to his situation. "I have not missed a roll call nor failed to stand guard at my time . . . since a week after the battle here and that is as much if not more than any other man in our co. can say." Henry then described the routine that he followed.

Every 3rd night I have to stand guard. This or something else has broken my rest at night—so I seldom ever get a good nights sleep. Probably it is attributable to my hard pillow—and harder bed; but more probably to my Spirit's restlessness and my troubled thoughts that are ever on the wing. But when "balmy sleep, tired nature's sweet restorer," comes upon me and I am blessed with a sweet oblivion from my troubles and hardships— when I am carried on fancy's wings to the fairy land of dreams, and meet up with you and am permitted to hold communion with you and have a pleasant play with Burlie or carried still further I meet with bro. Summer-field in the bright plains of vision and am blessed with a moment's rejoic-ing, then comes the sergeant or corporal of the guard and calls me, and lo, all the ills from which I had been resting come upon me again and I have to rise and return to my post. And when my two hours are out, I return to my hard bed to sleep, it often takes me an hour to get rid of the thoughts that filled my mind when I was on post. But I will say no more on this subject. Everything here is quiet."[56]

The calmness of Galveston and the routine of the Confederate garrison did not, however, constitute an ideal behind-the-lines situation. Rations for troops were becoming more and more scarce, and the shortages were becoming more serious. Henry had written to Mary about the problem, and, in her answer, she told him that she wished that she could share the food that was available on the farm. In his reply, written on March 2, 1863, Henry told her more about the shortages and described the reaction of the soldiers to the lack of good food. "Mollie, you seemed to be sorry for me on account of our fair [fare] in camps, our course bread and poor beef, and I know that you expressed what your heart felt when you said it would be a pleasure to divide your eatables with me. And I know it would be a pleasure for you always gave me the best piece in the dish and made me eat the little extras that you denied to all others but Burlie. I think of this every time I eat when the boys are busy in getting and almost snatching the best, if there is any best[,] for themselves." Describing his most recent meal, Henry told his wife that he had "just eaten a dinner of bread and molasses—a few less than a half dozen dipped into the same dish." Unfortunately, the situation showed no promise of any improvement; indeed, it appeared that it might become worse. Would the war never end?[57]

The Parson recognized the complexities of the conflict, and he was not optimistic about its early completion. "There is great talk here about peace;" he wrote, "men are proposing to bet large sums of money that the war will end in three months. But I am not so saguine [sanguine]. Yet the indications are favorable for the war to be ended soon. I am confident that it would end immediately if the Confederacy would agree to go back into the old Union. But that will never be done."[58]

The press, Henry reported, was relatively optimistic about an end of the war. "The papers give great news about the bad state of affairs in the North and the prospects for an early peace. It seems that the day is beginning to dawn. We hear that thousands are deserting from the Northern Army and coming into the Confederacy. But whether we hear the truth or not is the question I am not prepared to answer." The possibility of an end to the conflict between North and South reminded Henry once again of his brother Summerfield and his lack of information about him. "It seems a hard matter to find out what has become of the Arkansas Post Prisoners. I would be so glad to hear from bro Summer. How often have I thought of the words of David, when he said, 'Is the young man Absalom safe.' How glad would I be to know that my young bro was safe and among the living. I have studied more about him today than I have in a long time. There has no one gone to war that has carried so much of my affections as bro Summerfield."[59]

The lack of information about Summerfield had ominous implications, and Henry was no doubt more worried than he wanted his family to believe. The fact that the young man was a prisoner was not, in itself, a problem about which they should worry excessively. However, since neither Henry nor his parents had heard anything from him since his capture, Henry was beginning to develop a gnawing feeling that something was very wrong. His anxieties were soon to be fulfilled.

On June 10, 1863, Absalom and Levicy Renfro heard tragic news. Summerfield was dead of smallpox. The family was grief-stricken on hearing that their most dismal fears had been realized. In an effort to express his sorrow, Absalom placed the Renfro family Bible on his desk and wrote these words:

> We heard of the death of our beloved son Summerfield on the 4 of June 1863 but no particulars of it. Only that he died with that fatal disease, the smallpox. Away from home and all that was dear to him. O how I loved him I loved him I loved him. He died in defense of Southern Rig[h]ts aged 19 years. My youngest child, the darling of my old age. This will be read when the hand that makes illegible this scrawl will be cold in death. Wrote this 10th day of June A D 1863 by A C Renfro.
>
> My dear boy left home on the 5 of April 1862 to battle for his country's rights in an unholy war brought on by Northern fanatics.[60]

Like his father's grief, Henry Renfro's was such that he felt that he must put in writing his feelings concerning the death of his dear brother, Summerfield. Three weeks after hearing the awful news, he wrote a poem which he dedicated to "my dear old mother." Henry poignantly capsulized his feelings in the first verse:

> How lonely I feel when I think of the past
> And know that my dear brother is with me no more
> And the skies so bright are now over cast
> With a gloom I have not witnessed before.[61]

There is no record of what must have been terrible times for Absalom and Levicy Renfro. To have lost their youngest son must have caused grief beyond measure. Yet, what must they have thought about the continued danger to their sons Henry, Isaac, and James—all still exposed to the possibility of a similar death?

For Henry and Isaac, both still stationed in Galveston, the immediate possibility of an engagement with the enemy was unlikely, if not remote. Other campaigns in other theatres of the war were more important to the North than the retaking of Galveston, although a blockade of Union ships continued after the Federal loss of January 1, 1863. Henry reported on March 2 that "yesterday evening the Brooklyn got up steam and sailed up close to the bar and returned again to her anchorage and the early part of the night two small vessels crossed the bar and returned without doing anything." The blockade was to remain in place in an attempt to contain the Confederates, but another battle for Galveston was not to occur.[62]

Another struggle was looming on the horizon, but in this case it was one in which the Federal army would not be engaged. This fight was between the men in gray—a mutiny of some enlisted troops at Galveston against their officers. The cause was one that had been simmering for weeks, the lack of decent food combined with incessant drill. On August 4, Lieutenant-Colonel E. F. Gray reported to his brigade commander that "the only issue now given consists of beef, molasses, and corn meal. The latter, even when good, is exceedingly heating in its effects on the blood, and when, added to this, it is sour, dirty, weevil-eaten, and filled with ants and worms, and not bolted (and the troops without the means of sifting it themselves), it becomes wholly superfluous that it is exceedingly unwholesome." Gray then apologized at being forced into being a complainant, but he said that he deemed it to be "one of the first duties of a commander to watch with zealous care the welfare of those under his command."[63]

Other officers were not so sympathetic as Gray, however. His commander, Colonel and acting Brigadier-General X. B. Debray, commander of the Second Brigade, Second Division, Third Infantry, reported only a few days later to his headquarters in Houston that "the Third Regiment of Texas Infantry yesterday refused to drill and obey the orders of their officers, evincing tumultuous and riotous evidences of insubordination." Debray then ordered a dress parade on Broadway for all men, carbines loaded. In their front, Debray placed several companies of artillery with their cannons loaded with canister and then addressed the men. "I then advanced to the front of the regiment," Debray recalled, "and addressed a few words to these misguided men, assuring them that military discipline must be observed and respected, no matter at what cost of life, and that I was there determined and able so to preserve it." Debray then ordered the men to stack their arms, which they did reluctantly.[64]

The mutiny did not end with Debray's actions, however. Within days, Debray disarmed Luckett's Regiment after the men refused to drill. He depended upon Elmore's artillery regiment for support if the infractions became worse, but Debray noted that even that regiment was "of doubtful disposition." Debray said that "I am at every moment apprehending a collision between the men of Cook's regiment and them. Threats have been uttered." Griffin's Regiment, fortunately, was out of the city at the time the mutiny occurred, and as a result, Henry Renfro was not involved. His earlier complaints about the wretched quality of the food, however, lead one to believe that he and his companions would probably have been a part of the uprising had they been nearby. Debray noted that "the arrival of Gould's regiment and Griffin's battalion here would only add fuel to the conflagration." Continued firmness by Debray, however, effectively ended the mutiny by the end of August.[65]

As a result of the failed mutiny, the lack of *esprit de corps* among the troops, the unimproved rations, and the general disillusionment with the progress of the South in the war, the Confederates in Galveston had little to which they might look forward as 1863 neared its final quarter. It was a monotonous, uninspiring life for which many of the soldiers, including Henry Renfro, would gladly exchange one more exciting, even if more dangerous, if the chance should occur. Henry had little longer to wait before his opportunity would arrive.

Chapter 4

To Help Him Sing Dixie

Patience must have become virtue for Henry Renfro as he waited the almost endless months for word about a possible appointment to the chaplaincy. His hopes finally were fulfilled, however, and upon the return of Griffin's Regiment from the field to Galveston in late September 1863, orders were waiting which stated that Henry was to leave his present command immediately and report to Colonel J. W. Speight's 15th Texas Infantry, at that time on duty in Louisiana. At long last, after nearly a year of what seemed to be a fruitless labor, Parson Renfro had been appointed to the position of chaplain that had been filled since April 1861 by Rufus Burleson. Henry was over-joyed. In honesty, he had given up on the possibility of his selection for the post; now, he would actively serve as a minister once again. The bonus in the transfer was that Henry finally would be able to leave the much-disliked Griffin's Regiment and Evans's company even though the likelihood was almost certain that he would go to a much more dangerous region. The excitement and enthusiasm concerning the change were such for Henry, however, that his geographic location seemed unimportant.[1]

There is little question but that Henry Renfro's appointment was made by Speight solely on the recommendation of Rufus Burleson. Although the law provided that appointments were to be made by President Jefferson Davis, this was rarely the case. Without the benefit of knowing the religious denominations of men in the units, Davis no doubt would have appointed some chaplains whose religious preferences were different from those of the men in the field. Too, since chaplains usually associated closely with their commanders and other officers, it was said that "in nine cases out of ten, these officers prefer a good *companion* to a good *minister*." There is no evidence, however, that this had any bearing in the appointment of Henry Renfro to the chaplaincy of the 15th Texas.[2]

The official position of Confederate chaplains was relatively undefined. Although paid the same as lieutenants, $85.00 per month, chaplains were sometimes not treated as commissioned officers and lived instead in a sort of limbo between the higher and lower ranks. Although they occasionally were allowed to have horses while the men in the ranks walked, regulations specified that they draw the same rations per diem as privates. Their official position in battle situations also was unclear. One historian notes that "some fought, others did not. Others were good preachers, others were not. Some stayed on the front lines with their men; others did not." It is interesting to note that there was a shortage of chaplains throughout the Civil War, and it is surprising that Henry Renfro was not placed in such a position much earlier in the conflict. One Southern publication, the *Southern Christian Advocate*, noted that "there are enough worthy, intelligent and truly pious preachers serving as private soldiers to fill every vacancy in the army."[3]

Regardless of the delays, the theatre of operations, or the danger, however, Henry Renfro was glad to be chosen for the new duty, since an additional perquisite in his promotion was that he would be able to go home on a short furlough before leaving for his new position. If only for a brief time, he would be able to see his Mollie and little son Burlie once again. Within hours of his notification of promotion and transfer, Henry boarded a car of the Houston and Texas Central Railway bound for Millican, the northern-most terminus of the line. He then traveled overland to Johnson County. Although no record remains of the homecoming, there is little question that there were tears of joy as he arrived, unannounced, at his farm at the head of Crill Miller Creek northwest of Alvarado.

The days at home with his family passed quickly, however, and it was not long before Henry was on his way to Waco to confer with his friend and former teacher, Rufus Burleson, who had returned to Cen-

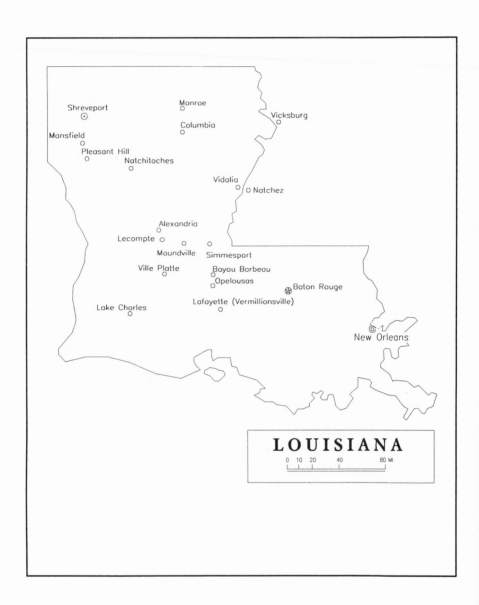

Figure 2. Louisiana during the Red River War.

tral Texas and Waco University from scenes of fighting in Louisiana only weeks before. Since Renfro was replacing his former teacher as the chaplain of the 15th Texas, he realized that he had to learn as much as he could in the short time available about his duties and his responsibilities. After a detailed briefing, the two old friends shared fond recollections of their happier days in Independence. With the knowledge that this short get-together might be their last meeting, farewells were sad and poignant when Henry left for Houston once again. In the Bayou City, Henry met and said goodby to his brother Isaac, who also had received a furlough to return home.[4]

Before leaving Houston on a Louisiana-bound train, however, Henry took time to write a short note to his wife. "My dear Mollie," he said, "I am now at the depot and Isaac will leave [for home] in a few minutes. I designed to write you a long letter but did not have time after writing Mothers. There is great talk of peace now, everybody says that peace will be made shortly. And I must close[;] Isaac will give you all the news. Goodby. May the Lord bless you and preserve you is my prayer." At long last, Henry's wish for a substantial position in which to serve the Confederacy had been realized.[5]

On September 8, 1863, the 15th Texas Infantry had been ordered to the area near the Atchafalaya River in central Louisiana to stem the possible advance of Federal troops toward Alexandria. Skirmishes with the enemy occurred every few days, but on September 22, an uneasy quiet prevailed as the regiment went into camp for nearly a week, enjoying the cool, pleasant fall weather.[6]

The relaxation of camp life was not to last, however, as intelligence was received that an advance contingent of Federal troops had occupied Stirling's Plantation at nearby Bayou Fordoche. On September 28, Speight's Brigade, along with other troops under the general command of Brigadier General Thomas Green, crossed the Atchafalaya River in a slow, drizzling rain. At sunup the next morning, the Confederates advanced toward the plantation, and they came under heavy fire about four hundred yards from the Union lines. Orders were given to charge, and an hour's heavy fighting brought victory to the 1,200 Southerners who were on the field. The large Federal force of 854 men counted 16 men killed, 44 wounded, and 453 captured. Casualties in Southern ranks were heaviest in the 15th Texas, which alone lost 15 men. Fifty-two men from Speight's Regiment were wounded in the conflict.[7]

A well-deserved and welcome five days' rest after the Battle of Stir-ling's Plantation was soon over, however, as the news that a new Federal advance up Bayou Teche might extend to Vermillionsville (La-fayette) and from there into Texas. The 15th Texas, along with the other Southern troops that had fought in the last fray, marched on October 6 to Moundville, three miles north of Washington, Louisiana. On the 7th and 8th, they continued their march on the Alexandria road passing through Ville Platte, then Chicot, a small village of "three buildings and . . . 4 hotel signs." They passed Belle Cheny Springs; then they reversed and marched north fourteen miles before reaching Jackson's Bridge. By the 12th, they headed north once more, then to the east through Cheneyville where they camped three miles below town. Evidently, the rumored Federal advance toward Texas was without foundation, and the constant debilitating marches had served little purpose.[8]

Colonel Speight, returning from Texas after a sick leave, reached the brigade at its camp site near Cheneyville on the evening of October 12. As Speight reassumed command, he was briefed on a new threat of twenty-five thousand Union troops under Major Gen-eral William Franklin which were positioned near the Texans at Caren-cro Bayou. In response to the peril, General Taylor, the commander of Confederate troops in the District of Western Louisiana, ordered an immediate concentration of Southern army units near Moundville. Speight's command therefore marched through Holmesville twelve miles south before stopping for the night. Early the next morning, October 15, they passed through Moundville before making camp near midday. A conflict seemed imminent as orders were received for troops to cook two days' rations. Yet, once again, the tension soon dissipated as marching orders were given, then canceled. It appeared that the troops would be in camp for a few days, at least.[9]

During the period of rest near Moundville, a major change in the structure of command was unveiled. A group of several organizations including the 15th Texas Infantry, the 22nd Texas Dismounted Cav-alry, the 17th Texas Consolidated Dismounted Cavalry, the 31st Texas Cavalry, the 34th Texas Cavalry, and the 11th Texas Battalion were merged into one brigade. Picked to lead the new combination was General Camille Armand Jules Marie, Prince de Polignac, a French-man who reported to Louisiana after serving under the commands of Generals Beauregard and Bragg. The Texas troops were not happy with the selection, and they wasted no words in saying so. Mutiny was a real possibility until Lieutenant General Richard Taylor promised to replace Polignac if he did not perform well in a combat situation. Unable to pronounce his name, the Texans nicknamed their new brigade commander "Polecat," then promised to give the new leader a chance, at least until he had the opportunity to prove himself in the next engagement with the enemy.

One of Polignac's first actions was to grant leave for Colonel Speight to return to Texas once again. Colonel James E. Harrison, who had substituted for Speight before as leader of the 15th Texas, assumed command. Summoned on October 20 by Polignac to give an assessment of problems among the Texas troops, Harrison cited absenteeism, lack of energy, failure to enforce discipline, and the failure of regimental officers to set examples to the men. Additionally, Harrison pointed out that the lack of shoes and clothing, combined with sickness and noncombat detail work, contributed greatly to the lack of morale. No doubt, Polignac resolved to do his best to find solutions.[10]

As is often the case in war, however, Polignac would have little or no time to put any changes into place, as orders were received the morning of the 21st to prepare to march once more. Traveling in darkness and in the rain, the Texans marched twelve miles up Bayou Boeuf to camp. All of the brigade except the 22nd and 34th Texas, which moved forward to support Tom Green's cavalry, were able to secure some much-needed rest until October 25. The brigade then went up the road to Holmesville, then to Cheneyville again on the 26th. Here, the unit's wagons and mess cart finally caught up with the men, and their arrival, according to one soldier, "afforded our mess pleasure similar to that experienced from a meeting with some old cherished friend."[11]

Among those who arrived with the brigade wagons and camp equipage was Chaplain Henry Renfro. Riding a horse he probably had purchased in Vermillionsville, Henry had followed the rumors, directions, and sometimes misdirections given by soldiers who had "heard" of the last location of the 15th Texas. He finally found the Brigade Supply at the old campsite at Moundville and resolved to stay with it until it caught up with the main command at Cheneyville.[12]

In the three days the brigade remained in camp until October 29, Chaplain Renfro took advantage of a time of full stomachs after a good meal to fulfill a promise to the men, made by the brigade commander before his arrival, of a religious revival. Although the open-air preaching was no doubt inspiring, a dismal rain poured down steadily. Despite the need of many of the troops in the brigade for spiritual reinforcement, particularly after the devastating engagements with the enemy that they had recently endured, Renfro preached to a small, yet enthusiastic, crowd. Besides the rain, however, another distraction began when a disagreement between some of the men and one Dr. Blanchard "resulted in a contemptible bombardment of his tent with potatoes and chunks." It seemed obvious that piety was difficult to find among many of the veterans of Polignac's Brigade.[13]

Fighting of a serious nature was not far off, however, as Harrison's 15th Texas was ordered on October 29 to report to General Tom Green eighteen miles below Moundville for picket duty. Upon arrival there, they were joined by the 18th Texas Infantry, detached from Walker's division and commanded by Colonel Wilburn Hill King. Four days later, the two regiments were joined by Colonel Oran Roberts's 11th Texas Infantry. It became obvious to all involved that the concentration of troops indicated a more serious purpose than picket duty, and when the cavalry brigades under Bagby and Major arrived, commanded by Tom Green himself, it was known by all that action was close at hand.[14]

After advancing toward Bayou Bourbeau, three miles from the camp of Federal troops under General S. G. Burbridge, Green ordered his brigade to halt while a plan of attack was formulated. "Major's brigade was to advance mounted over an open prairie to the west and strike the Union left flank;" wrote one historian, and, "Bagby's men were to move forward dismounted directly west of the road; while Roberts infantry were to charge south through a partially timbered area between bayou and road. Roberts aligned his men with the 11th Texas, 355 strong, on the left; the 18th Texas, 320 men, in the center; and the 15th Texas, 275 strong, on the right because its members had longer range Enfield rifles and would be more exposed to the advance. Two companies of the 15th Texas and one from the 11th Texas were thrown out as skirmishers. Green rode by and called for Harrison to 'run right over them and give them Hell.'"[15]

In a description of the role of the 15th Texas in the battle, Colonel Harrison recalled that his "command was in plain view of them [the Federals]. We drove them Back one mile and a half to their main encampment before which was a deep ravine. This was exactly to my front, and here thy [sic] made a desperate stand, and I too, for the first time was in the timber. It seemed to rain Minee [sic] Balls, grape and sheel [sic]. With out Counting noses, I sprang before my men and ordered a charge. A Shout and a rush then our Rifles told on their routed fleeing confused masses, and thy [sic] ley [sic] in heeps [sic]." [16]

The battle was a disaster for the Federal troops. After being told that the Union soldiers were about to flank his regiment, Harrison reversed his position and ordered his men to charge, "producing among them a scene of wild confution [sic], Men tumbling from Horses, screaming, Others throwing up their hands for mercy, Horses running wildly over the field without riders, others rooling [sic] and tumbling. Directly all was still." Losses in the Northern ranks included 25 dead, 129 wounded, and 562 missing. Most of those in the last category were prisoners of the Rebels. On November 4, "Confederate details buried the dead left on the battlefield and collected their wounded in the courthouse at Opelousas where sympathetic women of the area cared for them." [17]

The Battle of Bayou Bourbeau was a chilling baptism of fire for Henry Renfro. Despite the fact that he had participated in the Battle of Galveston on January 1, 1863, he had never been in such a pitched fight with extremely high casualties. There is little question but that his talents as a minister were in great demand from the dying and wounded as he moved from one to another, praying for those still alive and over those who were beyond help.

Yet despite the carnage of the battle, the surviving soldiers remained ready for continued action. Writing to a friend, Lieutenant Colonel Harrison noted that his "men are dirty and ragged—having been away from our [supply] train two weeks, but we are in good spirits and ready for another brush if occasion offers." Indeed, said Harrison, the Union soldiers were finding "the road to Texas 'a hard road to travel.'" [18]

By November 20, the nearly exhausted yet spirited Texans were on the road once again as Tom Green issued orders for Colonel Roberts to move his men to Simmesport, where they joined Taylor's infantry. They were not to remain there long, however, and they once again began their march in miserable weather, reaching Stirling's Plantation by December 5, Morganza on the 7th, and upriver to Bayou de Glaize on the 12th. By the 13th of December, they reached the small town of

Mansura; they then proceeded to Alexandria on the 14th. After a successful crossing of the Red River on December 17, they then proceeded to within two miles of Alexandria on the 18th and 19th. Yet, the Texans retained their morale and drive. "Notwithstanding our men are almost worn out by hard marches and extreme hardships and many of them bare footed," wrote Henry Renfro, "yet they are in fine spirits and as a general thing they disdain the idea of submitting to Yankee rule and authority."[19]

In a letter to his sister Margaret, Henry Renfro discussed his brigade's movements and the resulting reacquaintance with old friends. He reported on December 24, 1863, that the regiment "left Walker's Division [Colonel Wilburn Hill King's 18th Texas, detached from Walker's Division] at Sims Port in some 15 miles of the Mi[ssissippi] River, so I do not get to see my friends and relations in that division of the army." He pointed out, however, that there were many old friends from north central Texas in his regiment. "There are several men . . . that I am acquainted with," he wrote, " . . . one from Co. C, Nelson's Regt—Mr. Torbett of Buchanan. You can tell Mr. McAnear's folks that Dan is here and in tolerable good health."[20]

Upon leaving Simmesport, Polignac's Brigade and the 15th Texas were ordered north along the valley of the Ouachita, away from the scenes of action of the past months, and rumors among the troops suggested that they were headed for Arkansas and an engagement with Union troops there. Writing home about the possibilities, Henry related that it was "thought that Mouton's and Polignac's Brigades will meet [General Sterling] Price's army and fight the Yankees somewhere in Southern Ark." The Texans went through Winnfield on December 23rd, then moved toward Monroe the next day. In a letter written on the 24th from "Camp on the Road," Renfro noted that he did not believe that the brigade would remain in Monroe "over a day or two, but travel on towards Price's Army, which we hear is in or about Fulton, Ark. The boys do not like to march in that direction," he said, "but I do not care much where we go, yet I do not desire to go far into Ark.; but at this time last year O, how my poor heart would have leaped for joy to have been permitted to go to that state." Recalling that Arkansas was where his brother Summerfield was captured, Henry noted that he was constantly reminded of him. "And every day too I hear the boys talking about 'Camp Nelson, Little Rock, and Ark. Post,' all these places are dear to me yet sound dismal to my ear, and the animating notes of Dixie fall heavily upon my heart, when I remember that brother *Summer* wrote to me to help him sing *Dixie.*" [21]

On a more positive note, Henry noted that the regiment expected to have some of their best food in some time the next day. "We expect to have some good eating tomorrow on our *mess at headquarters.* We bought 3 turkeys and 6 chickens and about 75 pounds of pork and plenty of fine potatoes and other things which are not very common in camps." [22]

It is obvious that Henry's situation as a chaplain was much improved over that of a private soldier. He was treated as an officer of the regiment, he rode a horse, and he was accorded the respect normally given to a minister. Yet, his months as an enlisted man caused him to be extremely sympathetic toward the men in the ranks. Consequently, he sometimes looked for opportunities to be away from them because of his compassion. "I have been foraging," he wrote, "and enjoy it much better than traveling with the poor soldiers, unless I could let every one that is sick and tired ride my horse which is impossible. Indeed I enjoy myself better out of their sight. To see them marching along and panting under their burdens and falling by the . . . side makes me think of brother Summerfield and I invariably carry a gun or two and very frequently let them ride, and think to my self[,] did any body show my brother such kindness. I reckon not." Ending his note to his sister Margaret, Henry wrote that the regimental band sometimes played at night and often attracted sympathetic citizens from the areas around their tents. "Tonight," he said, "some ladies came into camps to hear the *Brass Bands.* Among the pieces they played [was] *Dixie.*" [23]

The rumors that Polignac's Brigade would march north into Arkansas continued as the infantrymen marched to Richardson Plantation east of Monroe on January 1, 1864. Despite freezing rain and ice, the brigade was moved again, this time to a new camp south of Monroe. There, the soldiers fought pneumonia and bitter cold, suffering because of lack of proper uniforms and shoes, a problem which was addressed on the 5th with the issue of new footwear to those in need. As no additional marching orders were received until January 17, the footsore troops had nearly two weeks to recuperate from the weeks of forced marches. [24]

The orders that were issued on the 17th did not, however, call for additional movement toward Arkansas as almost everyone had anticipated. Instead, Polignac's Brigade moved south along the Ouachita River to Columbia before crossing the river on the 20th and arriving in Harrisonburg on January 24. Soon, the reasons for their being there were clear; they were to act as a "covering force for Confederate engineers rebuilding the batteries on the river at Harrisonburg and at Trinity." Although the brigade must have appreciated the slower pace they enjoyed while camped, the location offered few if any amenities and a return to a structured military life. Daily drill practice no doubt brought grumbling from the men already exhausted from constant marches, and the lack of provisions and forage resulted in commonplace fare brought in from other areas.[25]

Boredom and tedium, therefore, were possibly a factor in General Polignac's request for permission from General Taylor to attack a Union outpost at Vidalia, on the west side of the Mississippi River opposite Natchez, Mississippi. Polignac hoped to replenish the Brigade's corrals of horses and mules, secure additional supplies, and provide an opportunity to capture the Federal garrison there. With General Taylor's blessing, Polignac took 550 men against the garrison on February 7 only to find that their advance had been discovered, and an effective barricade of cotton bales blocked the streets of the town. Polignac, however, chose to feign an attack rather than retreat and thus provide time for his men to round up livestock along the river. Unsheathing his sabre, Polignac yelled to his men, "Follow me! Follow me! You call me 'Polecat,' I will show you whether I am 'Polecat' or 'Polignac!'" The charge began with the Frenchman at the head of his troops and leading them toward the Union battlements.[26]

As Federal troops awaited the advance, they received able assistance from three gunboats across the river at Natchez which had been alerted to the Confederate attack. The combination of rifle fire and artillery from gunboats was deadly, and Polignac had no desire to lose men or equipment needlessly. Therefore, he pulled back in a guarded retreat to Harrisonburg, arriving there on February 10. The attack must be considered a success, however, as a count of livestock captured included four hundred horses, mules, and cattle. In addition, Polignac had erased any desire of the men to have him replaced. He had gained their respect.[27]

The movement of Polignac's Brigade for the next weeks was extremely demanding. After continued fighting with Federal troops and gunboats around Harrisonburg and along the Ouachita River, they occupied the town of Trinity on March 8, then moved to join Taylor at Alexandria to counter an expected advance up the Red River by the Union Army under the command of General Nathaniel Banks. There, the brigade was to become an active participant in one of the major Southern strategies of the Civil War—one that would lead to retreat and partial abandonment of Louisiana by Northern forces.[28]

When General Kirby Smith assumed command of the troops in the Trans-Mississippi Confederacy, he was convinced that if the Union Army wanted to move into western Louisiana and Texas, the only practical and efficient route was the valley of the Red River. Consequently, Kirby Smith made preparations to rebuff an invasion along that waterway. He erected fortifications along the lower Red River at Alexandria and Fort DeRussy. He fortified Camden and Shreveport, and he established arms depots along the shortest lines of communications between the river and Confederate troops in Texas and Arkansas.[29]

By January 1864, the Confederate commander's educated guess concerning the Union's intentions to invade the valley of the Red River was confirmed. The Northern armies planned to use the important Louisiana waterway as a springboard to the invasion of Texas. The Union commander, General Nathaniel Banks, decided to make the advance utilizing ships to carry troops to points along the Texas coast and up the Red River rather than risk an overland march that presented many hazards.[30]

Sherman arranged for ten thousand Union soldiers to join the Federal ships under Admiral Porter at the river's mouth. There, they were to meet Banks's army, which was to march overland to the rendezvous from the Teche. Together, the two armies were to move north on the Red River and arrive at Alexandria on March 17. From there, Union strategy called for a move up the river all the way to Shreveport, where they would conquer the last resistance from the Confederate command. Major General Frederick Steele, with another Federal army in Arkansas, would move south toward Shreveport and there join Banks's army in a pincer movement to defeat the Confederates. The Northern plan appeared to be a logical one; however, it had far too many variables to be effective, including a cutoff date, April 25, by which the task was to be accomplished or the expedition abandoned.[31]

Mouton's Division, to which Polignac's Brigade and Speight's 15th

Texas Infantry Regiment were attached, was to be a major player in the Southern effort to thwart the Union move to crush the Confederate armies and move into Texas. On April 8, the division joined that of Walker and Tom Green's Texas Cavalry, a combined force of about eleven thousand men, and waited for the arrival of Union forces three miles from Mansfield, Louisiana, at Sabine Cross-roads. There, Mouton's Division led the attack on Union lines supported by Major's and Bagby's brigades, and after fierce fighting, the Federals were routed. Only two days from Shreveport, the well-laid plans of General Banks were dashed. Even a Union victory the next day at Pleasant Hill, thirty-three miles west of Natchitoches, Louisiana, failed to slow the Northern retreat. It was obvious that all hope of reaching Shreveport by April 25 was lost. Nearly a month later, on May 18, another battle occurred at Yellow Bayou between Polignac's and Wharton's divisions and the rear-guard of the retreating Union army commanded by Brigadier General Joseph A. Mower. The Confederate loss was 452 killed; the Union lost 267 men. But the Red River Campaign was over. Although the North won the Battle of Yellow Bayou, it had lost the Red River Campaign. On the 12th and 13th of May, 1864, General Banks evacuated Alexandria, and the invading naval flotilla left the Red River for good.[32]

Late in the evening of July 28, 1864, Chaplain Henry Renfro was camped with the 15th Texas at "Camp Boggs," near Lecompte, Louisiana. He thought of home and Mollie, as usual, but he had no way of knowing that a momentous event in his life had occurred earlier in the day. Mary thought of Henry, too, and when the pains of childbirth began, she wished mightily that her chaplain husband could be with her. Not that she was alone. With her at the home that Henry had constructed near the head of Crill Miller Creek were friends and relatives who were familiar with the needs of a woman during childbirth. Her sister Martha, her mother-in-law Levicy, and her sister-in-law, Margaret Harris, stood by to provide the help that was necessary.[33]

Luckily, the birth was relatively easy, and the little girl and her mother survived the ordeal with few problems. Mary named the new baby Margaret Annette Renfro—Margaret, after Henry's favorite sister, Margaret Harris, and Annette, in remembrance of Mary's mother, Ann Ray. She would be called Annette, and as she grew up, she would become an attractive, vivacious, and headstrong young lady who was almost as legendary in the community in which she lived as her famous father.

Henry's desire to return to Johnson County was intense in the weeks that followed Annette's birth. The Southern cause was steadily deteriorating, and it sometimes seemed that the continued loss of life in service to a forlorn hope might best be ended once and for all. The complexities and ravages of war absorbed his thoughts, and he worried about the consequences of brigade commander James Harrison's rumored orders to send the 15th Texas with Walker's and Polignac's divisions far from Texas into battles east of the Mississippi River. He would be even farther from home, from Mary, and from Burlie. When the soldiers in the ranks heard of the proposed tactical movement, many were unhappy that they might be moved farther from home and family to support other armies in what many considered to be a losing cause. Henry was somewhat sympathetic to men in the ranks who objected to the march to the east, as he believed that their mission, as Texas troops, was to secure their state from the onslaught of Northern soldiers. To cross the Mississippi, they reasoned, removed their ability to do so.

Indeed, the objections to the new orders became so intense that talk of desertion was rife. By early August, the discussion changed to action, and over a hundred men of Polignac's Division were absent without leave. James Harrison, the commander of the 15th Texas, wrote that "there has been a greadeal [sic] of excitement in my Brigade. I have lost 123 deserted, [who] *won't cross the river*. There are many others who dislike it [the order] extremely." As a result of the desertions and the subsequent morale loss, General Kirby Smith suspended the disputed command on August 22, citing the problem of Union gunboats on the river as well as the mental well-being of the troops.[34]

As a chaplain, Henry Renfro had his hands full during this period. He could not in good conscience tell those who contemplated desertion that they had to stay. Like Renfro, many had problems and responsibilities at home that desperately needed attention. On the other hand, Henry believed that to give up the fight that already had cost so much would be almost a betrayal of those who had given all for the Confederacy. He appealed, then, to the individual conscience of those with whom he counseled, asking each to consider the consequences of his actions both to himself and to his country. Although he would have liked very much to have been among those who returned to Texas, Henry remained with the regiment, as he considered the chaplaincy a trust which he could not violate. He believed that the word of God desperately needed to be preached during the horrors of war, and that as the regiment's sole minister, he was the one with that responsibility.

For the South, the progress of the war became more and more discouraging, and less than a year after the Federal loss in the Red River Campaign, the Confederate States of America was a defeated nation. General Robert E. Lee, commander of the Army of Northern Virginia, surrendered to General Ulysses S. Grant at Appomattox Court House on April 10, 1865. But after the battles along the Red River of Louisiana, Henry Renfro was one of thousands of men for whom the war effectively had ended long before. Polignac's Division moved north to Arkansas and then marched back to Texas before disbanding in May 1865. The 15th Texas and Chaplain Henry Renfro went home again, this time for good.[35]

It is interesting to speculate concerning the reasons for the demoralization of the men in the 15th Texas and the South as a whole as the war came to a close. Without question, many of the Trans-Mississippi troops seemed to have a different view of the conflict than did those in the eastern battlegrounds. They saw their positions as protectors of their homes in Texas, and they were reluctant to go farther from home as the tone of the conflict seemed to turn decisively in favor of the North. Yet, there were also other seeds of discontent which no doubt had an influence on their actions. In Richard Berlinger's well-written treatise on the subject, *Why the South Lost the Civil War,* he cites other reasons as well. Declining morale in 1865, declared Berlinger, was a critical factor, and this was caused by uncertainty of the aims of the war. Whereas the continuation of slavery was, without question, one of the principal aims of secession in 1861, many Southerners saw it as a dead issue toward the end of the conflict, particularly after the Emancipation Proclamation. Berlinger also declared that nationalism faded as Southerners saw fewer and fewer reasons for making the ultimate fight. The arguments for state's rights and lack of centralized government were obviated, noted Berlinger, because the Jefferson Davis administration often did not appear to be substantially better than that of the Union. "Those who came to see states rights and a centralized government as the cause for which they fought," Berlinger noted, "were very often the same people who denounced the centralized despotism of the Davis administration." Yet, most Southerners recognized that it was important that Jefferson Davis and his government be strongly supported. The Reverend George Woodbridge sermonized in favor of the Southern leader when he noted that "Whatever has a tendency to destroy public confidence in [the leaders'] prudence, their wisdom, their energy, their patriotism, undermines our cause."[36]

It may well be argued that Southern religious beliefs were one of the most important factors that led to the outbreak of war. There was a strong feeling among Christians in the South that their cause was espoused by God, and therefore He would not allow them to be defeated. Southern historian James W. Silver summed up this philosophy with a statement that if, before the fighting commenced, "Southerners as a whole could be convinced that the Confederacy and the war were also of divine inspiration, they might well build up an indestructable morale. Because of the limited industrial resources of the South, the success of the Confederacy depended on the degree of intestinal fortitude developed by the man in the street and on the farm. He needed to identify himself as a member of God's chosen people and his country as a fulfillment of the destiny of history."[37]

Southern morale, however, was lagging on many fronts as the conflict neared its end. Although both North and South prayed to the same god, the tide of battle seemed to increasingly favor those north of the Mason-Dixon Line, and a feeling developed in many Southerners that if they were not winning, God certainly must not feel that they were in the right. "The devout," declared Richard Berlinger, "had no motive to keep struggling against God's will." As one Mississippi soldier wrote, "[W]e can never be conquered only by the ruling power of God but alas! if God is against us, we are ruined forever."[38]

Without doubt, however, there were many Southerners who would have continued the fight regardless of the circumstances. Many Southerners had no slaves, yet fought for slavery. Others little understood the war's commercial significance, the state's rights conflicts, or the battles for congressional turf; yet, they continued the fight for their homes, their families, and their regional chauvinism—a feeling that the South was worth fighting for. Some fought not so much for the South as they fought against the Yankees. Perhaps they simply gave up, for as historian Frank Owsley observed, "Anger and enthusiasm are too transient to serve as a basis of war." Yet, the tide turned and the war and the cause were lost, and the reasons for the defeat are largely debated today by few but historians and strategists.[39]

Chapter 5

Envy Loves a Shining Light

Whaen Henry Renfro returned to Texas in May 1865, it was not easy to forget the death, destruction, and hopelessness of which he had been a part in the fight for the Lost Cause. Yet he immersed himself in work, and his thoughts soon turned to spending time with his family, tilling his farm, and serving his church. All three would demand his best labors, and all received generous shares. Unlike many of his fellow soldiers from the deep South, however, Renfro returned to a home not too different from the one he left four years before, at least on the surface. No battles had scarred the landscape; no Union troops had scoured the land as they marched to the sea; the towns and houses were in place. Yet, changes had occurred. Faces of friends and kinfolk lost in the war were forever missing, and a new consciousness had begun to develop about the future. Slavery was dead, and the real or imagined perils of Reconstruction hovered on the horizon. The returning soldier and his family could resist the changes that were occurring and go to Mexico or Brazil, or they could endeavor to be content and accept the new order. Henry Renfro was one of those who chose the latter course of action.

Central to Renfro's decision to make the best of the situation at war's end was his family. Renfro's son, five-year-old Burlie, barely remembered the man who left to go to war so long ago, but he no doubt was thrilled to have a father again. Little Annette, soon to become her father's darling, was not yet one year old, and as a result she neither noted nor recognized the changes that began to occur when her father returned to Texas. It was Mary who was most pleased that Henry had at last come home. After all, their marriage had only begun when Henry enlisted with the Southern army, and despite having two children, she had desperately missed the communion of marriage and family. Too, she yearned to return to the life that she had planned for herself, expending her energies caring for Burlie, Annette, and Henry rather than worrying about planting corn, looking for lost stock, or thinking about the myriad of details that are necessary in the management of a stock farm.

During the first months after his return, Henry found labor to be a tonic, and he immersed himself in it. Although Mollie had done a creditable job in the management of the family business during his absence, Henry explored new opportunities to make the farming and ranching enterprise more successful. He repaired fences, cut weeds, built new buildings, and searched for high-value, low-price opportunities to buy cattle, horses, and sheep in order to replenish his stock and improve his breeds. He worked closely with brothers James and Isaac as all cultivated their adjoining lands, planting and harvesting cotton, wheat, and corn. If industry would make farming a success, Henry Renfro would become prosperous.

Yet, Henry's devotion to his family and his land did not affect his zeal for preaching the word of God. Within weeks of his return to Johnson County, Henry was asked to serve as the minister of the Alvarado Baptist Church, a congregation that was founded in October 1861 to serve the growing number of new settlers in the frontier town and the surrounding area. In addition to his Alvarado pastorate, Henry agreed to minister to the Shady Grove Baptist Church, a relatively new congregation also located in Johnson County. Finding little time during the week to write or practice his sermons, Henry rode horseback on Sunday morning in front of the buggy which carried Mollie and the children, reading his Bible and vocalizing the sermon for the day.[1]

The Alvarado and Shady Grove churches were not the only new ones in the region that had been established during and after the war. Religious growth had been an ongoing phenomenon despite the fact that most young to middle-aged men were away serving in the Confederate forces. To accommodate this expansion, religious leaders recognized the need to bring together the new congregations, all of which had common interests and were geographically close to each other. In October 1864, while Henry was still a chaplain in Polignac's Brigade in Louisiana, a new Baptist regional organization, the Alvarado Association, was formed to supplement the work of the old West Fork Association. Henry's father Absalom was one of those involved in its formation, and in 1864 he was appointed by Association Moderator James Jackson Sledge to serve on the Executive Committee. One year later, when the Association's annual meeting convened in September 1865, Henry was chosen to fill a leadership role that seemed to have been waiting for him. He was elected as the new moderator, or chairman, of the convention, and he enthusiastically preached the opening Sunday sermon for the assembled delegates. Like his father, he was chosen as a member of the Executive Committee for the coming year.[2]

Henry Renfro's energetic involvement with the Baptist Church was to increase in almost geometric progression as the months went by, and by the time of the 1866 meeting of the Alvarado Association in Shady Grove, he seemed almost to dominate the work of the organization. He served on a committee to redistrict the Association; he was one of two men delegated to examine, revise, and prepare the minutes; and he was appointed to the Domestic Missions Board. He was chosen to preach the missionary sermon for the next meeting. He was elected to the Divine Service Committee as well as the Committee on Schools and Education. One of seven ordained ministers in the Association, Henry continued to serve both the Alvarado church and the congregation at Shady Grove.[3]

When the Association convened in 1867 in Acton, Hood County, there was little change in Renfro's active commitment to the work of the church, and he once again served on several committees and boards. One, a group which was to make plans for the establishment of a new high school in Cleburne, was of special interest. Henry's support for a quality education for the youth of the region was to find a productive outlet.[4]

By the time of the 1868 convention of the Alvarado Association, this year held in the town of Alvarado, seventeen ordained ministers served the region's congregations, an increase of ten men in three years. Henry was recognized generally as an outstanding representative of the organization, and he was asked to serve as the delegate to the meetings of the West Fork Association and Richland Association, and to be the delegate messenger to the Baptist General Association of Texas. In 1868, Henry was chosen to become the pastor of the Bethesda Baptist Church, the pioneer congregation which he had helped to organize while a student at Baylor before the war. He was extremely pleased with his new situation, as he always had considered Bethesda, more than any of the others, as his home church. Henry felt that he had the best of all possible worlds. He had his family, his farm, and his church. What more, he might have asked, could any man want?[5]

Yet, the Parson continued to become involved in other organizations and causes. Because of its emphasis on schools, Henry was impressed with the work of the Masonic Lodge, and in 1867, he resolved to join the organization. He was granted a Demit by the Grandview, Texas, Lodge, Number 266, in December 1867. Seven years later, he was to be one of the founders and first officers of the Alvarado Chapter, Number 132, Royal Arch Masons. He was a member of the Patrons of Husbandry, a national organization devoted to farming and farmers, and by 1875 he was an active member of the Texas State Grange and was the Master of Number 564, a large organization which headquartered in Liberty Hill, Texas.[6]

In 1869, Henry Renfro was thirty-eight years old. He was highly respected within the Alvarado community, and he was generally considered to be a "rising star." But an event was to occur that was to have a very favorable impact on Renfro's reputation throughout Johnson County. February 13, 1869, was the day set for the laying of the cornerstone of a new Baptist educational facility in Cleburne, the county seat, named the Cleburne Institute. As a Baptist and a member of the Masonic fraternity, Renfro was invited to take part in the laying of the cornerstone of the new school. The participants gathered first at the Cleburne Masonic Lodge building, then marched to the corner of Buffalo and College streets where the ceremony was to take place. "The corner stone was . . . laid with grand demonstration," said the reporter for the *Cleburne Chronicle*, "showing that the order fully understood the business." Upon completion of the ceremony, the group "then marched in front of the school room for the purpose of placing the first speaker of the occasion, Prof. Jno. Collier, of Alvarado, in a position to be heard by all." Collier delivered a "chaste, elegant, and highly eloquent address, abounding with the most beautiful figures of Rhetoric . . . , giving a universal satisfaction to the auditors, and with great credit to himself." [7]

Rufus C. Burleson, then the president of Waco University, had been chosen to be the principal speaker for the occasion. Yet, after Professor Collier finished his speech, Burleson still had not arrived. The audience that had gathered to hear Burleson was somewhat uneasy and disappointed, and although Collier waited as long as was possible in the hope that Burleson would reach the gathering at the last minute, the respected Baptist educator and minister was nowhere to be seen. Turning momentarily from the crowd of from one thousand to fifteen hundred persons, Collier motioned for his friend Henry Renfro, who was scheduled as the alternate speaker should a need occur, and asked him to deliver an address in the stead of his friend and former teacher. Unhesitatingly, Renfro said that he would be pleased to speak to the gathering. The result was a speech on the importance of education which was far more forceful and eloquent than anyone might have expected on such short notice. [8]

As Burleson's alternate, the Parson knew that there was a possibility that he might be called upon to substitute for Burleson, and Renfro had worked many nights on a draft of an address. It would be a major speech on what essentially was a nonreligious subject, and he wanted it to be among the best that he had ever delivered. After stepping to the podium, Renfro began by extolling the virtues of men such as Henry Clay who started with nothing and secured education and fame. He then challenged others, especially the future students of the Cleburne Institute, to follow Clay's example and to recognize the importance of education:

> What man has done, man can do. To obtain a good education is an arduous work. It requires energy, patience and close application. It is an old and true saying that there is no excellence without labor. The indolent and slothful can never succeed. Poverty and ignorance and superstition will be theirs. It is for you to determine what course you will pursue. On this subject you are in a high degree the architect of your own dreams and destinies. Your welfare and happiness, your honor or infamy in the future depend on the impulse you now give to your desires & passions or the part you act in regard to these important affairs. By industry and patient cultivation and development of your mental capacities and powers you may become learned and wise and good and start on the high road to

prosperity and happiness. But by indolence and indifference you may allow these golden moments to pass away without improvement. You may join in with the giddy and gay and spend your youthful days in mirth and merriment, but the future will find you unprepared for its revelation and realities, incompetent to perform the work assigned you. Your lives prove vain and abortive and you at last will "go down to the dust from whence you sprung unwept, unhonored and unsung." I would that your minds could be impressed with the importance of an education. There is naught in earth or sky, in the bright day or strong night to compare with the riches of the mind, the splendors of the intellect. Nothing in the whole material universe [is] so vast as thought and so beautiful as love, [Joseph] Addison tells us. What sculpture is to a block of marble, education is to a human soul. The skill of the polisher exhibits the colors, makes the surface to shine. An education when it works upon a noble mind draws on view every latent virtue and perfection which without such helps are never able to make their appearance. The orator, the p[reacher], the statesman and philosopher often lie dormant in a poor ragged boy.[9]

The balance of the address also was well-written and delivered in a striking oratorical style that Rufus Burleson later was to say "had few equals." Discussion about the quality of Renfro's speech soon spread throughout the region, and there is no doubt that he was pleased with the compliments that he received from friends and acquaintances. But, as is so often the case during a period of good times, the vultures of despair were not far behind. The exhilaration caused by Henry's widespread recognition disappeared on August 27, 1869, when his mother Levicy died after a short illness. Less than three months later, on November 11, Henry's father Absalom also passed away. They were lovingly buried side by side in the little cemetery west of Bethesda Church, a place Henry later called "the most sacred spot on earth to me."[10]

The sadness of the burial of Absalom and Levicy Renfro did not, however, diminish the general enthusiasm for education that had been evoked by Henry Renfro's speech and the opening of the Cleburne Institute. Yet, the hundreds of dollars that had been pledged for the school's construction failed to arrive as they were needed. By October, all work stopped on the building with only the first floor complete, and a town meeting was called to address the problem. Evidently, the gathering did not produce the desired results, as a letter to the editor of the *Cleburne Chronicle* from "Interested 1" charged that although many non-Baptists had followed through on their offers of support, many Cleburne Baptists who had signed pledges were doing nothing. The letter writer believed that Baptists should "either start releasing their grip upon their money, or else stop feigning their support under false pretenses." The letter writer believed that the Institute likely would do better under secular control, and he noted that if the project were turned over to the citizens of Cleburne and Johnson County, the building "would go up so quick it will make your heads swim."[11]

Parson Renfro was one of those who had pledged support for the new institution, and he immediately answered "Interested 1'"'s letter with a letter of his own. He would not be included in any list of persons who did not fulfill promises, and he hoped to stir action from his fellow churchmen. "I will be one of 100 men," said Renfro, "to give $30; or one of 60 to give $50; or one of 30 to give $100. This I have done and this I will do." Despite Renfro's challenge, no evidence is found that it was ever answered. Nevertheless, the building was finally completed, but the Institute failed by 1875 for lack of continuing funding.[12]

The closure of the Johnson County Baptist school sparked the interest of many of the citizens of Alvarado who were unhappy with the inability of their own town to secure a permanent, high-quality school and who saw the demise of the Institute as an opportunity to locate a first-rate college in their town. Although Reverend John Collier had headed an institution known as Alvarado College since 1869, that academy evidently did not have the broad support sought by much of the regional population. The mistake of entrusting the task of building a new college to the Baptist Church, however, was not to be repeated once again. Knowing of the dedication of the Masonic Lodge to education, some suggested that the order should take over the entire mission of instruction. "Many of the citizens," wrote a historian of the period, "concluded that the Freemasons, being an organization of considerable strength at this place, and representing almost all phases of public opinion on all the questions of the day, religious and political, were the most eminently qualified to unite the discordant elements of a community in the interest of education." Because of this conviction, a community meeting was soon held in which the citizens of Alvarado "resolved to place the school interests

of Alvarado under their control, and pledged to give them their uni-
fied support." It is of interest that the consensus was achieved even
though no Masons voted in the referendum. Professor I. A. Patton,
formerly a teacher in Grimes County, was invited to come to Alvarado
and take charge of the new college. The Masonic Institute, as the new
school was called, was completed in 1875 and was located on "College
Hill," an eminence west of the city square. A two-story frame structure was constructed, and the new institution eventually boasted
forty boarding students from Johnson and surrounding counties. At
one time, it incorporated both a "normal" and a law department, and
it served as many as 168 pupils.[13]

Henry Renfro was as involved in the establishment of the new Masonic school as he had been in the building of the Cleburne Institute.
With two children who needed a first-class education, he had personal reasons for his support. Of equal or greater importance, however, was his energetic support of all institutions of learning, a philosophy that he had expressed so well in his speech at the opening of
the Cleburne Institute.

The needs of others, however, left little time for Henry to spend in
support of schools and education. One task that he assumed, far removed from the joys of learning, was one which must have been particularly arduous even to a compassionate minister. In early 1870, an
old friend of Renfro's came to his door, saying that he desperately
needed the support and advice of a man of God. Henry invited the
man into his home, and the two sat down to discuss the man's problem. Slowly, a story unfolded in which the man related that he had
been bitten by a rabid dog and that he knew that it was only a matter
of time before he, too, would suffer from the madness induced by
hydrophobia. Friends and family were anxious about what would
happen to the ailing farmer, and to ease their fears, he left them,
vowing to go somewhere else to die or recover. Knowing that his
chances of getting well were virtually nonexistent short of a miracle,
he asked Parson Renfro to assist him in making arrangements so that
he would not be a menace to others during his illness. Knowing that
time was short, Renfro immediately agreed to help. Near the Renfro
farmhouse was a corn crib, a log structure constructed much in the
same manner as a log house except that the logs were two to three
inches apart and notched so as to be secure. The victim asked Renfro
to "nail him up" in the corn crib to protect others from any actions

that he might take because of the disease. There, the visitor took up lodging, with Renfro providing food for every meal. Within a relatively short time, the toxic effects of the bite began to take effect, and the man did, in fact, lose his mind, alternately raving and becoming marginally lucid until he died. Henry preached the funeral of the unfortunate soul.[14]

Renfro's humanity for his fellow ministers also was intense, but he had little patience for those who, in the name of religion, practiced doctrines that he believed to be contrary to those he believed were taught in the Bible. As was the case with some other Baptist preachers, Renfro, on occasion, verbally chastised ministers from other congregations who disagreed with the tenets of the Baptist Church and who did not, as Renfro saw it, adhere to biblical teachings. Although no persons or religious groups were exempt from the possibility of scathing remarks, Renfro seemed to take special care to admonish from the pulpit the members of the Methodist Church in the area. The text of his sermons soon reached the Methodist clergy, and one preacher of that denomination, H. H. Sneed of Weatherford, responded vehemently to Renfro's attacks on the failure of Methodists to be baptized through immersion.[15]

When minister Sneed showed up at a Renfro sermon and attempted to make Renfro sign an already-written confession in which he would renounce his disparaging remarks about the Methodists, the quarrel deteriorated to violence. Henry refused to sign the document, and consequently, the enraged Sneed lashed out with a loaded quirt, striking Renfro's head and rendering a painful, bloody injury. Immediately after the incident, James Renfro rushed to his brother's aid. James urged that they make Sneed apologize, using force to do so if necessary. Henry declined to do so, however, and the resulting disagreement between the brothers caused an estrangement that followed the two men for the rest of their lives. Soundly condemning the altercation in a sermon soon after it occurred, Renfro claimed that Sneed's demand that he sign the document had been rejected by the Lord Himself:

Many can testify that devotion to the good old doctrines of the Gospel made me the unhappy object of a plot, which was doubtless to result in my death, or the ruin of my reputation. With feelings of pain and pleasure do I advert to that trying ordeal, which unholy men had ordered for my ruin, but which God overruled for my good. It was mine enemy's to abuse, to smite, to present deadly weapons, and demand my name to a libelous document on pain of death. It was mine to suffer, but to conquer, in that I handed back the libelous document, not with my signature, but all bespattered with my Huguenot blood. A little "blood-letting" in the defense of the truth gives one a martyr spirit. We should love the truth none the less because we have to suffer for it.[16]

Although Renfro was unrelenting in his attacks on Methodist doctrine, in the future he did his best to avoid public confrontations, violence, and bloodshed.[17]

Renfro's efforts to circumvent additional arguments with Methodist preachers were to no avail, however, as the Wesleyans determined to carry the fight to Baptist home ground. Seeking to gain new converts as well as to antagonize and humiliate Renfro, the Presiding Elder of the Weatherford (Texas) District of the Methodist Church, preacher T. W. Hines, called for a quarterly meeting to be held on August 3, 1873, in the shadow of the Shady Grove Baptist Church, a congregation which Renfro earlier had served as pastor. Through one "Brother King," Elder Hines had invited Renfro to attend, presumably to defend his beliefs in front of the assembled Methodists. Renfro declined with the excuse that he had already committed to preach that day at Mansfield, Johnson County.[18]

Nevertheless, the event went on as scheduled, and Hines took great delight in lambasting Renfro and the Baptist Church. He falsely told the assembled crowd that Renfro had promised to attend but had reneged. Hines then vehemently recalled the incident between Elder Sneed and Renfro, boasting and publicly celebrating that Renfro had suffered from the hand of a Methodist preacher. Hines noted that the attack by Sneed was justified because of the magnitude of Renfro's condemnation of Methodist doctrine. Finally, in an effort to use the controversy to advantage, the Methodist minister emotionally called for Baptists in the audience to renounce their former beliefs and turn to the Methodist faith.[19]

Upon Henry's return from Mansfield, he was met at his home by Baptist friends who related the afternoon events at Shady Grove. Renfro became extremely angry and concluded that the bitter invective offered by Hines that afternoon could not go unanswered. He rode to Shady Grove, immediately located Hines, and then berated him publicly in front of a Methodist audience, stating, among other things, that "for mercy and fair dealing, I would rather fall into the hands of common gamblers and drunkards than into the hands of Methodist preachers." The mood of the Baptist minister was such that Hines felt that it would be foolish to resort to the violent behavior that he had embraced only a few hours before.[20]

Four days later, on August 7, Renfro was still irate, and he resolved to write a letter to Hines in order to adequately express all of his feelings concerning his tormenter and the Methodist Church. "Sir, a few words to you now that the storm you raised has passed away," wrote Renfro. "I am full of regrets that I was under the necessity of noticing you as I did at Shady Grove on last Sabbath evening. Your conduct in the fore noon made it an absolute necessity. A proper degree of self respect and my many friends demanded that I set myself right before the people."[21]

Then Renfro attacked Hines's reasoning in selecting Shady Grove as the pulpit for his sermons. "You should exercise a little common sense of propriety; but your coming, as it were, to my door and belching forth such a torrent of abuse upon my devoted head, with the idea that it would be received by the people, and subserve the Sacred purposes of getting up a revival of Methodist religion, shows that you are egregiously green; and though you are acting as Presiding Elder you have not the capacity to make a decent class leader." Renfro continued by telling Hines that he was wrong in his supposition that he could turn Baptists into Methodists because of the incident between himself and Sneed. "I reckon you thought that I was, like Methodist preachers generally are, unpopular at home, but you found, to your sorrow, that you were simply mistaken."[22]

Renfro then addressed the actions that had led to the problems with Sneed and Hines. "It is coming to a nice pass, Sir, that a Baptist minister can not, even in kindness, preach his own sentiments and expose what he believes to be erroneous in the teachings of others, without endangering his life or reputation." In an allusion to the trials of those who followed Jesus, Renfro challenged Hines to "turn to the Acts of the Apostles and you will find that Peter and John were treated thus by the Jewish Sanhedrin, and Rome always dealt with the true advocates of the gospel and the opposers of her pretensions in the same manner and spirit you are now dealing with me! And you, Sir, are but showing your true lineage and descent from the Roman Catholic Church." Although Henry's letter seemed to be the "last word" in that chapter of the bitter dispute with the Methodists and their preachers, it was by no means the end of difficulties for the strong-willed Baptist preacher. Many more problems were to come that would be far more controversial.[23]

The Parson felt that the rancor created by the unhappy trysts with Sneed and Hines had no place in the hearts of those who called themselves Christians, and the two events provided additional fuel for Renfro's growing dissatisfaction with the interpretation of the Bible by men who claimed to represent the church, regardless of their denomination. Too, the charges made against him by men such as Sneed and Hines bothered Renfro much more than he publicly acknowledged. He viewed the bitterness of such men as a result of *man's* church rather than the church of God. More and more, the Parson believed that the basic message of God was love, and that man, in his orthodox church, was missing the point of Christianity and the word of God. Although he was not yet ready to verbalize these thoughts publicly, he expressed them succinctly in a poem written on July 24, 1877, to his daughter Annette on her thirteenth birthday:

You must not be too credulous
   Respecting to the Gospel plan
For much that's preached is treacherous
   Just the creed of recreant man
Of all that's taught by prophets old
   About the real gospel plan
Or that apostles too have told
   Is love to God and love to man[24]

Despite his misgivings about certain ministers he believed to be misguided, Renfro continued to work very hard for his own church and congregations. In 1869 he had served as pastor for the growing Bethesda Church, and by 1871 he was charged with the spiritual well-being of the churches at Shady Grove and Grandview. By 1872, Renfro was the pastor of the Pleasant Point Church, Johnson County, and the Eagle Hill Church in Tarrant County. In 1875, he was one of thirty-one ordained ministers, a dramatic increase from the seven men so recognized in the 1866 minutes of the Alvarado Association. Henry continued his breakneck pace in the work of the Association that he had begun ten years before. In 1876, he assumed the pastorate of two churches, was a delegate to the Association's Annual Meeting from Alvarado, chaired the Committee on Foreign Missions, and was chosen to preach to the assembled delegates at the Hood County meeting at its first evening meeting.

Yet Henry Renfro's energetic activity on behalf of the Baptist Church did not slow his interest in his farm and its expansion. He continued to be financially successful, and when two tracts of land adjoining the Renfro farm became available for sale in early 1874, the Parson moved quickly. One of the properties belonged to Thomas H. Neilson, a Philadelphian who had inherited the property from his father, Hall Neilson, the original patentee. The other was "The Russell Place," 160 acres of land adjacent to Renfro's belonging to one Hezekiah Russell. Russell, it will be recalled, was the one who declined to sell the same property to Mary Renfro while Henry was serving in the Confederate Army in Galveston. On March 22, Henry first wrote to Neilson, offering to purchase 160 acres of Neilson's property if a suitable price and terms could be agreed upon. At the same time, he approached Russell with the same proposition. Russell responded immediately with an offer to sell for $4.00 per acre, cash. Believing the price to be excellent, Renfro closed the sale on April 19 on Russell's terms.[25]

On April 13, 1874, Renfro also received an encouraging letter from Thomas H. Neilson regarding the possible purchase by the Parson of the Philadelphia attorney's Johnson County land. Although Neilson was not interested in breaking up the property into small acreages as Renfro had suggested, he made another proposition to the Baptist minister, offering to sell 640 acres at a reasonable price. Neilson had no idea of land values, however; his notions of price were unrealistic. As an absentee landlord, Neilson had experienced many problems in maintaining the large farm, and he felt that it would be in his best interests to get rid of it. "Could I get a reliable agent," wrote Neilson, "I would not sell my Johnson County land for $10 per acre, but as I have so much trouble with it & my other land I am willing to part with it below its value. I will not sell the tract in parcels. I will take $3520 currency cash for it, which is $5.50 currency pr acre."[26]

Neilson suggested to Renfro that he should buy all of the land and then sell the balance he did not need to others. "If you do not acquire the whole tract," continued Neilson, "you could sell what you did not want or could raise the balance of the money requisite to buy the whole by a mortgage on it. I have no doubt you can make a good thing out of it if you take it." Although he wished that he could afford the whole tract, Renfro did not feel that he could afford it at that time. Too, he was not convinced that it was an exceptional value at the $5.50 price. As a result, he wrote to Neilson and declined the offer, citing the price he already had agreed to pay Hezekiah Russell for adjoining property.[27]

Although continuing postal exchanges between Renfro and Neilson were amicable, Neilson made no move to lower his price for the property until nearly four years later. Perhaps one of the reasons that he did so was that he correctly guessed, from wording in Renfro's letters, that the Texan was a member of the Masonic Lodge. In a letter of February 5, 1878, Neilson remarked, "From a sentence in your letter I infer that you are a brother of the 'mystic tie' and that you 'have travelled.' Am I right? I too am a past master of the order," wrote the Philadelphian to his Texas correspondent, "so that you can be assured that I will act with you 'on the square.'" Consequently, in his February 5 letter, Neilson made two offers to Renfro. The first was a proposition to sell 250 acres at $4.00 per acre, cash, "provided you will have the deed prepared & the land surveyed, at your expense, or in case you do not wish to have it surveyed will guaranty the rest of the tract [the balance of the 640 acres] shall contain 390 acres & that you will secure me to that amount & dispose of the same at $4.50 per acre by next fall." In his second proposition, Neilson offered to sell Renfro his entire property. "Being desirous of disposing of the whole tract, I will sell you the same for $2755. viz $1000 cash & balance in one or two years secured by notes on the land, with 7% interest." Immediately, Renfro made a counter offer of $4.00, or $2,560 for the entire property, with a down payment of 50 percent and the balance of $1,280 for one year at 6 percent interest. In his desire to be sure that Neilson would have no question as to the proper handling of the sale, Renfro suggested that the City National Bank in Fort Worth would represent the Philadelphian in the transaction. Neilson was so eager to sell that he resolved not to raise any barrier, and he asked Henry to proceed in any way he felt best. "I have *every faith* in you," wrote Neilson, "& will do as you suggest & employ the agent you name, & sell on the terms *you propose*. If you will guaranty, the receipt of the money by me from the agent & will pay the expenses of bringing suit in case they [the monies received by the agent] are not paid."[28]

On March 19, 1878, Renfro paid Neilson $1,280 cash, then executed a note to Thomas Neilson for $1,280 to be paid in twelve months at 6 percent interest. Interestingly, however, there was one condition attached to the instrument relating to a cloud on the title to the land. "Now, if the said Neilson shall comply with his agreement, to have a certain deed (which is believed to be a forgery) purporting to have been made by Hall Neilson, deceased, to J. R. Barnes, stricken from the Land Records, of Johnson County, Texas, and thus remove, the cloud from the title, to the said tract of land, this note is to be and remain in full force and effect; otherwise to be null and void." Since Renfro paid the note in full on January 23, 1879, Neilson evidently was successful in clearing any irregularities in the title to the property.[29]

Although the purchase of the Neilson property by Henry Renfro went smoothly, the transaction caused a serious disagreement between the Parson and S. C. Roddy, a distant relative, one of his neighbors, and a member of Bethesda church. Roddy had been renting 160 acres from Neilson, and he wanted to lease that land for a number of years so that he would feel justified in making improvements. Eventually, Roddy wished to buy the property, and he wrote to Neilson with a proposition to that end. In reply, Neilson wrote Roddy that he did not want to tie up the property for long periods of time in a lease but that he would consider selling 220 acres. To be sure that Roddy understood his position, however, Neilson added that he was negotiating with Renfro for the entire tract and that Renfro "would act as my agent & that if . . . [Renfro] approved of it," he would sell the property Roddy had been renting. Clearly, Neilson had given the first option on the property to Renfro.[30]

Although Neilson's wishes were plainly stated in his correspondence, Roddy was extremely unhappy that Renfro had chosen to purchase all of the land. Also, he was not pleased that he was going to have to negotiate with the Parson if and when he wished to try to buy any of it. Roddy became even more distressed when, in 1878, he attempted to purchase the property and Renfro refused to sell it to him. Roddy chose to make the matter a public issue, contending that Renfro was obligated, because of Roddy's agreements with Neilson, to sell the land to him. He claimed, as proof, that he personally had a letter from Neilson which affirmed his right to purchase the property.

He then began a series of appeals in the *Cleburne Chronicle* in which he denounced Renfro and claimed that the Parson had not lived up to his promises. In an effort to make his case, Roddy presented three "witnesses" who said that Renfro, after reading Roddy's "letter from Neilson," had promised to sell the land to him. On Sunday, October 15, 1878, the entire matter was brought before the conference of the First Baptist Church of Alvarado, where Renfro was a member and former pastor, with the charge by Renfro that "S. C. Roddy, a member of Bethesda Church, had made and calculated charges detrimental to his christian character, and asked the church to appoint a committee to wait on bro. S. C. Roddy and ask him to attend the next conference meeting." After a vote was taken on the matter, Reverend J. R. Clarke, the pastor of the church and the moderator of the conference, appointed a committee consisting of church members J. J. Ezell, Isaac Kelly, and B. B. Prestridge.[31]

Although Roddy did not attend the next conference meeting on October 6 because of illness, he did appear at the meeting on November 3. The charges by Roddy were stated as follows: "That bro. Roddy was about buying a piece of land and he (Renfroe) interfeared [sic] with his trade and bought the land; and also that bro Renfroe promised to deed bro Roddy the portion he wanted at the same rates that he (Renfroe) purchased the land at, and then refused to do as he promised." The church conference was unconvinced by the evidence in the case. "After a statement from bro Roddy," Clerk W. A. Prestridge wrote in the minutes, "the church declared bro Renfro as standing clearly vindicated from the charges made against him by bro Roddy *as above stated* by bro Renfro." Unsatisfied with the result of the deliberations, Roddy made another charge in the case. "Bro. S. C. Roddy said he would make the following charge against bro Renfroe. That he, Renfroe, did promise me (Roddy) the portion of land on which I am now living, and that he has refused to do so, and denies ever promising it to me." Roddy delivered the charge in writing, and the church agreed to review it.[32]

In order to secure more information, the church conference asked two of its members who had discussed the case with both Renfro and Roddy, men named Gully and Reynolds, to outline any knowledge that they had of the affair. "After a thorough investigation of the case and finding no evidence of a promise by bro Renfroe," wrote the clerk in the minutes of the proceedings, "by a motion and a second the church dismissed the case."[33]

In spite of the findings by the Alvarado Baptist Church, Roddy continued to assail Renfro both verbally and in print. He then became infuriated when Parson Renfro placed another letter in the *Cleburne Chronicle*, denying once again that there had ever been an agreement between himself and Roddy concerning the land in question and challenging Roddy to produce the so-called letter from Neilson. Other correspondence followed from both men until Renfro wrote a scathing note which bore the heading, "S. C. Roddy, or Much Ado About Nothing." "I had thought," wrote Renfro, "to waste no more ammunition on 'dead ducks,' but having seen many readers of the Chronicle, I am advised to reply to Roddy's last publication, lest some man in his dotage, or little miss in her teens, might believe there was some truth in it." Then Renfro challenged his adversary's character and intelligence. "I know well," wrote Renfro, "that the public do[es] not relish the unsavory bills of fare Roddy and I have been giving them, and I do declare that I would be ashamed to meet a man of refinement, if I were the aggressor in this affair. Think of it. A man who cannot pay his debts, nor relieve the absolute wants of his family to pay ten cents a line to vent his spleen of hatred on a man who had been the best friend he had in the state. This deed alone is enough to show to all reflecting men the mental and moral status of S. C. Roddy."[34]

Regardless of the continued bombast by both parties in print, however, the decision of the Alvarado church in favor of Renfro effectively ended the dispute, although Roddy and his supporters were never quite the same in their relationship with Henry C. Renfro or the First Baptist Church of Alvarado. Some of Renfro's detractors insinuated, whenever an occasion presented itself, that a minister had no business being able to purchase such large tracts of land in the first place. Ministers, they said, should be poor and have no interest in the things that are of the world. Commenting on this suggestion, Renfro wrote that "gossiping, tattling, and envy . . . are at the bottom of these troubles. If I were a common drunkard and gambler, neglecting to provide for my family, parties would not be so up in arms against me. But I am a preacher . . . ; I am prospering in the world, and envy loves a shining light." Henry noted that there were those who felt that he should do nothing and own nothing. "He should be as unambitious and gentle as Mary's little lamb," noted Renfro, and "as to the goods of this world, he should be able at all times to sing, 'No foot of land do I possess, no cottage in the wilderness.'"[35]

Interestingly, some of those who saw fit to criticize the results of Parson Renfro's business acumen went one step further and stated that with his obvious success, he should cease to be on the payroll of any of the churches of which he served as pastor. What they did not know was that Renfro had long ceased to take a salary for his work as a minister, although he did take an occasional donation when offered. Those church members who were in leadership positions already knew this fact, but the uninformed began to whisper that Renfro's wealth was somehow derived from religious revenues. To squash the rumor, the members of the Rehobath Baptist Church in Tarrant County, a congregation served by Renfro at that time, issued a written statement in defense of their minister. "We the members of the aforesaid church [Rehobath Baptist Church] hereby certify that there has never been any stipulated price for H. C. Renfro's services as pastor of this church and that in his preaching among us his course indicates that he has been activated by other than a moneyed consideration." The statement was signed by W. A. Saey, Church Clerk, and six members of the congregation. With this note in hand, Renfro was able to crush any further innuendo on that issue.[36]

Although Henry was sometimes impatient with some "men of the cloth," Baptist and otherwise, his friendship with his old teacher, Rufus Burleson, remained warm over the years. The two men kept up an unremitting correspondence, visiting whenever occasion allowed, with each giving whatever support he could give to the other, sharing troubles and triumphs. On his celebration of twenty-five years as a university president, for example, Burleson wrote his former student that he was well in health and in his work. "The university is . . . in so fine a condition. Over 200 students and new ones coming in daily. As this year ends my first quarter of a century in the president's chair, I am anxious to matriculate 400 students." Also, Burleson encouraged Renfro to continue his support for the university, something he had done since Burleson became that institution's president. "I send you a few catalogues for circulation and trust you can send us a few recruits. We especially want those young preachers you speak of. I sent them our catalogues." Finally, Burleson thanked his former student for a contribution of farm produce and informed the Parson of his plan for picking it up and transporting it to Waco. "Our mutual friend Algernon Daniel says he has a friend who wants to come to Waco with a team and will haul it cheaper than I can send a team for it. I hereby authorize it and ask you to contract for the hauling and I will pay the price he agrees upon on delivery to Waco."[37]

It was in part due to the influence of Dr. Burleson that Henry Renfro put aside nagging questions that had begun to develop concerning orthodox religion, and he continued to be extremely active in his church. His agenda for the 1881 convention of the Alvarado Association at Eagle Hill, Tarrant County, was as hectic as it had been fifteen years before. As a delegate from the Alvarado Baptist Church, Renfro was appointed to both the Committee on Foreign Missions and the Committee on the State of Religion, which he chaired. He was one of those chosen to preach to the assembled delegates. He was one of thirty-two ordained ministers in the Association and was appointed, once again, to the organization's Executive Committee. Finally, he was appointed as the messenger to the West Fork Association.[38]

Renfro continued to be a popular speaker at local and regional events, and he often met with and supported other ministers and laymen whom he believed to have exceptional merit. One such person was a Reverend F. M. Law, with whom Parson Renfro conducted a "Partnership Meeting" at the Burton School where "a multitude congregated to hear the unsearchable riches of Christ." Henry Renfro preached an 11:00 A.M. sermon, after which "a delicious and bountiful dinner was served, in prairie style." By 1:30 P.M., Law presented "a long and interesting discourse," after which the two ministers "consolidated their testimony upon the subject of election and the final preservation of the saints."[39]

Although he remained popular with local churchgoers such as those who gathered at Burton School, Henry Renfro also was considered at the beginning of the 1880's to be among the leaders of the Baptist Church in Texas. This was reflected in his participation in church functions which included some of the most important figures in the state. In the "Programme for Missionary Mass Meeting to be Held at Grandview, Johnson County, Texas, November 4th, 5th, and 6th, 1881," Renfro is shown to have preached six ten-minute sermons alongside such pillars of the Baptist community as Rufus C. Burleson, R. C. Buckner, and B. H. Carroll.[40]

Too, the Parson continued to be active in his relationships with Waco University. In the 1882 meeting of the General Association of the Baptist Church in Sulphur Springs, Texas, after the properties of Waco University were transferred to the Association, Renfro was appointed one of the thirty-two commissioners throughout Texas charged with the responsibility of raising $60,000 for the Waco school. The following year, 1883, Renfro was appointed to the Board of Visitors for Waco University. Both jobs the Parson carried out to the letter.[41]

In his ministry on the Texas frontier, Henry Renfro demonstrated his capacity for exceptional achievement. He had become a force in the Baptist community. He had proven himself to be an extremely capable minister. He had established himself as an outstanding orator. In addition, he was a leader who demanded the respect of persons both in and out of the congregations which he served as a minister. Also, however, Henry Renfro had shown that he was and would be controversial—a person who would not always accept the status quo and who would sometimes go to extremes to demonstrate that he was firm in his convictions, religious and otherwise.

Chapter 6

Fate Plays Her Hand

Like the bluster of a Texas storm, Henry Renfro's life resembled the erratic movements of dark and threatening clouds. Succeeded by sunshine and infinitely clear skies, the somber billows inevitably reappeared and stormed again at first opportunity. Although Henry's family—including Mary but especially Burleson and Annette—had been spared much of this cyclical movement in the past, all of them occasionally found themselves sucked into the tempests of controversy as the decade of the 1880's approached.

During the final years of the 1870's, however, life at the Renfro home on Crill Miller Creek was almost tranquil. Burleson—"Burlie"— was everything that his father and mother would have wanted him to be. Hard-working, honest, and caring, Burlie loved the farm and everything that went with it. As he approached twenty years of age at the beginning of the 1880's, he began to take on many of the everyday farming and ranching tasks that heretofore had been done by his father. Friendly and companionable, Burlie treasured his friends, and he had many of them. Annette, four years younger than her brother, was not a typical preacher's daughter. She was somewhat pampered, and her mother did everything that she could to be sure that the blossoming young lady had all of the advantages that social position and more-than-average wealth could provide. Annette's dresses were always at the crest of fashion, and she always was able to sport a new broach, a shiny gold watch, or a new lace shawl. A pretty girl who sported fashionable ringlets of curls over her forehead, Annette had more than her share of beaus, and what she might have lacked in striking beauty she more than made up in coquettishness and an independence that in itself attracted the young men of the area. Upon learning to play a piano that she received as a present from her father, Annette further enhanced her standing as a lady of the world. Already, she had gained a reputation in speech and declamation, delivering addresses to the local reading club with titles such as "Should Females be Equally Educated with Males?" and "Patience."[1]

The ability of Henry Renfro to provide well for his family was a result of sound business practice and hard work. Yet, even with those qualities wealth is not inevitable. Sometimes fate plays her hand and extraordinary events occur, providing good fortune when unexpected. This was to happen to Henry Renfro in 1881 when the Missouri, Kansas, and Texas Railroad began construction of a new line into Johnson County. As was their practice, the line's management decided to establish a new community midway between Fort Worth and Cleburne to capitalize on the use of rail for transportation and movement of farm produce. The property chosen by the railroad land agent Major Grenville M. Dodge was another of the tracts which Henry Renfro had purchased as his business prospered. In the beginning, Renfro did not wish to sell the land, believing that it would increase in value substantially as increased settlement followed the railroad. In a conciliatory move, the Parson offered to donate every other lot in the proposed town tract if he could retain the others as his own property. Although this proposition was refused by Dodge, Renfro finally agreed to sell when offered a price for the property which exceeded what Renfro believed he would be able to demand for years to come. Dodge freely made one concession, however; he allowed the Parson to name the new town. Remembering the man who had more influence on his life than anyone else, Renfro specified that it be called "Burleson" in honor of his friend and former teacher at Baylor University, Rufus C. Burleson.[2]

Yet, the additional wealth that was created by the sale of the land for the new municipality of Burleson was not all sweet, as there was renewed criticism of the Parson because of his business acumen and his financial success. Notwithstanding, the disapproval of some who were jealous of Henry Renfro's wealth had but little effect on the everyday life of the Renfro family. They continued to live much the same as always, with the Parson looking after the needs of the ministry and of the farm. There was one change, however, as the additional resources provided by the land sale allowed Henry and Mary to initiate a program that they might not have been able to begin without it.

The Parson and his wife had long wished that they could provide substantial moral and financial support to young men who, for one reason or another, had no families to care for them. Mary had been raised an orphan herself, and she knew something of the loneliness that a youngster can feel with neither mother nor father. Therefore, the Renfros decided to bring to their home several young men with no families and scant future. Believing that self-respect was the foundation upon which productive lives would be built, Henry and Mollie provided each new arrival with meaningful chores to be completed and paid a real wage for the results. In turn, the foster children who were "adopted" by the Renfros developed a love that was analogous to that felt by family members with blood ties.[3]

One young man named Ira Bishop recalled, many years later, his busy but happy days on the Renfro farm. "Fall of '82 he hired me, only a lad—to feed 90 head of cattle penned at home. I chopped up about 15 bushels of corn night and morning. He had lots of stock to see after," recalled Bishop, "a bunch of horses running at large in and around . . . on the prairie—big pastures of cattle. Also young mules and mares in another pasture—had to be fed during cold snaps. Oh, plenty of work for a boy. I was young and strong and ready to go." Speaking of his fortune at being taken in by the Renfros, Bishop recalled that he was "lucky by divine guidance to get such a home. An orphan boy being tossed about with the wind. Was wild & rough. Coming in contact with his [Renfro's] fatherly advice changed my prospect of life. I had caught a new vision. He was a leader of men and of boys—a father to the fatherless and [he] made it his business to see after the needy. A finer Man Never lived, A real pioneer—."[4]

Bishop recalled with equal tenderness his memories of the Parson's wife, Mary, during his years at the home on Crill Miller Creek. "Had a hard chill one cold day and my fever must have gone high. Slept upstairs. Cold winter night. That angel wife of his came twice that night to my bed and laid her motherly hand on my brow—Slipping away—leaving the hot tears running down my cheeks. My only regret," said Bishop nearly fifty-five years later, "is I let her die without telling her that I was not asleep. I was young then—now am 77 but these impressions still live and grow." [5]

The names of most of the others who were given a home at the Renfro farm are lost, but all were as closely attached to the Renfro family as was Ira Bishop. Another who found a refuge there, John Gilmore, visited with his "family" over a fifty-year period after he went off on his own. He returned to see the Renfro family time and time again, the last visit occurring when he was eighty-eight years of age. [6]

All of the youngsters who lived at the Renfro farm, including Burlie and Annette as well as some of the "adopted" sons, attended the Crill Miller School. It was located east of the home place of one Pleasant Inman at the foot of a hill where "there was a deep well and free camp ground where the roads crossed, one going up the hill to the east and one going up the hill to the west." Despite the fact that Johnson County was on the edge of the Texas frontier in the 1870's and 1880's, all of the students received a satisfactory education while studying such classic texts as *McGuffey's New Fourth Eclectic Reader*. When the Masonic Institute opened at Alvarado, Henry Renfro saw to it that both Burlie and Annette were enrolled as boarding students at the new educational facility on "College Hill." Later, Annette would refer to the school as "the dearest spot on earth to me, for it was there that the strongest attachments and tenderest associations of my life were formed." [7]

Attending the Masonic Institute at the same time was a young man named Julius Baker. A fun-loving and intelligent student, Julius had moved to Johnson County from Louisiana with his parents, Darius and Margaret Ann Baker, soon after the Civil War. Darius was vitally interested in education and served as the president of the Masonic Institute's school board from 1880 to 1881. Julius was a classmate of Burleson Renfro, and after both completed their studies at the school in early 1881, they continued to be close friends. Although Annette had no shortage of beaus, Burlie saw qualities that he liked in his friend Julius and determined to introduce him to his little sister. The decision, however, was made only after Burlie first considered the possibility of a match between Julius and his cousin, Dora Coody, in Arkansas. In a letter to Dora, Burlie discussed Julius's sterling qualities but feared that his relative's recent acquisition of a new boyfriend in Searcy made his intentions moot. "Cousin," wrote Burlie, "I have found a fellow for you at last, but then I guess I am to [sic] late, his name is Julias [sic] Baker, he is one of my classmates." The letter was soon forgotten, as the distance to Arkansas precluded any possibility of Dora Coody and Julius Baker getting acquainted.[8]

However, Burlie was sufficiently impressed with Baker that he soon arranged an introduction to his sister. Burlie's hunch that the two would like each other was a good one, and seventeen-year-old Annette and twenty-one-year-old Julius were attracted to each other from their first meeting. It was not long before letters from the young man assumed a serious tone. Julius first wrote to Annette on November 24, 1881, and said that he would like to "take this means of telling you that your benevolence, kindness, and good looks have completely captivated me, and that my heart is entirely yours." Five days later, on November 29, 1881, Julius wrote another tender note in which he told Annette that she was "the only one that I ever did care anything for." When he received a less than enthusiastic response, he penned an answer which pointedly stated that he was "trying to carry on a flirtation" and that he wanted to call on her and "talk privately." By mid-December, Julius professed that he was "never contented, unless I am in your presence."[9]

Although fascinated with the possibility of having a serious new suitor, Annette was somewhat reluctant to give up her image as an alluring Southern belle, attracting all of the eligible young men in the countryside. She admitted in later years to having been engaged to three men at one time with none knowing about the others. A railroad man and distant cousin named Buck Satterfield was her favorite, but Buck was usually far away, and Annette was of the nature that their occasional meetings were insufficient for the companionship that she craved. Also, Buck was the nephew of S. C. Roddy, Annette's father's antagonist in the dispute over the Neilson land. Parson Renfro would have nothing to do with Satterfield personally, as he was known to take a drink of hard liquor from time to time. Besides that, he had no desire for his Annette to become too close to the Roddy family. The would-be romance was quashed completely when the Parson told his daughter, "Just don't come home again if you marry Buck Satterfield." Annette was so thoroughly disappointed that she told her father that he "might as well ask for her life." The young lady proved to be more resilient than she would have liked to appear to her father, however, and she soon began to consider, once again, the other young men who might be a part of her future. Her interest in Julius Baker soon increased, and it was not long before he and Annette began to see each other frequently. She continued to be a boarding student at the Masonic Institute, sharing a room with a young lady from Waco named Mintie Roberts who became a life-long friend. Julius, on the other hand, completed his studies and entered the business world, borrowing about $3,800 from his brother Darius to open a grocery store at the Missouri Pacific depot in downtown Alvarado.[10]

When Annette returned home at the completion of the school term, however, the would-be courtship became more difficult. Accustomed to having her way, Annette often took offense when Julius did not acquit himself according to her definition of a proper beau. Her letters upbraided him for lack of seriousness and for failing to make the drive to her father's farm to see her as often as she would like. As a result, many of Julius's letters to Annette were filled with apologies for real or imagined wrongdoing. In a letter of February 10, 1882, Julius noted that he was sorry that he had been unable to call on her because of heavy rains. Two months later, the young merchant apologized once again for playing a "game," and admitted, probably without real cause, that he had been "rude" to her. Yet, the romantic feelings between the two were mutual, as Annette admitted in a September 1882 letter that "hours seem like days when you are gone," and that she could not even "enjoy the company of her best friends if he were not present." So, the sometimes troubled courtship continued, and by July, Julius wrote Annette asking her to "accept the ring with our selected initials." In her answer, Annette wrote that she "was pleased. . . . It is all that I could ask. Let them remain forever unchanged and the sentiment indelibly written in our hearts."[11]

A long siege of bad weather did little to help the situation, and in August 1882, Julius lamented that "providence intends to keep us apart by continued rain." After Annette professed illness, probably in a play for sympathy, Julius wrote that he was going to visit her the following Sunday, weather permitting, and penned, "I am going to ask your parents if they have any objections to our marriage." Obviously nervous about the prospect of petitioning for the hand of Parson Renfro's daughter, Julius noted that he did not "expect any thing else than your father's taking a gun to me (?) but, however, I cant help it, I am going to ask him." Again, however, Julius was unable to keep his date, but he wrote and reiterated that he wanted to see Annette's father for "special business."[12]

By late September, Julius finally was able to make the trip to the Renfro farm to see Annette and to discuss the subject of their marriage with her father. Although there is no record of exactly what the Baptist minister said to the young man, the two became good friends during the days that Julius visited the Renfro family, and no objections were offered to the proposed marriage. Parson Renfro drove Julius to the depot for the train ride back to Alvarado, and the two cemented their friendship during the trip. Even so, on October 4, Julius wrote Annette that he had worried about "boarding" with her father so long, and he expressed concern about being away from his store during the time he spent at the Renfro farm.[13]

Julius knew that financial success would result only from close attention to business, and he was reluctant to make a habit of closing the grocery to make the ten-mile drive to the Renfro farm on Crill Miller Creek. He had many customers who depended on him, and he knew that if he stayed away too long, they would be forced to find new sources. His likeable manner, however, made many friends, and even the press supported his business efforts. The following note appeared in a news column of *The Alvarado Bulletin:* "Our young friend, Julius Baker, has launched out into the commercial world, all solitary and alone, and is now the proprietor of a first-class staple and fancy grocery house on the south side of the square. He is a very deserving young man and we wish him his abundant prosperity. See his card." Baker's beginning advertisements were abrupt but straightforward: "Go to the Mo. Pacific depot for cheap groceries. JULIUS BAKER, Prop." As both business and competition increased, however, his space in the *Bulletin* grew progressively. By November, his ads were much more sophisticated and informational. "JULIUS BAKER," read the headline, "Dealer in Staple and Fancy Groceries, at the Missouri Pacific Depot, Alvarado, Texas. A new, full and complete stock of groceries, canned goods of all kinds, tobacco and everything kept at a first-class grocery house. Your patronage is respectfully solicited."[14]

Meanwhile, Annette's brother, Burleson, now nicknamed "Dr. Burleson" by his friend Julius, also had met a young lady with whom he was infatuated. Burlie's new love was a pretty girl from the nearby community of Egan named Kittie Miller, and the two, along with Annette and Julius, were often seen together at outings and events in and around Alvarado. Although for unknown reasons Kittie was never embraced by the Renfro family in the same manner as was Julius Baker, it soon became a well-known secret that eventually the two couples would marry, and speculation was rife as to which pair would make the decision to do so first.[15]

Yet, the petty bickering that sometimes ensued between Julius and Annette threatened their courtship. On October 14, Julius once again wrote a letter of apology to Annette, asking her not to "think hard of me for telling you that you had neglected answering a simple question. It was all a joke, and very frivolous." Another note of November 2 was similar and concerned a misunderstanding between the two. Despite the problems, however, the off-and-on love affair between Annette and Julius was to have a positive ending, for they soon set a date for their wedding.[16]

Upon learning that Annette and Julius were to be married on December 7, 1882, Burlie and Kittie determined not to be outdone, and they mischievously set their wedding date for December 6, one day sooner. On November 19, Annette wrote Julius that Kittie had purchased her wedding clothes and that she would do so the next day, "for the great occasion." The time for the two ceremonies soon arrived, and the announcement of the marriages was reported in a newspaper article entitled, "Hymen's Harvest":

> At the residence of the bride's father near Eagen [Egan], Texas, on the night of the 6the [sic] of Dec. 1882, by the Rev. J. J. Davis, Mr. J. B. Renfro, son of Rev. H. C. Renfro, and Miss Kittie Miller, all of Johnson County.
>
> By Elder J. R. Clarke at the residence of the bride's father, Eld H. C. Renfro, Dec. 7, 1882, Mr. Julius Baker and Miss Annette Renfro. Their many friends wish them great prosperity and happiness.[17]

The Alvarado Bulletin reported the event in more detail, noting that "Mr. Baker is a thrifty and highly respected young merchant, doing business at the Missouri Pacific depot. He was raised up in this community by highly respected parents. The lovely bride is the daughter of the Rev. H. C. Renfro, for a quarter of a century a resident of this county, and universally esteemed as one of the most eloquent of ministers. He is one of the few of his calling who by diligence and industry has amassed a fortune." Continuing his description, the reporter for the *Bulletin* noted that "the table groaned beneath the load of luxuries, and the family had the felicity of making each guest feel at home."[18]

Henry Renfro was pleased with the choices that his daughter and son had made in their selection of spouses, and he soon took the opportunity to write to his friend Thomas Neilson in Philadelphia with the news. In a reply written on February 20, 1883, Neilson expressed his congratulations "on the marriage of yr son & daughter & am delighted to learn that their choice meets with yr thorough approbriation [sic], for it is so hard for a father, after having lavished love & every earthly comfort on his children & often too, at the expense of much self denial, to see them throw themselves away on unworthy objects & requite his care & tenderness, by disappointment & heart ache."[19]

Neilson's discussion of disappointment and heartache was almost a foreboding of things to come, for despite the desires of Henry Renfro and his wife Mary, neither prosperity nor great happiness were to be the result of the wedding of Julius Baker and Annette Renfro. Julius's worries about being away from his business and the resultant decline in earnings were confirmed by March of 1883. At that time, the promissory note that the young man had given his brother Darius for the dollars needed to establish his grocery business was due. Although Darius likely could have allowed his brother an extension in his debt, he chose for unknown reasons not to do so, and he made a demand for all of the principal plus interest. When Julius was unable to pay, the brother chose legal recourse. On March 23, 1883, the *Alvarado Weekly Bulletin* reported that "Mr. Julius Baker, doing business at the Missouri Pacific depot, was closed out by writ of attachment last Tuesday, in favor of D. Baker for $3,800." The sadness of the interfamily squabble was heightened because of the death, on January 13, 1883, of the father of both of the men.[20]

The shutdown of the grocery store in Alvarado had a pernicious effect on the new bride. Accustomed to being successful and at the forefront of every venture she had ever begun, Annette was depressed by the foreclosure of the business by her brother-in-law. She did not understand how brother could treat brother in that manner, and she began to express her dissatisfaction concerning the event in her relationship with others, including Julius but principally with Darius and the rest of the Baker family, whom she blamed for the legal action. Words were exchanged between Annette and Darius which were to have tragic and long-lasting effects. Too, Annette's disposition suffered because of the conflict, although it is unlikely that she herself realized the magnitude of the change. Her morose attitude was compounded by a long siege of foul weather, and rain fell day after day, creating a sense of the blues in Annette that she was unable to shake. She lamented her new position in life, complaining that she had to cook, to keep house, and even work in the fields. Yet, Annette's duties were no more than any other young lady starting a home, and there is no question but that she was looking for reasons to be unhappy. The Parson's daughter never enjoyed the chores of a housekeeper.[21]

Although Parson Renfro and his wife Mary knew of the superficial effect that Annette's problems were having on her personality, they had no inkling of the extent of the problem, although they could not have helped knowing that Annette was not herself. Yet, whatever their knowledge of the unhappiness that their daughter was experiencing, they were determined that it would not affect plans for a vacation which Mary had made months before. Ida Coody, Mary's niece from Searcy, Arkansas, visited in Johnson County during the last of April and the first part of May 1883. When the time came for her to return home, Mary Renfro as well as another niece, Fannie Ray, accompanied Ida back to Arkansas.[22]

Mary's first letter home was received on May 24. In it, she revealed her concern about Annette, specifically asking how her daughter was getting along in her role as a homemaker. In an answer written on May 26, Burlie included a short reference to his sister's problems. "Well Ma you asked how Annette was getting along with housework, she is getting along well enough, Julius and John [Renfro] helps her. Julius milks & churns for her. John says he wants to see Aunt Mary, and so he does, he misses you very much." Henry Renfro was surprised at the extent of his daughter's depression, and he immediately set out to find ways to solve the problem. He and Annette always had been very close, and the Parson talked to Annette privately about her unhappiness and searched for a solution. One was not immediately forthcoming, however, as Annette told him that she did not really know what was the matter—only that she was disappointed with the Baker family and that she had not yet achieved the happiness that she believed that her marriage would bring. Renfro also discussed the situation with Burlie and with Julius, but neither of the men could give a clear-cut explanation of Annette's mood. It was almost as if both were trying to deny or minimize the problem in the hope that it would go away.[23]

On June 5, for example, Julius wrote a letter to Mary Renfro in which he said nothing about Annette's problems; he wrote positively about his new wife and gave no indication of marital difficulties. Instead, he discussed the activities at home. "Annette has just finished me a nice every day shirt[,] the first she ever made for me, she thinks she has done wonders. We are going to gather grapes this eve[;] we have postponed it long enough. Pa thinks it is a bad way to make a living, but we will 'steal a march' on the old fellow and gather them while he is gone to the Fort [Fort Worth]. Blackberries are getting ripe and the woods are full of them[;] we can put them up too cant we?"[24]

A few days later on June 17, Julius acknowledged that Annette had been having difficulties but concluded that they were in the past. "Annette is not afflicted any now and she seems to be a great deal better satisfied, she put up seventeen 1/2 gal. cans Blackberries[;] dont you think that is very commendable[?]" Julius likely was restricted somewhat concerning what he could say, as his wife as well as his father-in-law planned to enclose letters in the same envelope with his. He ended his correspondence with the comment that "Pa and Annette are going to write so I will close."[25]

Henry was reluctant to correspond with Mary about the problem, as he was sure that she would want to shorten her long wished-for visit with Chellie and return to Texas. However, he felt that he had to tell her of the situation. "Annette is having a hard time," he wrote on June 17, "and Julius deserves great credit for his kindness." The Parson noted that he knew that Annette's attitude would be difficult to change, but said that if she did not do so, she might well endanger her marriage with Julius.[26]

Recognizing that part of Annette's problem was Julius's temporary lack of the means of making a living, Henry and Mary determined to remedy the situation, deeding to each of their children and their spouses, as a wedding present, a tract of over one hundred acres of farmland. Furthermore, they provided funds for each couple for a new house, thus giving Annette and Julius and Burlie and Kittie an extra degree of independence, a measure of security, an honorable profession, and a profound boost in confidence. The gift, which allowed Julius to become self-supporting once again, was important to Annette. Her disposition, although far from being what it might have been, began to improve somewhat, and with the change came a partial but welcome return of harmony between Annette and the Baker family.[27]

Yet, even with the problems which surfaced in the first three years, the first four years of the decade of the 1880's were good ones for the Renfro family. Henry's associations with persons both within and without the Baptist Church had proved to be reasonably serene and without the conflicts that had characterized past years. Too, the financial position of the Renfros was secure because of sound business practice and the continued acquisition and sale of lands. The creation of a loving extended "family" of homeless young men was of value to both the Renfro family and to those who were given jobs and opportunities. The marriages of both Burlie and Annette appeared to be improving steadily, and the couples seemed to be on their way to long-term happiness. The special relationship that had developed between Henry and Mary in their twenty-five years together continued to be strong, and love was ever present in the Renfro household. Yet, the bright beams of happiness were to be darkened by black clouds of bitterness and storms of hate that lurked just beyond the horizon.

Chapter 7

A Heart Warm Fond Adieu

Parson Renfro enjoyed the reading, research, and study that were necessary to be thoroughly conversant with the Bible, and he always made time for that effort. He spent long hours studying the Holy Scriptures as well as such works as John Laurence Mosheim's *An Ecclesiastical History, Ancient and Modern*, Vincent L. Milner's *Religious Denominations of the World*, and *Theology: The Philosophy of Religion*. Occasionally, however, he found the time to go beyond the religious and investigate and analyze literature, philosophy, and history. During short periods, usually late at night, he pored over his "well-worn" copy of *The Poetical Works of Robert Burns* as well as *Moore's Poetical Works*. He even read, in Latin, the works of Juvenal, a first-century Roman satirist. Yet, Renfro longed for the leisure that would allow him to inquire more deeply into the meaning of life and his relationship to the Supreme Being. He was to find the time to do so, but the result would be the undoing of his career as a Baptist minister. In the meantime, however, he was to continue the hectic schedule that he had set for himself.[1]

At the beginning of the 1880's, Henry Renfro was almost as busy in the work of the church as he had been twenty years before. The minutes of the Seventeenth Annual Session of the Alvarado Association of September 15, 1881, note that he was a delegate from the Alvarado Baptist Church. He served on the Committee on Foreign Missions and was the chairman of the Committee on the State of Religion. Renfro was once again elected to the Association's Executive Committee, and he was appointed as the messenger to the West Fork Association. He was asked to preach to the assembled delegates. Although not listed as the regular preacher of any particular congregation, Renfro was one of thirty-two ordained ministers in the Association.[2]

Renfro's devotion to his faith, combined with the intense effort that he had always put into the management of his farmlands, allowed little time for additional activities. The hours necessary for reading of books other than those needed in his ministry always had been almost nonexistent. With his increasing success in business ventures, however, came the opportunity to break that pattern. Land purchases and sales, combined with the profitable operation of the Renfro stock farm, provided for the first time the financial well-being which allowed the Parson to slow his personal pace of work and secure additional help for his farming operations. With the newfound leisure which became available to the Parson, he began to do more of what he personally wanted to do and less of what always had been demanded by his church and his profession. In September 1882, for the first time, he was hardly mentioned in the minutes of the annual meeting of the Alvarado Baptist Association. The lack of participation of one formerly so active in the Association's affairs, however, soon generated questions in the minds of those who by their nature searched for fault.[3]

Yet, despite the fact that there were some persons who thrived on dissension and rumor, most persons in and out of the Baptist Church still considered the Parson to be one of the outstanding men in the Central Texas area. When a new courthouse for Johnson County was completed in Cleburne in November 1882, Henry Renfro was selected as the principal speaker for the occasion. After an elaborate ceremony in which the cornerstone was laid with full Masonic ceremony, the Parson "made a short and happy speech, choosing for his subject the rise and fall of civilization in general, and Johnson county in particular. He was frequently applauded during the remarks." The *Bulletin* reporter concluded by saying that the "ceremony was deeply impressive and the audience extremely attentive."[4]

Renfro's active participation in the affairs of the community made him one of Johnson County's most prominent citizens. His years of active participation in the Baptist Church, his enthusiastic promotion of schools and youth, and his success as a farmer and stockman established the Parson as a respected leader. Yet, the public which puts its citizens on a pedestal often is quick to criticize and condemn their leaders when they perceive what they consider to be a weakness. Henry Renfro was aware of this possibility, particularly from those in the church with whom he worked on a daily basis. As a result, he must have realized that his study of some of the more controversial literature of the day, if generally known, would raise eyebrows among those whose beliefs allowed no questions regarding the divine inspiration of the Bible. An unremitting curiosity, however, impelled Renfro to study with great interest the works of Spinoza, Thomas Paine, and Robert G. Ingersoll. These books, the contents of which contained passages which challenged orthodox religion, raised additional questions in Renfro's mind as to the role of the church and its relationship to humanity. Inevitably, some of the concepts and ideas questioning orthodox religion that Renfro studied became a part of the sermons that he preached on a regular basis. Although the Parson did not deliberately try to change the beliefs of those to whom he spoke, the concepts discussed in his sermons raised questions. Many parishioners were alarmed at what they heard, particularly in regard to Renfro's denouncement of some clergymen who he believed were "fleecing the flock" and promoting orthodox religion as a way of enriching their own pocketbooks. By fall 1882, rumors concerning Renfro's lack of devotion to orthodoxy had begun to impair his credibility with some elements within the church. Old adversaries such as those who had supported Roddy during his trouble with Renfro as well as some who were critical of Renfro's personal accumulation of worldly goods began quietly to take aim at the Parson, and whispers and innuendo began to supplant trust and friendship.[5]

It should be noted, however, that Henry Renfro was not the only minister in the Central Texas area who was criticized because of his thoughts or because of the content of his sermons. Indeed, the philosophy of what was known as "Liberalism" had spread throughout the state. Seven years earlier, in 1875, Dr. Levi James Russell of Heidenheimer, Bell County, Texas, was expelled from both the Masonic Lodge and the Knights of Pythias for "heresy." Russell was the president of an organization known as the "Association of Freethinkers of Bell County," and as such, he was the subject of derision from almost all churchmen in the area. On the night of October 6, 1877, Dr. Russell was called out at midnight, supposedly to treat an extremely sick woman, but the false emergency was only a ruse to isolate the doctor from any possible assistance. A mob of men from Bell County who called themselves Christians first stripped the physician, then flogged him "unmercifully," applying one hundred lashes to his bare body. There is no doubt but that Henry Renfro recalled the incident with some apprehension as his own beliefs edged closer and closer to those of the assaulted man.[6]

And yet, the threat of violence and the recollection of the assault on Russell deterred neither Renfro nor others from doing as their consciences dictated in regard to Free Thought and their relationship to the organized church. In September 1882, the same week that Julius Baker stayed at the Renfro home and asked the Parson for the hand of his daughter, a news item appeared in *The Alvarado Bulletin*, titled simply "Special to the Dallas Herald from Waco." It reported the content of a sermon made by the Reverend James D. Shaw, the minister of the venerable Fifth Street Methodist Church in Waco. The news report detailed Shaw's presentation to his church with the comment that the minister "boldly took a new departure from theological creeds and placed himself abreast with what is known as the advanced thought of the present day. He rejects the absolute inspiration of the scripture, the atonement, the saving power of faith, etc., and accepts the teachings of Christ as a higher human philosophy." Approached by a reporter from the *Waco Daily Examiner*, Shaw denied any hint that he was heretical and recalled that in his sermon he "said not a word that is in violation of our 25 articles, or my obligations to the [Methodist] church." Yet, Shaw realized that an explanation was in order. "A long and critical study of the claims of Christianity," stated Shaw, "has forced me to reconstruct my religious beliefs to some extent, and how far this may go I am not now able to say." Shaw promised that if he found it "necessary to antagonize the doctrines of the church," he would "not use her appointment in the pulpit to do it."[7]

Henry Renfro read the article about Shaw, and he felt an immediate kinship with the Methodist minister. Although he had never made a public statement concerning his ever-increasing doubts concerning the spiritual direction of the orthodox Baptist Church, Renfro knew that the complaints that had been raised concerning the content of some of his sermons had reached proportions that would eventually compel him to do so. The Parson was impressed by Shaw's courage in making public his views, and he soon began corresponding with the Methodist minister. Shaw's examination of biblical questions would cause Renfro to examine further the tenets of those who challenged the orthodox church. Although Renfro was sympathetic to ideas questioning the inerrancy of the Bible and the saving power of Grace, he was not yet ready to go as far as Shaw in questioning the bedrock of Christian belief.

Shaw, on the other hand, already had made statements that placed his standing with the church in a dubious position, and as the months went by he found himself, more and more, on a collision course with orthodoxy. Upon completion of his four-year term at the Fifth Street Methodist Church, Shaw preached a farewell sermon with the expectation that he would be transferred to a new congregation by the upcoming Northwest Conference, to be held in Cleburne, Texas, beginning November 1, 1882. Shaw's deviation from conventional Methodist doctrine, however, precluded such a move, and after his attempt to state his beliefs in open conference was denied, a motion was made to refer Shaw's case to a committee. This group of three men would then make a decision as to the course the Conference should follow in regard to the questionable minister. In a forty-five minute defense of his beliefs, Shaw addressed several facets of his creed including the inspiration of the scriptures, the divinity of Christ, the vicarious atonement, and the punishment of the wicked. Although Shaw spoke to the committee in a "very able and persuasive manner," it was recommended by its members that Shaw be asked to surrender his credentials as a clergyman. The reason given by the committee was that Shaw's views were "detrimental to religion and injurious to the church." On November 4, Shaw returned his documents as a minister to Methodist authorities.[8]

Despite the dishonor of his disenfranchisement, Shaw returned to Waco not in disgrace but in general approbation of the town's citizens. His decision to remain there was heartily welcomed, even by the press, and he returned to that city more in an air of triumph than in despair. "Rev. J. D. Shaw is at home," one article began. "It is hardly necessary to say that his greeting on all hands, was of the most cordial in nature." Finally, the editor noted that if Shaw "ever had any doubt of the estimation in which he is held by the people, the greetings he received yesterday must have assured him that Waco needs him."[9]

Shaw was not long idle, and by December 2, only a month after he had been stripped of his church credentials, he announced the formation of the Religious and Benevolent Association, "organized to unite all those who wished to enjoy religion without any sacrifice to religious freedom." The group "met twice each Sunday for lectures, songs, and discussion" in Waco's district courtroom. Primary among the new organization's missions was the "determination to collect and dispense funds for the education of orphaned children and to disseminate knowledge among all classes." Although there were those who attacked Shaw, including one small-town newspaper editor who labeled the fledgling organization the "Hell and Damnation Society," the membership of the Religious and Benevolent Association was entirely respectable, including some of Waco's well-known attorneys, doctors, merchants, and educators. With their help, Shaw soon was able to begin the construction of a new building called Liberal Hall, designed to be a permanent home for the new organization.[10]

It was not long before Shaw announced in the *Waco Daily Examiner* the plans for the publication of *The Independent Pulpit*, a news magazine that would "satisfy the growing demand in this state for a publication which will voice the views of our most liberal and independent thinkers on the moral, intellectual, and social questions of the day." The announcement was picked up by the *Alvarado Weekly Bulletin* of March 2, 1883, and no doubt it was read by many who were beginning to believe that Henry Renfro was following the same errant path as Shaw. Rumors continued to be rife concerning the changes in the religious beliefs of the Baptist minister.[11]

One of those who heard the whispers about Renfro's supposed infidelity to the church was Rufus Burleson, serving as the president of Waco University. Burleson was alarmed at what he heard about his friend and former student, and on September 15, 1883, he composed a long letter to Renfro, urging that they correspond about the questions that had been raised and to plan a meeting as soon as possible to discuss the rumors and to try to resolve them. But the letter was misplaced and did not arrive, and the Parson had no hint of his friend's deep concern until much later.[12]

The continuing and growing controversy about liberalism provided ammunition for some Baptists who believed in the inerrancy of the Bible to charge that Henry Renfro was the Johnson County equivalent of J. D. Shaw. Discussion fueled gossip, and it was not long before even some highly respected church leaders began to repeat a story that Renfro was a confirmed infidel who remained in the pulpit in order to convert all Baptist Christians to his beliefs. The matter became so urgent that at the conference meeting of the Alvarado Baptist Church on October 6, 1883, charges officially were made against the Parson. "There was read a Preamble and Resolution," stated the minutes of the meeting, "against bro H. C. Renfroe [sic] for advocating and Preaching the Doctrine of Infidelity." Then the moderator of the conference, J. R. Clarke, appointed a committee of three men, J. A. Baugh, B. B. Prestridge, and S. H. Jack, to "see bro Renfroe [sic] . . . and report at our next meeting."[13]

Renfro felt compelled to answer the charges publicly, and within days he wrote a long letter to the editor of *The Alvarado Bulletin* which outlined his position and his doubts. "I find that the rumor has gone from Dan to Bursheba that I am a confirmed infidel, to all of which I plead not guilty. The wise and good," continued Renfro, "are profuse in their regrets and earnest in their appeals for me to retract my footsteps while the religious fanatics, ignorant and superstitious, are pouring upon me the vials of their wrath, saying that this is proof that I am always a hypocrite and bad man." Showing an understanding of the reasons that some persons pursued the rumors of the changes in his philosophy so diligently, Renfro noted that "the heresy of a minister is a sweet morsel, especially for the ignorant multitude, many of whom can scent the breeze and track the steps of a heretic with all the infallibility of an inquisitor."[14] Renfro admitted that he had "been doing a little independent thinking of later years, and my frail bark is now dashed upon the breakers of doubt." Yet the Baptist minister appealed for patience, asking his questioners to "'deal gently with the young man, even with Absalom,' for I am not right certain what is the matter with me. When I understand the true diagnosis of the disease I will then apply the remedy. . . . I want a fair chance," he said, "and as my church has an intelligent membership, and in her pastor [J. R. Clarke] the Henry Clay of the Texas pulpit, I have no fears of being dealt with in a summary or harsh manner." Renfro then outlined some of the thoughts that had surfaced in his studies.[15]

I may state that one result of my reading and observation is that all religious denominations have egregiously blundered in making such a great ado about the things necessary to be believed, and paying so little attention to the moral conduct of their respective membership. I sometimes think it would have been better if no religious creed had ever been written. They have been prolific sources of strife. Christ never wrote a creed, nor did he ever command anybody to write one. He who believes in God and hopes for immortality, with moral conduct corresponding thereto, is certainly not far from the kingdom of God. I am almost sure that orthodox christians have exalted faith into undue proportion and to [too] much ignored the office of reason in matters of religion.[16]

Continuing his letter to the editor of *The Alvarado Bulletin*, Renfro noted that his many supporters and friends had urged him to "leave off further investigation of these vexed questions." The Parson then noted that he had recently "received a long and suggestive letter from a Methodist brother . . . which was so kind, so touching, so gentle and loving, and contained such mighty appeals to my heart and conscience that I was tempted to lay the whole matter of my defection upon the blues, ascribe them to a diseased liver, and rid myself at once of the whole business. . . . I am not indifferent," stated the Parson, "to love and friendship, kindness and gentleness. These warm and touching appeals hold a mighty influence over my heart and weaken my resolution in the course I am pursuing."[17]

Yet, Renfro felt compelled to resist the temptation to drop his investigations, and he noted that he felt stronger, morally, than he had ever felt in his life. "But then," recalled Renfro in his letter to the editor, "I ventured into the path Spinoza trod, and to tell the truth I have an almost irresistible temptation to follow on a little farther. Strange to say, that while my late investigations have [been] somewhat disturbed by theological opinions, they have in no way lessened the force of moral obligations upon my heart. Never before in my life did I ever have such complete control of my wild and impetuous nature. Never before less enmity and ill-will toward my fellow man. Never before more patience, humanity, gentleness, kindness, forbearance, and forgiveness." All Henry Renfro desired at that time was the patience of those who questioned him. "Now I love my church," he said. "All my predilections, all the memories and associations of my life cluster around her, and I am willing to become a very beast of burden in the performance of moral duties and obligations, if she will slacken the reins, and give me a little more latitude on the theological questions." Finally, Renfro promised that if, after his "investigations and researches," he should not be "in harmony with the doctrines and teachings of the denomination," then he would "strengthen myself as best I can for the 'irrepressible conflict,' and 'with melting heart and brimful-eyes,' pass the ordeal separated [separating] me from the church."[18]

The committee appointed by Alvarado Baptist Church minister J. R. Clarke called on Henry Renfro at his home near the end of October. Although the three members of the committee were charged with ascertaining whether or not the church should continue with its charges against its former pastor, all of the men were friends of long standing, and none wished that Renfro might be separated from the association that he had held so many years. Therefore, when Henry questioned the damning preamble and resolutions that were read in charges against him at the October 6 meeting, the committee agreed to ask the conference to repeal them and continue its investigation in a more unbiased mode. In exchange, Henry assured his friends that he would refrain from preaching until the investigation against him was completed. At a meeting at the Alvarado church on November 3, the preamble and resolutions of the previous meeting were rescinded, thus softening somewhat the charges against its former pastor.[19]

On Saturday, December 2, the conference of the Alvarado Baptist Church met once again to discuss the case of Henry Renfro. Since the committee report was not, in itself, sufficiently severe that the conference could take any punitive action, the committee suggested that the Parson be allowed to testify in his own behalf before the church. Accordingly, the motion was made and carried that "the church request bro Renfro to attend our next conference and give some satisfactory statement in regard to his investigation of the Scriptures."[20]

Although Renfro was willing to address the conference in the attempt to have the charges against him dismissed, the next meeting was not held until January 6, 1884. Renfro still had not by that time been told of the desire of the conference that he should attend, but when the matter was discussed, a definite date finally was determined. "The case of Elder H. C. Renfro was brought before the church," read the minutes. "Moved and carried that bro Renfro be notified to attend our next conference meeting, Saturday before the first Sunday in Feb. and answer to the charge of Infidelity in not believing in the inspiration of the Scriptures." In an extraordinary move, the conference decided to ask that leaders from other churches be requested to attend also. They were "requested to send three or more to meet with us, on the first Saturday in Feb to assist us in our deliberation." Churches in Cleburne, Grandview, Mountain Peak, Union Hill, Sand Flat, Pleasant Point, and Bethesda were asked to send representatives.[21]

On January 18, 1884, only days after the date was set for the trial of Henry Renfro, Rufus Burleson opened an old memo book that he last had used in the months before the opening of the fall semester of Waco University. In it, much to his chagrin, he found the letter that he wrote to Renfro in which he expressed his concern for his former student. Having learned that the hearing was to be held on February 2 and realizing the urgency of the situation, Burleson quickly wrote another letter in which he explained to his old friend what had happened. "No pen nor pencil can express," wrote the university president, "the surprise and regret that I feel at this moment—just half an hour ago opening an old memorandum book . . . I found stored away the letter herein enclosed which I firmly believed I mailed to you at Alvarado Sept. 15, 1883. Oh how many thousand times I have wondered and grieved that you made no reply." Burleson emphasized that he often had wanted to try once more to change his former student's mind, but he felt that Renfro may have preferred to leave the situation as it was. "I sat down several times to write you again," wrote the Parson's old professor, "but I thought no[,] it may only give pain to your sensitive heart to urge a correspondence and a meeting. But now the mystery is all explained."[22]

Fervently, Burleson explained his feelings for Renfro and noted how much he had wished for a change of heart. "Oh, how many times have I grieved and wept and prayed for your deliverance from the bondage of doubting castle and that your last days may be your best days for Jesus and his cause." Speculating on the reasons for Renfro's doubts and on immortality, Dr. Burleson noted that "perchance He allows you to suffer temptation darkness and doubt that you may know to succor them that are tempted in these dark days. If I die before you emerge from under the clouds my last prayer will be for you and at the pearly gates of the New Jerusalem I will be waiting and watching for you and will expect to see you coming up with many sheaves with you of your last gleaning."[23]

In an effort to have Renfro understand that he was not abandoned by everyone in the church, Burleson discussed the correspondence of one person within the church that was favorable to the Parson. "You have probably seen a letter from Bro Martin V. Smith referring to your present and past condition. In his expressions of love and affection for you he echoes the feeling of thousands in Texas." Then Burleson described his own efforts to keep Renfro's reputation beyond further question in the Baptist community. "You will see a letter I have written on the same subject showing that though you did receive aid from the churches [while at Baylor] you had refunded it all. I feared that some one might reflect on your honor if this point were not clear." Then, Burleson expressed the desire to see his old student and discuss all that had happened. "I now repeat I want to come up to Burleson and preach and spend a night with you and talk over all things old and new joyful and sad." In closing, Burleson noted that "Wife and daughter and son join in love to you and family."[24]

But the good will and encouragement of one of the most important figures in the Baptist Church in Texas did little to slow the heated controversy that was due to boil at the next conference meeting of the Alvarado Baptist Church. The morning of February 2, 1884, was to come all too soon. The sun dawned exquisitely, and it seemed almost incomprehensible to the Parson that a day that began so beautifully might provide the setting for anguish and distress. For weeks, he had endeavored to be mentally ready for the ordeal, and he believed that he had been successful. "My face was, as I thought, steeled against the weakness of weeping, and my tears dried up, so I felt at times like Job's war horse, ready for battle." Then the invited representatives from other churches, persons described by Renfro as "the old brethren I had known and loved for twenty-five years," filed into the church sanctuary and "took their seats as gravely as if they had assembled to hear Gabriel preach the funeral of the universe." Once everyone was seated, the organ began the notes of "How Firm a Foundation," and for Renfro, it was "a time for memory and for tears." The reminiscences continued as J. R. Clarke began his sermon entitled, "Will ye also go away?"[25]

Upon completion of the address, the case was called, and moderator Clarke rose and read a telegram from Rufus Burleson in which the educator and minister asked that the hearing be postponed for a month. The request was denied; however, Clarke did agree to allow Renfro to read several letters that he had received from his friend and mentor. Uncharacteristically, Renfro verbally stumbled as he recited the contents of Burleson's correspondence. The reading was done "as best I could," he would say later, "though in a very stammering way." Then, moderator Clarke began his interrogation, which Renfro answered freely, "expressing my doubts about the truths of all orthodox teaching." In his answers to Clarke's questions, the Parson did not at first deny the inspiration of any part of the Bible. Pressed, however, he did admit that he did not believe the statement that was recorded in the last verse of the last chapter of John:

> And there are also many other things which Jesus did, the which, if they should be written every one, I suppose that even the world itself could not contain the books that should be written.[26]

Describing the events that followed, Renfro noted that "this wicked denial of such a precious passage of scripture was considered by the moderator, and another minister, who was sent to assist the Alvarado church in the work of purging out heresy, as sacrilegious and downright infidelity, for which I was then and there excluded." "Others will bear me witness," wrote Renfro within days of the event, "that I did not absolutely deny the inspiration of a passage of the bible, but that last verse of that last chapter of that last gospel; and I think it was this that turned the tide against me, for motions and seconds came current forthwith." The minutes of the Alvarado Baptist Church recorded the event simply with the statement that "The case of Elder H. C. Renfro was brought before the Church. After a thorough investigation of the case, the church sustained the charge of Infidelity in not believing the Inspiration of the Scriptures. The charge being sustained by motion & second the church withdrew fellowship from bro Renfro."[27]

Upon the completion of the vote, Renfro was asked to surrender his certification as a Baptist minister, an act which provoked the emotion against which he believed he had steeled himself. "Then came the hardest part of all," Renfro recalled, "—giving up my credentials, which I did with many tears. How hard it is to rid ourselves of the powers of first impressions, and the sacred memories and associations of early life. Even when the mind and judgment are completely convinced and converted, as mine was, the heart clings on with unyielding tenacity and refused to be divorced from the objects of its earliest love." But he gave them up, then asked for a few minutes in which he might address the assembled conference. He was told icily that he could not, as it was a Baptist meeting, and Renfro was no longer a Baptist. Recalling the event, the former parson noted that he was "truly sorry when on surrendering my credentials, and taking occasion to speak of what sorrow of heart I felt in giving up a document I had held so long . . . and giving my brethren and sisters 'a heart warm fond adieu,' to be told that I was out of order, when that was the fact only because I was out of the church." His first request denied, Renfro then asked the assembled delegates for the opportunity to utilize the church at a later date to "give the facts that led me into doubt," but once again, the appeal was refused.[28]

At home again by Saturday afternoon, a depressed Renfro looked for solace in the poetry of Robert Burns. "Turning almost intuitively to this melancholy dirge, 'Man was made to mourn,' I read it in a more realizing way than ever before." He compared the Scottish Bard's work with the Bible, noting that "if every sentiment in the Bible was as pure and grand as the sentiment in this poem, written by a poor Scottish peasant, I would have never had one hour's trouble with the inspiration of the Bible. . . . Here," said the disenfranchised minister, "is inspiration pure as a snow flake."

Man's inhumanity to man
Makes countless thousands mourn.[29]

After contemplating time and time again the proceedings of the conference, Renfro decided that it was incumbent upon him to express his view of the day's events in writing, lest any think that his will was defeated by the trial or that his determination was subdued by its verdict. In a letter to *The Alvarado Bulletin,* he detailed the agenda of the meeting, pointing out the frustration that he experienced and the distress that he felt at the lack of insight shown by those who sat in judgment. First, however, he expressed disappointment that they had not even considered the plea of Rufus Burleson to delay the proceedings. "I was sorry," he wrote, "that the church refused to grant the kind request of Dr. Burleson, to postpone my trial for a month, if for no other reason than to honor a noble veteran and venerable minister, who has done more for the Baptist denomination, religiously and educationally, than any man who has ever made a track on Texas soil. He knows me better than any other man on earth, and in his great warm heart he wished to shield me from rash and hasty discipline."[30]

In further reference to the swiftness of the proceedings, Renfro hinted that the outcome of the trial might have been different if more time had been allowed and if persons eager for his expulsion had not been so influential. "I have thought," Renfro related, "that if the church had been let alone she might have dealt with me with more tenderness and been in less haste for final action." Yet, in a note of conciliation, Renfro wrote that "she is a noble church, and I love her still. Our relation has been of the tenderest character, and our separation was in kindness."[31]

Renfro realized, however, that a powerful change had occurred in his life and that his relationship with the church and those in it would soon change significantly. "But the days of our meeting and greeting are ended," he said, "and when she [the church] meets and sings her hymns of lofty cheer, she may now and then 'send a wish or thought' after one who served her to the best of his abilities, out of pure love and not for filthy lucre's sake. My preaching, Sunday School picnic, Christmas tree speaking are over. Nor shall I meet again the blushing bride and groom at the hymeneal altar, and feast on wedding cake, all of which has been pleasant enough. Adieu to all of these."[32]

Without question, Renfro understood what the future would hold for him from some who in the past had held out their hands in friendship and good will. "Welcome hatred, persecution, and abuse," Renfro wrote, "I now bear my bosom to the storm I have dreaded so long. I have lost the fellowship of a good church and brought against me the abuse of the unthinking; but I have kept my conscience. I have not dishonored my manhood by disguising my sentiments. . . . This," wrote the former parson, "has been the great struggle of my life. God knows how many honest tears it has cost me, and the sleepless hours I have spent in reflection. . . . I know," said Renfro, "that though my doubts were not of my own seeking, and would not down at my bidding, that others would see it differently, and I would be censured."[33]

As far as he personally was concerned, however, Renfro wrote that he continued to believe that he did the right thing at the meeting in conference with the members of the Alvarado Baptist Church. "The only bright side I now see to this picture, is that I am free, and can express my sentiments untrammelled. I must confess that this consideration is somewhat refreshing, as I had felt so long that my utterances had rendered me obnoxious to the church. To tell the truth, I have grown to [too] liberal in my feelings and sentiments to make a right good landmark Baptist, and any other is regarded as unworthy of the coldest seat in the average Baptist church."[34]

Renfro ended his "Open Letter" with a statement of appreciation to those who supported him, an expression of what religion really ought to be, and a mild censure of those who place faith over qualities he considered to be more important. "Many thanks," he said, "for the good ladies and gentlemen who showed me so much kindness and sympathy while I was passing through my ordeal, and which proved a very cordial to my heart. Honor, honesty, and truth make a trinity of essentials in the warfare of the world. That is pure religion that leads a man to make his living by the sweat of his brow; to owe . . . man nothing, to attend strictly to his own business, and let the business of everybody else alone; to deal justly, love mercy, and walk humbly before God. And he who is wanting in these grand prerequisites, and labors for the exclusion of a doubter—well, what is he?"[35]

In the same issue of *The Alvarado Bulletin* in which Renfro's open letter appeared on February 8, a news article appeared which reported the convention at the Alvarado Baptist Church at which Renfro surrendered his membership and ministry. In bold lettering the paper proclaimed the event with the headline, "Excommunicated. Elder H. C. Renfro Dispossessed of Credentials." It is of interest that the news article said nothing of the line of questioning concerning the last verse of the last chapter of John; rather, it stated only that Renfro was asked if he believed in the resurrection of Jesus Christ. "Mr. Renfro," the correspondent of the paper wrote, "took the floor and endeavored to explain himself when he was called to order and was seated. Another motion was then made to dispossess him of his credentials, and after some discussion, the motion was carried by a rising vote."[36]

As a result of his expulsion, Henry Renfro was now free to pursue any course that he saw fit in relation to the orthodox church, the Bible, and his own conscience. He heartily believed that the direction that he had set for himself was correct, and he resolved to pursue it even further. He was convinced, furthermore, that the travail which he had recently endured had not alienated him from his true friends, of which he had many, and that there were scores, perhaps hundreds, of persons in north central Texas who also nourished the same doubts and concerns as he. The next months would prove this assumption.

Chapter 8

The Paper Debates

Two decades after the end of the Civil War, the Baptist Church in Texas and in the South remained extremely conservative. In contrast to churchgoers in the West and the North who had experienced, since 1830, "vigorous religious experimentation and revolution . . . ," Baptist Southerners "remained intensely orthodox, more orthodox than the conservative leaders of southern evangelicalism who were visible in a wider world." These churches, according to historian David Edwin Harrell, Jr., zealously guarded "their local independence and doctrinal purity." In addition to their defense of orthodoxy, members of churches during the decade of 1880 saw their religious institutions as more than a place for development of spiritual well-being; they also became the center of social life for the entire community. "For some persons," concluded one study, "involvement in their church's program is the core of their existence. Meaning and purpose of life, values to live by, encouragement in the face of constant adversity, are given through their church associations." Thus, any attack on orthodoxy became, in essence, an attack on a way of life—an assault on the entire rural social structure. Therefore, when a public debate on the subject by way of letters to the editor of *The Alvarado Bulletin* commenced, there were those among the faithful that felt compelled to state the position of the orthodox church in the strongest terms.[1]

As a result of the orthodoxy of the Baptist Church and the relationship of that orthodoxy to the whole idea of community and social values, Henry Renfro was condemned and expelled. In the eyes of many of the faithful, a decision not to do so would have endangered their way of life as well as constituted a serious threat to their own faith. Despite the condemnation and expulsion of Henry Renfro by the Baptist Church for infidelity, however, he welcomed the freedom that accompanied his separation from orthodox religion. If he had been expected to disappear and be heard from no more, those who would have desired it would be sorely disappointed. Less than a week after the trial, the pages of *The Alvarado Bulletin* once more were graced with a long letter from the former minister in which he detailed his expulsion and offered his version of the convention at the Alvarado Baptist Church. On the whole, the letter was kind toward those who had opposed him so doggedly. Renfro made no personal accusations; no names were called, yet he offered no excuses for his position. Instead, he attacked the system of orthodox religion and those he termed fanatics who created the difficulty in the first place. "Here is evil under the sun:" wrote the disfranchised Parson Renfro, "If a man investigates, from turret to foundation stone, any system of religion founded on revelations, miracles, and prophecies, he is very apt to get into doubting castles, and if he fails to investigate for himself, and pays somebody else to do his thinking for him, he is very liable to become a religious fanatic; and I have an idea that the history of the church would reveal that the pious doubter has been an angel of light compared to the religious fanatic." [2]

Renfro continued his "Open Letter" with a plea for men to use their minds and to question all teachings about which doubt arises. "The time will come," he said, "when every man will do his own thinking, and not pay another to do it for him—when every man will be his own pope, his own priest, and his own preacher. The time will come," continued Renfro, "when men will be controlled less and less by blind faith, and follow more and more the lamp of reason. The time will come when men will preach and practice the religion of the heart—the religion of deed rather than the religion of creed. The time will come when churches will not check, but demand their ministers to investigate all important questions, and give to them and to the world their honest thoughts." [3]

It soon became obvious that his expulsion by the Baptists did not turn the citizenry against the former minister. One week after Renfro's "Open Letter" of February 8, the following note from him appeared in the *Bulletin:*

> By request of the citizens of Alvarado, I will deliver a lecture on Sunday, February 17, 11 a.m. at the opera house, giving the statements and concessions of christian write[r]s that led me into doubt.[4]

Even before the scheduled lecture, however, questions concerning the reasons for the dismissal of Renfro from the pulpit and from the church were forthcoming. On February 15, one "Citizen" wrote a letter to the editor in which he asked "Uncle Jerry," one of the editorialists of *The Alvarado Bulletin,* to "give us an exegesis of the last verse of John." In an extremely long answer to the question, the newspaperman reasoned that men do not know the reasons for everything that God has inspired to be written in the Bible, and that the last verse of the last chapter of John was but an example of our failure to understand.[5]

Although there were, no doubt, persons who believed (or wished) that there would be no real interest by the residents of the area in the philosophies of Henry C. Renfro, his reception the following Sunday erased that uncertainty. The reporter from *The Alvarado Bulletin* noted that "Mr. Renfro lectured . . . to a large concourse of people last Sunday. It was perhaps the largest audience ever assembled at the opera house."[6]

The text of Renfro's address was "For a Man to be Mentally Faithful Unto Himself," and it was reported that the "surrounding country" was well represented in the audience, as well as "many from neighboring towns." The reporter from the *Bulletin* who attended the meeting noted that "the services were opened by singing, and a beautiful prayer by Mr. Renfro." The former parson explained to the crowd the reasons for his change in perspective, noting that his studies had made it "irresistible" to him. Paradoxically, Renfro told the assembled congregation that as his belief in orthodox religion had grown less and less as time went by, his religious consciousness had actually "reached a higher plane than formerly."[7]

Renfro pounded on the theme that he believed that "errors and corruptions" had been introduced into the Bible, not only by "the negligence of the transcribers," but also "by the boldness of those who ventured to strike out, add, and change the word of God, to suit their convenience" and who "openly avowed and defended the practice of falsifying and forgery to promote the interest of the church." Moreover, Renfro stated to the assembled audience, many of the most celebrated reformers, such as Luther and Calvin, "not only doubted certain books of the new testament but [also] denied them."[8]

Although Renfro obviously believed that the Bible contained many flaws and errors, he made a sincere effort to emphasize that the fallacies that he pointed out did not invalidate most of what the Bible said. In closing his lecture, the former minister noted that the Bible "abounded in good, wise maxims and sayings . . ." and that he "did not doubt the inspiration of every Bible lesson that taught men to do justice, love mercy, and walk humbly before God; that men ought to be guided by the lamp of reason and common sense in religious matters as well as everything else." Finally, Renfro asserted that he would do nothing to "demoralize or encourage the young in evil, and warned all young men to stand aloof from all the contaminations of the times."[9]

In a review of the opera house lecture published in *The Independent Pulpit*, former minister J. D. Shaw reported that Renfro "delivered a very eloquent discourse, saying in the conclusion that he did not want to be the champion of his own cause, but to exercise his free rights as a thinker." Shaw continued his praise of Renfro's first public lecture since his removal from the Baptist Church with the statement that "We have known Mr. Renfro for many years, and rejoice at his freedom from credalism and ecclesiastical bigotry. He has no superior in the Baptist church in this state, as an able, eloquent, and dignified speaker, and against his moral character there is not one jot or tittle. He is an honorable acquisition to the ranks of Liberalism. We hope ere long to have the pleasure of listening to him in Liberal Hall. Who will be the next to come from under the galling yoke?"[10]

Neither the large crowd which gathered at the opera house in Alvarado nor the generally sympathetic press reviews that his lecture received stymied those who neither understood nor approved of H. C. Renfro, however, and questions and criticism were quick in coming. One "Uncle Johnnie" wrote a letter to the editor in which he sought a source for a statement in a February 17 address in which Renfro said that the Epistle of James was "an Epistle of straw." In an effort to answer all questions quickly and succinctly, Renfro immediately answered, noting that he had secured his information from the "distinguished christian, Le Clerc," who wrote in his *Disquisition on Inspiration*, that "the Protestants have not called Luther a heretic for saying that the Epistle of James is an epistle of straw." Renfro's response, and especially his reference to ancient writers that most had never heard of, probably added to the frustration of some without the educational advantages of the former parson.[11]

Within the Alvarado community, the expulsion of Henry Renfro from the Baptist fellowship was the talk of the town, with some praising him and some persons saying publicly that the action of the church was a just one. Some who never met Henry Renfro or knew of his character were quick to denounce the man who had spent so many years promoting the orthodoxy that he now condemned. Yet, there was one journalist with considerable power and influence who did not take kindly to the abuse that was being heaped on the head of Henry Renfro, and he penned an eloquent defense of the man that he had known as a friend for eighteen years. F. B. Baillio, a correspondent for *The Alvarado Bulletin* from the community of Grandview, Johnson County, compared Renfro with the martyrs of old.

" . . . [T]he blood of the martyrs is the blood of the church," and the men who suffered martyrdom, suffered because they were not in sympathy with the orthodoxy of their day—they were the advanced thinkers of their day, and were, as some in these latter days, "born before their time." Men have in all ages suffered for opinion's sake. In olden time by violence, bloodshed, the fire, the rack, by every ingenuity fanatics could invent, and perpetuated in the name of religion. The heart of man continues the same—it is eminently errant, and though civilization has eliminated physical violence there still remains the more refined but more cruel, to a sensitive mind, of social ostracism and mental torture for all who dare to question so-called orthodox teachings.[12]

Continuing, Baillio noted that he did not know what Henry Renfro believed. "I don't know that he is right—I can't say that he is wrong; but I do believe that he is honest in his opinions. I know he has the courage of his convictions and withal is as good, true and trusty a man as we have anywhere; he is a good man and the church militant has lost one of her most gallant knights—one who, as Tennyson says, was 'From spur to plume a star of tournament.'" As a conclusion to his defense of the former minister, Baillio noted that he hoped that "this [the removal of Renfro from the ministry] is only a temporary loss, and let us who fear not investigation and free thought—that is mental liberty—but the stupidity of atheism and craze of infidelity—let us hope that he will not use his fine talents in tearing down that which the best years of his life were spent in building up and beautifying."[13]

Renfro appreciated the support of someone as well-respected as F. B. Baillio, and all he had ever asked was the right, so eloquently stated by his friend, that he be allowed to believe and think what he wished without being condemned by those who feared "investigation and free thought—that is[,] mental liberty." As a result, the former Baptist parson believed that it was necessary to answer accusations against him and to rebut published innuendo that he believed would reflect upon his right to do so. Consequently, after the long article by Uncle Jerry about the meaning of the last verse of the last chapter of John was published in the *Bulletin* on February 22, Henry could not resist writing an answer. In a letter published in the same publication on March 7, Renfro, with tongue in cheek, congratulated Uncle Jerry for his adroitness in "covering up the defects in exaggerated statements, and showing that things impossible are nevertheless true." Renfro continued his letter by saying that in the early days of the Christian church, many eminent theologians such as St. Augustine and "John, the Apostolic Father Papias [the author of the Gospel of John]," made changes in the scriptures as a matter of course. "The fact is," Renfro ended his correspondence by saying, "that was an age when ridiculous fables, forgeries and pious frauds were universally practiced among Christians, and no inspiration could deter them from the cherished habit."[14]

Uncle Jerry wrote a very long answer to Renfro titled "INNOMINATA" for the *Bulletin,* and it was published the next week. Rather than try to answer Renfro's accusations of fraud and forgery by early theologians, he termed the former Baptist's beliefs as "silly" and faithfully defended the doctrine of the inspiration of the scriptures, contending that the destruction of man's belief that the Bible was the word of God would destroy hope. As for the writer's intent in the last verse of the last chapter of John, Uncle Jerry noted that "the education of the people of that day was of such character that it required such language as John used to make them understand the magnitude of Christ's ministry." He then accused Renfro of "getting all wrong" and ridiculing the Lord's Supper. Also indicting F. B. Baillio in his rebuttal of Renfro, Uncle Jerry first implied that both were supporters of J. D. Shaw of Waco and Free-Thinker Robert Ingersoll, then reaffirmed his support for the inspiration of the scriptures, giving the following reasons for his invective:

> But when the Bible is attacked, I expect to defend it to the extent of my humble ability when called upon to do so. For, destroy, uproot or undermine our faith in the Bible—lay it on the shelf as an unreliable book, and where are we—what are we or what have we to hope? What rule of conduct have we in this life—what hope for the future? A ship at sea without chart, rudder, or compass would not be a more pitiable object. I did not try to show that "things impossible are nevertheless true," but simply tried to account for a particular form of figurative language.

Then, Uncle Jerry gave as further affirmation of his belief in God and the Bible's inspiration a series of accounts of deathbed scenes in which the dying revealed, in their own way, that they were on the way to heaven and that they had seen, while yet in this world, a glimpse of the great beyond.[15]

F. B. Baillio was very displeased that his colleague had chosen to lambast his support of Renfro and to include his name as an adversary in his last letter. In his "Grand View Items" of March 21, Baillio noted that Uncle Jerry "hops on me like a jay-bird on a june bug. Just why I can't tell, unless it was because I tried to say something nice about a good man. I don't endorse Mr. Shaw or Mr. Ingersoll; I don't admire them; I don't endorse Mr. Renfro's teaching, and never did, but as a man I respect him and even admire him, for he is a good man, if he ain't orthodox." Continuing, Baillio said that he did not endorse the teachings of "any man or any set of men. Like the heathen, I am a law unto myself. But I am no teacher." He then called upon Uncle Jerry to end the controversy. "Let's quit: let's have peace. If I ever won any laurels, or if I ever do win any, they are yours. You write for hog and hominy. I plow for it; but the laurels are yours. Let's have peace."[16]

It almost would appear that the management of *The Alvarado Bulletin* also had decided to end the debates, as a reporter did not appear to report on the second lecture by Henry Renfro at the Alvarado opera house on March 16, supposedly because of a rainstorm that passed through Alvarado that morning. However, in "Bulletin Briefs" of March 21, a short explanation was tendered. "Mr. H. C. Renfro filled his appointment at the opera house last Sunday morning notwithstanding the inclement and threatening weather, to a fair audience. On account of the bad weather our reporter was hindered from attending, hence the non-appearance of a synopsis of this gentleman's lecture." [17]

The *Bulletin's* failure to cover the lecture was more than overcome, however, by its publication in its March 28 issue of a long and detailed letter by Renfro in which he followed up on the articles of both Uncle Jerry and Baillio. Entitled "A Soft Answer Turneth Away Wrath," the missive attacked Uncle Jerry with kindness. "I am led to believe," commented Renfro, "that from some expressions in his article that there is something loving and gentle in his nature, and that he [Uncle Jerry] would a thousand times rather help a poor gloomy doubter along life's weary way than to needlessly wound and crush his feelings by angry and abusive epistles." Continuing, Renfro noted that he liked Uncle Jerry and felt "assured that on better acquaintance we might meet and talk and debate questions, and though we might be poles apart in benefit, in heart, and feeling we would be 'like kindred drops.' I love this kind of man," the former parson stated, "and though I may be called an infidel, knave, and hypocrite, my heart turns instinctively to the spirit that is kind, gentle, loving, forebearing and forgiving as the magnetic needle turns to the pole. I have often wondered why it was that men possessing godliness suffer themselves to become the willing victims of hatred, malice, and revenge." [18]

From the tone of his letter, casual readers might have surmised that Renfro was referring to someone other than Uncle Jerry, but the tone of the missive left no doubt among those who had been following the debate toward whom his disguised barbs were directed. Satirically, Renfro continued his attack by saying that he knew men "who profess to be guided by the book that directs us to not let the sun go down upon our wrath, who are great sticklers for the creeds and confessions of the churches, and who never fail to get real happy at every revival meeting, who have let more than a thousand suns go down upon their wrath, and now in a cool sly way take great pleasure in giving an opponent a stab in the fifth rib when convenient. My experience and the experience of thousands would develop the fact that such men, to say the least of it, are not a blessing to the cause they have espoused."[19]

Renfro was convinced that the roots of persecution of persons not considered orthodox were emotional rather than rational. Noting that, he continued his "Soft Answer" by saying that "Anger and hatred are not the best. They soil the soul. 'They harden all within and petrify the feeling;' and I am striving with might and main to not let them have dominion over me. I have been astonished at the cruelties of the churches toward those who innocently get into doubt and scepticism [skepticism]—how they beat and pelt and abuse them." Renfro then referred to his friend J. D. Shaw of Waco, "of whom Uncle Jerry speaks in such terms of reproach." The former parson presented a spirited defense of Shaw and a condemnation of the treatment that his Waco friend had been given by many orthodox Christians:

> How patiently and heroically has this good man borne his bosom to the storm of fury brought against him by his former friends and brethren, all too for an intellectual conviction, and not for any immoral conduct. I have been a close observer of passing events and truth compels me to say that J. D. Shaw has exhibited the fruits of the spirit all the way, and his traducers have manifested the works of the flesh in trying to crush him—and yet they are the children of God on their way to heaven, and he is the child of the devil and on his way to hell; and they only mean kindness in beating and pelting and abusing him in order to harden him for his fate.[20]

Renfro was also upset with Uncle Jerry for his remark that he had ridiculed the Lord's Supper. "I may be all wrong," he wrote, "but I have not ridiculed the sacrament of the Lord's supper. Madam Rumor has a great many hard things to say of me, and she may, on other rounds, have told Uncle Jerry some such thing, but he is old enough to know that Madame R. is not valiant for the truth. Uncle Jerry will defend John in telling an unreasonable story, but is not set for the defense of the Fathers or any other set of informed men who follow in John's footsteps." Renfro then recalled the statement of Uncle Jerry in his March 14 letter: "The education of the people of that day' was of such character that it required such language as John used to make them understand the magnitude of Christ's ministry." "This," attacked Renfro, "is an unfortunate statement. It is precisely upon this principle that Papias and St. Augustine, and indeed all the Christian fathers openly avowed and publicly defended the practice that it was right to deceive and lie in order to promote the interest of the church, and that consequently, lying, deception, imposture, forgery and pious frauds were everywhere practiced among the early teachers of Christianity." Renfro then summed up his thoughts in the matter by concluding that it "was an easy thing for these old fathers to delude the ignorant people with their pious frauds yet they brought disgrace and infamy upon themselves and injured the cause they espoused; for by all honorable literature they have been branded with the shameful conduct of lying."[21]

Renfro then ended his "Soft Answer" by lambasting Uncle Jerry's allusion to deathbed scenes to prove the divinity of the Bible and the redemption of the soul. "As to death bed scenes and sayings . . . the happiest person I ever saw die had never complied with the terms of salvation as expressed in the New Testament, and the good man whose funeral I preached, which subjected me to the criticism of my brethren, met death most heroically, and fell asleep as calmly and placidly as a babe sinks to rest in his mother's arms." Renfro then ended his letter with the same plea as his friend Baillio saying, "Let us quit. I want no controversy." Uncle Jerry was not yet willing to end the contention, however, and he wrote a long column in the *Bulletin* for its April 4 issue entitled "Was Christ Essentially Holy." The arguments he presented were much the same as before, yet Uncle Jerry did not this time personally attack either Renfro or fellow correspondent Baillio.[22]

In the same issue of the *Bulletin*, a letter to the editor appeared from a reader identified as "E. K.," who noted that "it appears that Uncle Jerry has lost a part of his laurels." While not mentioning either Baillio or Renfro, "E. K." supported the former minister's line of questioning in reference to possible changes in the translation of the Bible and posed several questions, noting that if he wanted to gain other laurels, Uncle Jerry should answer questions such as where King James got his authority for the translation of the Bible, whether or not the translators were inspired, and whether the "late revision" of the Bible was inspired. There is no record of a response from Uncle Jerry. The journalist probably felt that he was ahead in the paper debates between himself, Baillio, and Henry Renfro, and saw no reason to invite anyone else into the fray.[23]

In Uncle Jerry's "Squib No. 23," he again took the offensive against Baillio, suggesting that one of the best ways to resolve any movement toward liberalism was to reinstitute the tried and true "Old Camp Meeting" as a way of gaining converts to Christ and in bringing in those who might have been lost from the fold of the church. If so, said the writer for the *Bulletin*, he hoped that Baillio would be "one of the first fish caught. . . . I want to see Baillio securely hooked, squirming at the end of the line, and launched into purer waters the very first one." [24]

Yet, on May 2, an article appeared which had all of the hallmarks of a truce when it appeared that Uncle Jerry made an attempt to reconcile himself with his fellow journalist. In an article entitled "Then and Now," Uncle Jerry noted that "the article by B." in the last issue of *The Alvarado Bulletin* "was worth a year's subscription in itself. It was in truth an artistically arranged bouquet of literary flowers—pleasing, instructive, restful." No explanation was offered as to whom Jerry was referring, but as there was no other article or letter in that issue signed with "B.," Baillio assumed that it was he to whom his fellow writer was referring, and he responded in his column of May 16.

> I have won my first laurels. To Uncle Jerry I present that beautiful bouquet of literary flowers, so artistically arranged. I promised Uncle Jerry that if I ever won any they should be his. I now stand by the agreement. Take them my dear old Uncle, you bind them up and if there is a "poison leaf" among them you should know it. But honestly, my dear sir, I did not know you had so much "taffy" in your makeup. Indeed, sir, you spread it on with a master hand. [25]

Then, Baillio returned to the subject of the inspiration of the Bible, saying, "It can defend itself. We can't understand all the Bible, it was never intended that we should, but we can understand enough to make us all good men and good citizens—and enough, too, if we live up to its good teachings, to make this earth, as far as man is concerned, a perfect paradise." [26]

Baillio noted, however, that the Bible itself must keep up with the progress of the world. "In the old days religion led and civilization followed—now civilization leads with her steam-engines, telegraphs and even her 'reapers and sulky plows' and religion must keep up."

Ending his letter, Baillio expressed, once again, his wish that the debates would end. "But I don't enjoy this kind of fun, it isn't my trade."[27]

The statement by Baillio that Uncle Jerry should be careful that there was no "poison leaf" in the "laurels" that he was returning miffed the editorialist for the *Bulletin*, and an obviously unhappy Uncle Jerry denied that the accolades that he had given to "B." referred to the correspondent from Grandview. Jerry then continued to stir the waters of discord, first with an ungrounded interpretation of Matthew 13:12 which Henry Renfro immediately attacked, then with questions about Baillio's statement that the church must change with the times. The passage from Matthew appears as a quotation from Christ that notes that "Whoever has will be given more, and he will have an abundance. Whoever does not have, even what he has will be taken from him." Uncle Jerry took the quotation literally. "How true to the letter," he expounded. "Who ever heard of a poor man receiving as costly a present as often bestowed upon the rich. How many costly gems are bestowed upon a poor girl when she marries? It is the millionaire's daughter that is honored with bridal gifts, that aggregate a sum that would be a fortune to the eyes of many a poor girl."[28]

Answering caustically, Renfro wrote that he was

slow to believe that Christ ever uttered a word to favor the rich man and to oppress the poor, and that he would much rather ascribe all such expressions to those who, according to one Christian historian, "exercised the boldness to strike out, add or change some words which they thought necessary to be omitted, added or changed" in the Bible. If Uncle Jerry has no better evidence for the divine authenticity of the Bible than this expression of Christ wherein he endorses a wicked practice of giving to the rich and taking from the poor, if indeed these are his words, then he is not set for the defense of the gospel, and should consider well the closing sentiments in his squib.[29]

Like Renfro, Baillio was quick to respond to Uncle Jerry's continued criticism in regard to his statement that the church must change with the times. He discussed the manifold variations that have occurred over the centuries in the church, then noted that "Wesley might not even recognize a modern Methodist circuit rider." With the contention that man's quest for power was one of the principal reasons for the many faces of the Christian church, Baillio noted that "the church was nearly a unit until the death of Christ and then like the Empire of Alexander, it was divided among ambitious leaders and religion pure and undefiled was subordinated to sectarianism."[30]

The quick and effective rebuttals that were offered by Baillio and Renfro seemed to make Uncle Jerry even more unhappy with both of his adversaries, and he continued to heap invective on the two men, especially Baillio, mainly because of his fellow journalist's backing of the former preacher. As a result, Baillio decided that the time had come for a less polite answer, and on May 30 he made yet another able defense of Renfro and of his right to defend him. "My platform in this free country is—to let every man think as he pleases. I am for free thought—free speech. But I am forced to the conclusion that my 'able eulogy' of Mr. Renfro hurts you worse than you would like to admit even to yourself. I did try," said Baillio, "to say something nice about the *man* Renfro, and I could say some things about him yet—nicer things than I have said. I said I believed him a good and true man. I say so yet. I said I like him—admired him—I say so yet. I said I did not and never had endorsed his doctrines. I say very positively I knew nothing of his doctrine. I do not care to know. His doctrine did not interest me one particle and does not 'til yet but I do hate to see every man that can shove a pencil jump on a man because he declares his true thoughts." Concluding his defense of Renfro, Baillio told Uncle Jerry that he "did not like to see the man abused, and his doctrines passed by in silence." It was the man that he eulogized, said Baillio, and not his doctrine.[31]

Baillio also was unhappy about Uncle Jerry's continued implications that he (Baillio) had himself said that the Bible was not inspired. "Point out to me," interrogated Baillio, "in all my scribbling where I have put even a dirty finger print on the sacred pages. Show me a man who has ever heard me say one word against the Bible. But you are or seem to be more anxious to call me among those who doubt the Bible and your arguments are or seem to be based on your apparent suppositions. Put on your eye glasses and scan my items closer." Concluding his attack, Baillio intimated that Uncle Jerry might even be envious of him because of his support of Renfro, and then he theorized that his good words in defense of the former minister might be the source of the entire controversy. "And now in conclusion," continued Baillio, "I fear very much that my able eulogy of Henry C. Renfro—a naturally good man—lies at the bottom of this whole trouble and has furnished matter for lo these many 'Squibs.' Christian charity can't stand an able eulogy."[32]

Although Baillio had provided an outstanding defense of Henry Renfro, the former minister was well able to take care of himself, and in "An Open Letter" to the *Bulletin* of June 6, he lambasted Uncle Jerry for what he said were misstatements of fact. Renfro noted that he had been misquoted in the *Bulletin*'s synopsis of his last lecture, but that he had decided not to make an issue of it until it was picked up by the "argus eye of Uncle Jerry." Renfro said that he "did not say that the miracles of Christ were forgeries, but I said this: There is not a testimony outside the disciples of Christ to support the wonderful miracles he is said to have performed, and the startling events that attended his death and resurrection that had not proved to be a forgery." Continuing, Renfro noted that he "did say that it is a strange sad thought that Christ who came into the world to save the lost never wrote a word of the New Testament, and never commanded anybody else to write a word of it; and that we had good reasons to believe that the New Testament, and especially the four gospels, were not written till so late a date as the year 182, or more than 150 years after the death of Christ, and then it was written by men who knew nothing of the facts[,] only what they had heard from the open mouth of tradition."[33]

Believing that Uncle Jerry was really dodging the issues that had been raised in much of the letter-writing between the three men, Renfro then raised four questions which he challenged Uncle Jerry to consider. "And now I turn to Uncle Jerry," said Renfro, "and ask him to 'gird up his loins like a man' and answer the following questions."[34]

The first query posed by Renfro concerned Adam's quandary upon facing temptation in the Garden of Eden. Renfro stated that Adam was faced with a dilemma that would have caused him to make a fatal error regardless of what he did after being tempted. If Adam had withstood the snare offered by the devil, Renfro contended, the scheme of the entire creation would have had to change and "the eternal purposes of God [would have been] thwarted and himself [Adam] undeified." On the other hand, if Adam yielded to temptation, it would fill the world "with woes and wants and miseries," and the next world (hell) would become "a lake of fire and brimstone in which nearly all of his children are to be engulfed." Renfro asked Uncle Jerry what Adam should have done "when perfect obedience would have dethroned Jehovah and undeified the Eternal."[35]

Renfro's second question to the journalist questioned the authority of the Bible in relation to the miracles which are attributed to Christ. Contending that no secular historian ever supported the claims of the Gospels, Renfro asked Uncle Jerry "for the testimony of any profane historian in the early stages of christianity in support of the miracles of Christ that has not proved to be a forgery foisted upon his writings by the Christian fathers."[36]

The third question posed by Renfro compared the veracity of secular versus Christian historians. "Why was it," queried Renfro, "that in the early stages of christianity profane historians had established the character of being truthful and reliable in narrating events, and that christian historians had established the character of being guilty of resorting to pious frauds, impostures and absolute forgeries?"[37]

Finally, in a fourth question, Renfro asked Uncle Jerry to explain why early Christians, in their defense of the Bible, concluded that it was "not able to stand on its own mercies, its own divinity, its own inspiration," and that they then resorted "to trickeries, falsehoods, civil penalties and corporeal tortures to impress the people of its divine authority."[38]

There is little question that Renfro knew that his questions were rhetorical and that they would be difficult if not impossible to answer. Yet, he asked them because he knew that they would force Uncle Jerry to explain his positions to the newspaper audience more clearly. The journalist's arguments, Renfro believed, were the result of emotional feelings rather than concise and logical thought, and he was confident that Jerry's answers would make that clear.

Despite Renfro's questions and criticism regarding the divine inspiration of the scriptures, he declared in his June 6 "Open Letter" that the Bible was still an extremely worthwhile book. "Know all men by these presents," he said, "that I have not thrown away the Bible, as a book, but have been speaking of things which have led me to doubt its full inspiration. There are many grand sayings in the Bible, tender sentiments, wise proverbs, good laws and wholesome instructions, which I admire and shall endeavor to practice in my life.

I dislike its wars of extermination, its indiscriminate slaughter of men, women and children, its subjecting the pure maiden to the debauchery of soldiers, its slavery, polygamy, tyrannies, barbarities and obscenities; and especially when these crimes are laid at the door of an infinitely loving God—and I do not believe that the Allwise Jehovah is guilty of the crimes and cruelties alleged against him by the writers of the old Testament and the orthodox pulpit of today." Renfro continued by avowing that he loved "every word, sentence and sentiment in the Bible that makes men wiser and better, and insist that we should read the Bible as we read all other books, and whatever commends itself to our hearts and minds we should accept, and practice; and whatever is clearly repugnant to right, reason and common sense, and absolutely abhorrent to the best impulses of conscience, we should reject, and ascribe the error, not to God, but to a cunning priest or a deceptive Christian Father, who openly avowed that it was right to deceive and lie, if by that means the interest of the church might be promoted."[39]

Finally, Renfro stated that "There is no moral quality in belief. A man cannot help his belief. Thousands of men believe all the Munchausen stories of the Bible and are bad men still, and thousands disbelieve them and are good men. . . . Now," said Renfro, "I'm so simple as to believe that one insult patiently borne and kindly forgiven, one cup of joy put to the lips of sorrow, one burden gently lifted from the heart of the fallen and forsaken, one kind word to assuage grief and cheer loneliness, or one unselfish deed in feeding the hungry or clothing the poor is worth mountains of faith in a mysterious being and mysterious doctrines we cannot understand. On this rock I stand."[40]

In the same issue of the *Bulletin* in which Renfro's "Open Letter" was printed, Uncle Jerry had his first opportunity to answer F. B. Baillio's article of May 30 in which Baillio suggested that envy of his "able eulogy" of Renfro was the cause of the continual verbal sparring between Uncle Jerry and himself. Uncle Jerry believed that he was winning the debates and took time to say that he now had Baillio "against the wall." "It would not afford me half as much enjoyment to pin an ordinary man to the wall," boasted Uncle Jerry, "but it is so seldom that I can manage to shove an intellectual Sullivan against that useful impediment, that I really enjoy it." However, Jerry was stung by the implication that he *envied* Baillio, then noted that he himself had said "nice things" about Henry Renfro in previous writings. "I am sorry, though, that Baillio made the insinuation that I *envied* the praise he bestowed upon Mr. Renfro. Such a *thrust* was unworthy of a man of his calibre to say nothing of its subject. When I become so mean spirited as to envy any fellow pilgrim the full meed of praise he deserves, I want the boss to break his left hand–crutch over my head. . . . " In defense of himself, Uncle Jerry then noted that "in the same number of the BULLETIN—I think—I wrote a piece which the boss kindly permitted to pass as editorial, in which I said perhaps as many 'nice things' of Bro. Renfro as he did, and palpably with as good motives, as I did not expect it ever to be known to any one but the editor. I tried to cheer him up and make him feel that the community were not down upon him *as a man*, but upon his position, and expressed the hope that he would yet come off of the fog. So what about envy now?" [41]

One week later, however, Uncle Jerry was likely not feeling as charitable toward Renfro as he attempted to answer the questions raised by the former minister in his last missive to the *Bulletin*. "I will have to look after that 'open letter' in the last BULLETIN, or run up the white flag, an article I rarely have on hand." Beginning with question number two, he noted that it was of no importance whether or not a "secular writer" ever testified to the miracles of Christ. "Everyone who understands the laws of evidence must be satisfied with the testimony of the Apostles." Then, Uncle Jerry noted that there were "writers" who testified to the fact that miracles were performed, and he included in his list the Jewish Talmud, "The Acts of Pilate," and a letter by one Publius Lentius, governor of Judea during the time of Christ. "Will Bro. Renfro show this is a forgery also[?]" [42]

In continuation of his answers of the former parson's queries, Uncle Jerry considered Renfro's third question asking why profane historians had the reputation for being truthful while Christian historians had "established the character of resorting to pious frauds, impostures and absolute forgeries." With some validity, Uncle Jerry made no answer, asserting that the wording of the question made it impossible to answer and noted that if he could have worded the sentence, it would have had a completely different context. However, Uncle Jerry chose not to answer Renfro's fourth question at all, perhaps recalling that he himself had made excuses in his "Squib No. 17" for those who made changes in the Bible in order that "the people of the day" would "understand the magnitude of Christ's ministry."[43]

Renfro's first question, answered last by Uncle Jerry, posed a question as to what Adam would have done had he "known all about the eternal purposes of God," with the clear implication that had Adam not sinned, the entire universal plan of God would have been thwarted. In answer, Uncle Jerry stated, with no explanation, that for God to have created a man "who was essentially and constitutionally holy, and could not disobey . . . would have been a mere machine, without merit." The second Adam that Uncle Jerry envisioned would have been "essentially and constitutionally malignant and could not avoid disobeying," and would have been "unworthy of the workmanship of a Thrice Holy God." The third Adam that could have been created, according to Uncle Jerry, was "one who had the ability to obey, and the ability to disobey; one who could remain loyal or prove disloyal, at his option, fortifying the one with the promise of life, and deterring the other with the promise of death. Thus endowed," said Uncle Jerry, this third man "was thrown out into the world to be tried—to be acted upon by motives, influences and temptations, and as a free agent exercised his ability to do evil and fell, and the responsibility of his condition rests upon him, and him alone." Thus, Uncle Jerry, in a long and eloquent reply, still avoided answering the first question posed to him by Henry Renfro.[44]

The debates were continued in the pages of the *Bulletin* yet another week as the June 20 issue went to press. In it, Baillio jumped back into the fray, making fun of Uncle Jerry's implication that the Grandview writer had been licked. "Where," queried Baillio, "did Uncle Jerry bury my men of straw? Uncle Jerry's complacency is gargantuan—alarming. He demolishes my men of straw—he silenced me and presto he has whopped me. 'What a glorious victory.' It was a glorious victory! A finished scholar—an old veteran of orthodoxy has licked a poor illiterate clodhopper. If it affords Uncle Jerry any comfort I will acknowledge that I *have been silenced*, but not by force of your arguments but by the length of your squibulums." As he continued, Baillio argued, "I can't admit I was *whipped*." Making one last attack, Baillio charged that his nemesis was "a great writer but mistakes a multiplicity of words for convincing arguments. He is a fine writer but not a fair opponent . . . ; he jumps at conclusions and argues from unwarranted premises." Then Baillio ended his column with slight praise of his debate opponent: "I have not said aught to ruffle his feelings. What I have said and do I said in a Pickwickian sense, for my Uncle, personally, I have the highest regard. I am tired of the tiresome subject and expect the Boss is. And Uncle dear I do not think we should monopolize so much space. I do not suppose anyone cares to know our peculiar views—let's quit and give the balance of the corps a chance and the Boss a rest. I am silenced because I was talked to death—only this and nothing more." [45]

In the same June 20 issue of the *Bulletin*, however, another man who also called himself "Clodhopper" had no intentions of putting aside his thoughts and vehemently attacked Renfro for his "Open Letter" of June 6. "I have been meditating some, upon that characteristic letter of Mr. R. C. [sic] Renfro, and am ready to exclaim with thousands of my countrymen, Alas! *How hath the mighty fallen.* A few fleeting years ago," continued Clodhopper, "he had the confidence, love, and esteem of all the christian people that knew him. . . . What is it," said the Clodhopper, "that has so suddenly come over the spirit of his dreams?" [46]

Perhaps Henry Renfro must have wondered the same thing at times, and although his mind was set and his course was underway in the sea of liberalism, he missed the church—the institution to which he had devoted much of his energy for so many years. Perhaps for himself, perhaps for his wife Mary, or perhaps for his children, Henry resolved in mid-June 1884 that he would attend church services once again at Bethesda Church, the institution that he had supported in its beginnings and where so many memories still lurked to renew the days of "Auld Lang Syne." In a letter to the *Bulletin* of June 20, Henry recalled that he "gratefully and reverently appeared in the old church where my sisters and many relations meet monthly to worship." On the way to the church, said Renfro, he considered what might be the subject for the day, and noted that "I indulged the hope that I would be treated to a sermon on practical religion. That as there were many in the church and settlement not on speaking terms . . . I really wanted the preacher to dwell on the importance of love, kindness, patience, forgiveness and Christian forbearance." Renfro found all lacking, however, and as a result indulged in a sting-

ing denouncement of orthodoxy. "No harm is meant by this criticism
of the ministry," wrote Renfro, and "such men as Drs. John Collier
and R. C. Burleson are exempted." [47]

Although Baillio had unilaterally declared an end to the paper debates in his June 20 column, Uncle Jerry could not resist making a
final blast against his fellow correspondent and Henry Renfro in an
article entitled "Declaration of Principles. Squib No. 28." published
in the *Bulletin* on June 27. He defended his approach to the entire
controversy with the implication that his attacks had been misunder-
stood—that they were not inspired by dislike, but by honest disagreement. "Some way I shall always believe that there is standing room
somewhere, between enmity for a man and *disbelieving in his teachings*,
and that at least a mile and a half intervenes between *abuse* of a man
and *a refutation of his views*. I will continue to claim that it is a laudable
ambition to desire to try your axe in good timber, or to cross lances
with none but a foeman worthy of your steel." [48]

Baillio's insistence that he was through with the debates combined
with Uncle Jerry's final words in the June 27 *Bulletin* convinced Henry
Renfro that he, too, should end the controversy. This decision was
made despite the fact that he had compiled an eight-page salvo concerning what he considered to be illogical answers from Uncle Jerry
to his questions. In a letter entitled "Uncle Jerry in the Dark," Renfro
considered every point that his adversary had tried to make, then
ended it all with this statement:

> For my life I cannot see the consolation of a gospel that for the last eighteen
> hundred years has not saved more than one out of every hundred of the
> human family. A gospel that teaches us that God before the foundation of
> the world determined to consign nearly all of his children to an endless
> hell certainly is not very consoling. We apply the wrong word. It should
> be consternation of the gospel, that is, according to the teachings of the
> New Testament and orthodox theology. Now I believe that the good and
> loving God will save untold millions that the creeds, and confessions of
> faith condemn to a never ending hell. Which is the more comforting
> doctrine! [49]

Yet, Renfro's letter was never published. Instead, the former minister drove his buggy to the office of *The Alvarado Bulletin*, offered his
hand to Uncle Jerry, and quietly and gracefully ended a year of re-

criminations and hard feelings between intelligent men who happened to feel differently about the interpretation of the Bible. Although Renfro's feelings about the scriptures, about liberalism, and about the failure of orthodox religion had not changed, he filed the letter "Uncle Jerry in the Dark" among other writings, sermons, and speeches he had compiled over the past quarter century. Finally, the paper debates were at an end.[50]

Chapter 9

Without a Murmur or a Frown

As was their custom, on New Year's Day 1884, the Renfro family gathered together for recollections of the happiness of past years and an expression of their hopes for the ones that were to come. Henry Renfro opened his copy of *The Poetical Works of Robert Burns* and read aloud the verses transcribed by the Scottish Bard entitled "Auld Lang Syne," a poem which seemed particularly poignant as Henry's final confrontation with the Baptist Church approached. Had any of the family known what the future would bring, the celebration of the beginning of the new year would have been dismal, indeed. Although the Renfro family had faced problems in the past, their earlier tribulations would appear trivial when compared with those they were to endure in the future. The year of 1884 brought the Parson's confrontation with orthodoxy, an ordeal all had expected to be traumatic, but none of the family had any concept of the additional condemnations, recriminations, sadness, and death that were to devour their lives in 1885.[1]

Nevertheless, an announcement made that New Year's Day of 1884 as the family gathered at the farm on Crill Miller Creek provided considerable consolation for everyone's worries and apprehension. Annette was expecting a baby! It would arrive in July or August, the soon-to-be-mother announced, and she and Julius were tremendously excited about the coming event. Clearly, any lingering problems between the two had vanished, and Annette and Julius were the happiest they had been since their marriage. Their joy in the anticipation of the coming birth tempered the worries that they felt for Henry as the days and weeks went by. Yet, an illness that accompanied her pregnancy incapacitated Annette. She spent much time in bed, and Julius did whatever he could to be sure that Annette had every need fulfilled.[2]

As a result of Annette's disabilities, she was unable to provide active support for her father, the Parson, as he confronted the Baptist Church in Alvarado and was found guilty of infidelity. Julius, however, supported his father-in-law with a vengeance, and during that period the two men grew closer, more like father and son than in-laws. Julius studied the Parson's writings and attended his lectures, and he became convinced that Renfro's positions relating to orthodoxy were correct. Their mutual anticipation of a new baby in the family helped both Henry and Julius maintain a measure of excitement for the future. The baby would soon arrive, but the enthusiasm would be short-lived.

On July 28, 1884, Annette's twentieth birthday, a little girl was born. Named Ida Mintie Baker after one of Annette's best friends and her former roommate, Mintie Roberts, the new arrival was a source of great joy and pride to the family. It was Henry and Mary's first grandchild and the first niece for Burlie and Kittie. A happier father than Julius could not have been found. Yet, the baby was not healthy. For reasons that were not known, she could not properly digest her mother's milk and, as a result, the health of the youngster gradually faded. Less than a month after being born, on August 24, Ida Mintie was dead.

Annette was devastated by the loss of the baby, and she put some of her thoughts into a one-page manuscript she titled, "The Loved and the Lost." In it, Annette expressed her intense grief concerning the death of her first-born child: "My sweet babe born on the day I was twenty years of age, and was called my birth day present staid [sic] with me but four short weeks which were weeks of joy to my mind though my body was in pain. I vainly thought she had come to stay and comfort me through this weary life. . . ." Annette then questioned whether or not she would see the little one again. "Is there a sweet beyond where my loving babe and I with loving friends shall meet and pluck the ambrosial fruits of paradise and live forever.[?] Then let me rest in hope."[3]

The loss of Ida Mintie was also very painful to Henry Renfro, and he wrote of the tragedy, as well as the problems with the church that had plagued him and his family, to his Philadelphia friend, Thomas Neilson. In a reply written on November 27, Neilson offered his sympathy, noting that "Truly we all have our troubles in this life! We indulge in honest toil & well spent time, a harvest of barren regret. Am sorry to hear of yr family troubles & the loss of yr little grand daughter, but does not the philosophy of life teach us rather to rejoice at [rather] than regret, the death of the little buds who escape the trials & cares of those who tread the wine press of life."[4]

Continuing, Neilson wrote his Texas friend that he hoped that he was satisfactorily surviving his problems with the church, and he urged him to continue his adamant stance.

> I trust your mind is easier, now that you have taken the step & the vials of wrath have been exhausted on you. You can now pursue the "even turn of yr way" & snap your fingers at yr tormenters & traducers. Be brave & fear not & yr persecutors will leave you. Remember the lives of Lucile.

> If a man once lets the world see that he feels
> Afraid of its bark & twill fly at his heels,
> Let him fearlessly face it, twill leave him alone,
> But twill *fawn* at *his feet*, if he flings it a *bone!*"

Ending his note, Neilson asked Renfro to "present my regards and sympathy to yr daughter & with same for yrself [yourself] & wishing you every happiness & success & hoping to hear from you soon."[5]

Despite the problems that he had endured, Henry Renfro had no intention of doing anything other than heeding Neilson's advice and "fearlessly" facing the world. During a visit at his farm with a Burleson friend, "Old Man" Tom Mills, noted that everyone and everything around him could see the positive difference in him since his problems with the church had come to an end. Waving his hands toward two old hounds that belonged to him, he said to Mills that "even these old dogs can tell the difference in me." Renfro sincerely believed this to be true and that "excepting the bitterness and persecution of my former friends, I have never been so free from care and sorrow since the early days of my boyhood."[6]

On February 2, 1885, one year to the day after his dismissal from the ministry and the Baptist Church, Henry felt it would be fitting to write a letter to his friend J. D. Shaw for publication in *The Independent Pulpit*. Entitled "Mr. Renfro's Anniversary as a Liberal," the essay was a philosophical reflection on the events of the past year as well as an overview of the beliefs that Renfro had expanded and developed in his search for a personal truth.

> I have concluded to celebrate the first anniversary of my separation from the Baptist church by writing a letter for the PULPIT. Some of your readers may wish to know how I am getting along in the ranks of the Liberal army. A year ago today I stood before my church, with fear and trembling, and with many tears, freely confessing that I was a "Doubting Thomas" and bewildered to know what to do. The brethren soon taught me that he that doubteth is damned, and though I asked for bread, they gave me a stone. That was an hour of struggle between early impressions of truth and duty, with love and smiles on one side, and hatred and frowns on the other. And I have never regretted the choice I then made, unless it was for an hour or two when I was smarting under the ecclesiastical lash, and drinking the wine of the fierceness of orthodox hatred.[7]

Discussing the period after his dismissal when he attempted to explain, through lectures and letters, the reasons for his change, "the hue and cry went up from all this hallowed ground that I was crazy, a crank, a hypocrite, blasphemer, child of the devil, and all those kind and loving words so peculiar to those people who profess to love their enemies, to overcome evil with good, and to restore a fallen brother in meekness." Then Renfro struck out again at those within the church who would harness free speech and expression. "Think of it! In this land of equal and inalienable rights, under the stars and stripes, for exercising a right vouchsafed to me, not only by heroic valor and patriotic blood, but by the very charter of my creation, the right of freedom of thought and speech, I am followed with hatred and abuse, by the only people who claim to be born twice, and to be on their way to heaven."[8]

Renfro noted that the animosities were not confined to criticism of the content of his speeches but also included threats of physical violence. "A few," he remarked sarcastically, "who have made unusual progress in the divine life, and are going on to perfection, have stated that they would not go to hear me lecture, but would go to see me hung." One lady, Renfro noted, went so far as to say that "if she could find a few choice spirits sufficiently imbued with the loving influences of orthodox religion, they would mob me." Yet, Renfro said in his anniversary letter that "none of these things move me. I have gone to my appointments without even a body-guard, as hero-ically as Paul went up to Jerusalem and Martin Luther put in his ap-pearance at the Diet of Worms."[9]

Despite his making light of the hazards he faced from those who might do him harm, he knew of the dangers and was apprehensive about the possibilities of physical attack from those adamants who saw him as a serious threat to orthodox religion. "It is true," Renfro commented, "in traveling through the long and lonesome lanes, com-posed of thick bushes and briars, I would now and then think of the fate of Dr. Russell, of Bell County; but, relying upon the justness of my cause, and the sincerity of my intentions, I would persevere, and never failed to meet a respectable crowd and honest hearers." Rus-sell, it will be recalled, was abducted and given one hundred lashes be-cause of his Free Thought and estrangement from Christian beliefs.[10]

Summing up his feelings concerning orthodox religion and its ada-mant stand for the inerrancy of the Bible, Renfro continued his letter to the *Pulpit* by saying that

> The whole system of orthodox theology seems strange to me now. It is wholly unaccountable why an infinitely wise God, who had an eternity in which to fix his purposes concerning man, when he determined to raise apples and children, and set more store by his apples than by his children, should have put them in the same garden, and allowed them to get mixed; that he should have doomed the whole human family to an endless hell, because the first pair, at the suggestion of a reasoning serpent, that [he] himself had made, ate a little fruit, solely for the purpose of knowing good from evil, which taught the woman modesty, and placed them both among the Gods in knowledge, is what I do not understand.[11]

Ending the letter to J. D. Shaw and *The Independent Pulpit*, Henry Renfro reasoned that the Bible should not be man's "infallible guide in matters pertaining to truth and duty. . . . We should follow the lamp of reason," he said, "and ask the aid and guidance of common sense and conscience in all things." Conscience, the former minister declared, "may not infallibly lead us in the right way, but I am satisfied that it is a safer guide than a book that is flatly contradictory and conflicting. When I was a boy, my father told me conscience was God's preacher, and I remember even then how it exercised its office in exhorting, reproving and rebuking me for my youthful follies; and all along life's journey it has pointed almost as infallibly to the pathway of duty as the magnetic needle points to the pole." [12]

At the same time that he wrote the letter which was entitled "Mr. Renfro's Anniversary as a Liberal," the disfranchised parson wrote a private letter to J. D. Shaw in which he expressed a strong interest in becoming a part of the Religious and Benevolent Association which Shaw had founded, and he inquired about setting up a similar organization in Johnson County. "I am longing for the time when I will be able to cease to 'serve tables' and give myself wholly to the work of teaching free thought doctrine. What about the Religious and Benevolent Association? and are you pleased with its workings, etc.? Do you think we could establish one at Cleburne or Fort Worth?" [13]

Renfro had determined that he wanted to spend much more time in the pursuit and teaching of the doctrines of Free Thought, and he told Shaw that he wanted to go to Waco "in order to be 'regularly ordained' to the work of teaching Liberalism, provided it is not done 'by prayer and the imposition of holy hands,' as I sometimes feel that I am 'called,' if not qualified, for this business." Then, tongue-in-cheek, Renfro noted that he was due special support from Shaw because of the backing that he had given the former Methodist. "I must claim a little partiality from you," said Renfro, "as probably no other man in the State has had more hard fights on your account than I have. I have distributed the PULPITS you sent me, and think I will be able in a short time to send you some subscribers, though money is exceedingly scarce. Send me a few more, if convenient, and I will scatter them broadside." [14]

In a letter written on February 15, Renfro apologized to Shaw for his inability to accept an invitation to go to Waco on February 22 to address the Association at Liberal Hall. "It will be impossible for me to be in Waco on the 22nd instant, as I have a lot of beef cattle to dispose of, and the time is at hand for me to act in the matter." Yet,

Renfro believed so strongly in the cause for which he had dedicated himself that he pledged to visit Shaw at as early a date as possible. "I would be glad," continued Renfro, "if it was so that I could be present at your next meeting and render you any assistance in my power. I firmly believe that the cause in which we are engaged is the cause of truth and humanity, and is destined to take the people out of the hands of the priests and elevate them in the scales of moral, intellectual, and social existence. I am so much persuaded of this fact that I am willing to spend and be spent in the work. But I am here almost alone. They have dug down the altars and killed the prophets, and I am left alone and they seek my life. There is a power in union and an influence in association that I need. I have much to discourage me, and yet I have no idea of giving up to the enemy." Finally, Renfro promised to come to Waco in the future to discuss their mutual interests. "I intend to pay you a visit at my earliest convenience, and we will have a long talk and lay some plans for the future." [15]

Indeed, Renfro was unable to visit Waco because of the pressing need to sell some of his cattle, and he considered driving them to New Orleans for the World's Industrial and Cotton Centennial Exposition scheduled for March 1885. In fact, the Renfro family planned to make a grand affair of the trip, with several members of Henry and Mary's families attending. In a news item in the February 1 issue of *The Alvarado Bulletin*, it was reported that "quite a number of persons in this neighborhood [Marystown] think of taking in the World's Fair in March. Among the number are H. C. Renfro, wife and daughter, B. B. [E. B.] Ray, wife and daughter, E. D. Renfro and T. W. Hollingsworth." Renfro wrote J. D. Shaw about the possibility of his making the trip, saying that he would likely take his beeves there for sale. As an aside to the plans, Renfro told Shaw that when he sold his cattle, he had a "notion of sending you the money for five or six PULPITS and send them to friends who ought to read them, both to enlarge your purse and expand their brains." [16]

Yet, as he thought of the long distance involved in driving beef cattle overland from Johnson County to New Orleans, he began to wonder if possible higher prices in the Crescent City would be worth the discomfort and time that such a trail drive would require. Instead, he began to think of driving them the short twenty miles from the ranch to the Fort Worth stockyards for sale. The price might not be as good as that he might receive in New Orleans, but the change in plans certainly would let the visit to the Exposition be a well-deserved vacation rather than a demanding chore.

Thus, the change in plans was made, and on Monday morning, February 23, Renfro, his son Burlie, his son-in-law Julius, and the "hands" began the roundup of the animals to be sold. A stiff north breeze made the task difficult, but the work was soon done and the cattle penned at corrals near the windmill on the hill by the Renfro home. Before sunup on Wednesday morning, the herd was on its way. The day, which began cold and crisp but with clear skies and little wind, gradually deteriorated as a norther swept down from the plains into the Cross Timbers. The sky became overcast, the wind rose, and a driving snow began to pelt the cattle and the cattlemen as they made their way to Fort Worth. The stock bawled at being forced into what became a fierce, biting wind, and a cattle drive that ordinarily would have been completed in one day was stretched to two. By Thursday morning, however, Henry Renfro complained that he was not feeling at all well, and he left Julius with instructions to take the cattle to the stockyards, then meet him and Burlie at the boarding house of William E. McBride on East Weatherford Street. By midday Friday, the cattle were penned, and Julius proceeded to the McBride house as soon as possible. He found that Henry was critically ill and trembling with chills and fever. One Dr. Burts already had been called, and he quickly diagnosed the problem as pneumonia, aggravated by severe exposure.[17]

Since his father was rarely sick, Burlie was extremely alarmed at the severity of the illness. Therefore, he and Julius decided that the family should be informed. Accordingly, Julius went to the telegraph office and sent a message to his wife and mother-in-law to come as quickly as possible—that he was very apprehensive about Renfro's condition. Both arrived before noon on Saturday, February 28, and they were followed by a host of other kinfolk and friends who were concerned about the former minister's illness. By Sunday, however, Renfro's breathing had become shallow, and the alternating chills and fever became more and more severe. Dr. Burts declared that he could do nothing other than hope that the sickness would break on its own. The Friday edition of *The Alvarado Bulletin* reported that it had learned from J. B. Renfro that "his father, H. C. Renfro, is lying in Ft. Worth at the point of death."[18]

Although miserable because of the severity of the pneumonia,

Henry Renfro was lucid. He realized that he was dying, and he did his best to console those at his bedside. Renfro declared that he had made peace with himself, and that if he should die, he was ready to go. He told Annette that she should tell his sister Margaret, who had made many efforts to induce Henry to retrace his steps to the Bible, "that he was happy by his late change in faith, and that all he hated to die for was that he wanted to . . . help rid the world of so much ignorance and superstition."[19]

On Sunday night, the ordeal became progressively worse, and Annette and Julius began a vigil at the bedside at 9:00 P.M. Julius attended to his father-in-law's needs as well as he could until early Monday morning when he called for all of the family to come. Henry Renfro was near death. Mary was there, as were Burlie and Kittie. The McBrides, owners of the boarding house and old friends of the former parson, were also in the room together with others who had come to admire the fortitude that Henry had shown during the ordeal of sickness. The former minister died calmly, "without a murmur or a frown," at about 7:30 on Monday morning, March 2, 1885.[20]

The Tuesday edition of the *Fort Worth Gazette* offered the following obituary:

> Elder Renfro, as he was called, at one time was a prominent Baptist preacher in Johnson, Hill and Tarrant counties. His father was one of the pioneers of Johnson County and he entered the ministry when quite a young man. He conducted services in Fort Worth when the place was a mere hamlet and probably was known by almost every man in Tarrant County. He was about fifty years of age at his death and for the last few years of his life his religious views had undergone a change and he could probably have been classed among the "Free-thinkers." Those who know him in this city say he was a man of wonderful vitality and energy, and that he was universally liked and admired. He leaves considerable property and was always in easy circumstances. His remains will be taken to Johnson county on the south-bound train this morning, followed by his mourning wife and children.[21]

On March 5, three days after Henry's death, J. D. Shaw penned a personal note to Mary Renfro expressing his dismay at the death of his fellow liberal. "My Dear Friend," he wrote, "I am distressed at the news of the sudden death of your husband, and write this note to assure you and your family of my sincere sympathy in this hour of sadness and sorrow."[22]

The planning for the funeral then began. Despite the long-time friendship between Henry Renfro and Rufus Burleson, no one knew whether or not the Waco University president would be willing to preach the funeral of one who had so criticized the Baptist Church and orthodox religion. Despite sure condemnation from some of his fellow churchmen, however, Burleson did not hesitate when he received the news of Renfro's death with a request that he preside over the services. He immediately agreed to preach the funeral sermon of his former student and friend, and the date for the funeral was set.

In the midst of the grief at the Renfro farm on Crill Miller Creek, another burden was added to those already being shouldered as Burlie was forced to bed by an illness which seemed to be the same as that of his late father. By Wednesday, March 4, it became evident that Burlie's condition was worsening to the point that he would not be able to attend the funeral of his father. Would troubles never end?[23]

On Sunday, March 8, the earthly remains of Henry Renfro were returned for the last time to Bethesda Church, and no doubt he would have been pleased with the crowd. Over one thousand persons, friends and former friends alike, arrived to attend the former parson's services and to hear the sermon by Rufus C. Burleson. The church was filled, and scores of persons clustered near the doorway to listen to Burleson's funeral oration. The Parson was buried in a ceremony conducted by the Alvarado Masonic Lodge in the cemetery adjacent to the church in a plot near that of his father, his mother, and his granddaughter, little Ida Mintie Baker. Few words derogatory of Henry Renfro were heard that day.[24]

Writing in the March issue of *The Guardian,* a church-related magazine of which he was Historical Editor and Contributor, Rufus C. Burleson was profuse in his praise of his old friend and offered hope that Renfro would yet be saved. "We are called to mourn the death of Rev. H. C. Renfro, for so many years a leading citizen and Baptist preacher in Johnson County. He entered Baylor University in 1853 and continued four years. He was a model student in every department, but excelled in oratory. As an eloquent preacher he had few equals." In an evaluation of the reasons for Renfro's fall from the grace of the church, Burleson noted that "it has been known for some years [that] he has not been able to give much time to preaching and studying the word of God on account of his great and absorbing financial plans. In consequence of which he became involved in doubt and gloomy fears. But all who knew him longest and most intimately, believe it was only as the sun under the dark eclipse, and if he could have lived longer and had leisure for reading God's word and prayer, he would have emerged from the eclipse and been as before he became immersed in secular pursuits, a burning, bright and shining light." Then, Burleson stated that "in his last hours, he said, 'if it is the will of my Heavenly Father to take me, I am ready to go.'" Burleson concluded his article with the statement that "Waco University has lost a devoted friend, and our literary family, a bright star."[25]

The day after Henry Renfro's funeral, March 9, the family suffered yet another tragedy when James Burleson Renfro passed away with the same disease that had stricken his father. One newspaper reported that it was thought by some that "the strain upon his mental powers, during the illness, death, and burial of his father, was too great for his physical condition already weakened by exposure. He was young, in the prime of manhood, had plenty of this world's goods, his domestic relations were all that heart could wish, yet he had to answer the summons of the death angel." The loss of a husband and father, then of son, husband and brother, was almost too much for the survivors to bear. Burlie was buried next to Henry Renfro on March 11, only three days after the interment of his father. One reporter who covered the event wrote a doleful narrative of the sad proceedings:

> As we stood by and heard the clods rattle upon his coffin, listened to the broken sobs of a mourning mother and sister, who loved him dearly, as we listened to the wail of anguish that burst from the lips of a loving wife as she gazed for the last time upon the husband of her youth, and if angels are acquainted with the passing scenes of earth, Burlie Renfro, in his bright home, treasures the look of infinite love his wife bestowed upon his clay ere she resigned it to its resting place.[26]

Although the burial was accomplished quickly after Burlie's death, both his wife Kittie and his mother Mary Renfro wanted Rufus Burleson, the man for whom Burlie was named, to come once again to Johnson County to preach a memorial funeral sermon for the young man. On May 18, Burleson wrote Mary Renfro that he had received three letters requesting him to do so—one from Kittie Renfro, Burlie's wife, another from William Jack, a good friend of the family and a relative of Julius Baker, and finally, a postal card from her. All had asked if he could be there on the fourth Sunday, the 24th of May. In reply, Burleson said that he could be there at that time, but that it would fit his schedule better if it could be postponed one more week to the 30th. "I am ever ready [and] anxious to do anything and everything to comfort those who weep for the dead whom I loved so tenderly. I *can* come on next Sunday (4th) but it will be more convenient to come on the 5th Sunday and preach the funeral at Burleson *provided it will suit you just as well*. Please telegraph me at once your wishes and I will conform to your wishes." Concluding his letter, Burleson said, "All well and join in much love to you and family. My wife always loved your husband as a son." A marginal note on Burleson's letter from one J. C. Jones confirmed the fourth Sunday date, however. "I have just received a telegram from Bro Burleson stating he would be there next Sunday (4th) to preach Burlie's funeral at Bethesday [sic]. Received this letter in one to me. So have it published that Bro. Burleson will be here next Sunday." [27]

On Sunday, May 24, Rufus Burleson once again preached a sermon for someone who was dear to him. In this case, the funeral was extremely touching to Burleson as the epitaph was for a young man who bore his own name. This, added to the fact that he had preached the services for James Burleson's father only weeks before, provided a poignant setting for the crowd of family and mourners. An *Alvarado Bulletin* reporter covering the event noted that when he viewed such scenes at funerals, and

> look around and see tear drops glistening in the eyes of friends, we are forced to the conclusion that the happiness of man is insecure, and if we learn no other lesson it should impress upon our mind the great truth set forth in Gray's Elegy, that—
>
> > The boast of heraldry, the pomp of power
> > All that beauty, all that wealth o'er gave,
> > Await alike the inevitable hour.
> > The paths of glory lead but to the grave. [28]

Within a month of the death of Henry Renfro, an article appeared in *The Texas Baptist* which purported to give evidence that the minister-turned-freethinker had repented while on his deathbed. The article stated as fact that "H. C. Renfro, who was once a Baptist minister, and then switched off into Infidelity, died at Fort Worth a few weeks ago. In his last moments he said: 'Nothing but the words of Jesus will do me any good at this hour.' Infidelity will not do for a dying man." The report may well have been triggered by Rufus Burleson's statement in *The Guardian* that Renfro had said, "if it is the will of my Heavenly Father to take me, I am willing to go." Yet, Burleson made no claims that Renfro had repented on his deathbed. Indeed, the Waco University president stated in the same article that he and others believed that his former student was under a "dark eclipse" and that had he lived, he would have "been as before he engaged in secular pursuits, a burning, bright and shining light." Commenting on Burleson's statements, J. D. Shaw wrote in *The Independent Pulpit* that Burleson "did not corroborate the statement of the *Baptist*, and all who know the Doctor as well as we do, know that he would have made good use of any such confession as a further illustration of his recent rehash of the long exploded falsehood concerning the death of Thomas Paine. . . . Dr. Burleson," continued Shaw, "was too kind to damn so good a man as his old pupil and 'son in the gospel' so he is reported to have said in his talk at the grave that if he [Renfro] was truly converted when he professed Christianity he might be saved. He was kind enough to express the opinion that his reason was dethroned, and he would not therefore be accountable for denying Christ. If the statement of the *Baptist* is correct, the Doctor should then and there have shown that at last he returned to Christ." [29]

Several months later, Rufus Burleson wrote a note to Annette Baker that unequivocally established the fact that Burleson did not believe that Henry Renfro had returned to the church before his death. "Thirty four years ago," wrote Burleson, "your noble father then a very young man, became a student of mine in Baylor University [at] Independence. For noble bearing piety and eloquence he had no superiors and few equals. I loved him as a son and ever regarded him as the very soul of honor. And I am sure that sad eclipse of faith, which has often happened to the greatest and wisest Christians in all ages, would soon have passed away had he lived on earth[,] but he is now above the clouds and beyond the sun where all is light and life and love." [30]

However, Baptist publications did not ask the opinion of Rufus

Burleson in the matter, and publication and republication of the story of Renfro's reputed deathbed conversion continued to be printed. In his efforts to show that the writers in *The Texas Baptist* and other newspapers had fabricated the story, J. D. Shaw went even further, securing a certificate "signed by C. McBride, at whose house Mr. Renfro died, Mrs. S. P. Johnson and Mrs. N. C. McMillan, who waited on him from time to time." According to Shaw, the paper that was signed by McBride and the others noted that all were present during Renfro's illness and death and that "he bore his illness with remarkable courage and fortitude, and died calmly." In the last minutes before Renfro passed away, they attested, "he was asked if all was well." The reply from Renfro was that "All is well, I am ready to meet the great monster, Death." [31]

In further proof of his claims that Renfro had not recanted his beliefs, Shaw told his readers that he had a letter from Renfro's son-in-law, Julius Baker, who stated that Renfro's "son and daughter were with him during his illness, and they say he never called on or had anything to say about Jesus Christ or any other God. I was with him," continued Baker's letter, "from 9 o'clock on Sunday night till half past 7 o'clock Monday morning, when he breathed his last, and during my stay he never said anything about Jesus, although he suffered untold agonies. Many others can testify to the same. So you see that the *Baptist* has 'switched off' into a positive falsehood." [32]

"Thus we see," Shaw continued in his article in *The Independent Pulpit*, "that the pious fabrication by the *Baptist* or its informant is without any foundation, and this effort to misrepresent the death utterances of an unbeliever is only in keeping with the practice of the church in past ages. If the *Baptist* was misinformed on the subject, and stated what it had a right to believe, of course it will now correct the error; and we hope the pious journals that have so readily caught up the falsehood and repeated it, will entitle themselves to the claim of honesty and fairness, by making a public correction of the same." In conclusion, Shaw spoke a simple eulogy of his friend and expressed his feelings for the mourning family. "It appears that our dear friend died just as he lived, an honest, sincere man, whose convictions were unshaken by any fear of God or a future hell. We deeply sympathize with his afflicted family, who have since been called to give up his only son, who died one week after the death of his father." [33]

Shaw's pleas that the religious journals set the record straight concerning Renfro's "death-bed confession" on the basis of the proof that he had provided were of no avail. The *Good Samaritan*, another Baptist publication, soon featured an article written by preacher R. C. Buckner in which the story was again repeated. Julius Baker read Buckner's "local" and was incensed. He immediately wrote to J. D. Shaw stating that "if you have not read it get a copy and read. All the devils in the bottomless pit could not have conceived of a more villainous ltr [letter]. If the editor of The Tex. Bap. calls on you for any proof I can supply you with some of as honorable men as there are in the country who saw H. C. Renfro die, and will sign a document that the ed of the Tex. Bap. is a liar." But the mold was set, so far as the orthodox publications were concerned. The statements, once made, were there to stay for all time.[34]

Yet, even if Julius Baker and others were willing to carry on the fight for a lost cause, Henry Renfro's old friend Thomas Neilson recognized the futility of it all. "I and those who knew & loved him," wrote the Philadelphian,

> will care little for the slanders of the religious journals, which assail him, their shafts will not hurt the living & cannot now vex or worry the dead. It can truly be said of him,

> > His life was gentle & the elements so mixed
> > in him. That nature could stand up
> > And say to the world. *This was a man.*

Neilson, in a letter to Julius Baker written on April 22, wrote an elegant elegy of his long-time correspondent:

> I am grieved and shocked beyond expression & tender to you, to his widow & daughter my sincerest, heartfelt sympathy, for if I (who never had the pleasure of seeing his kindly face, or hearing his winning voice) learned to respect & love him, simply from corresponding with him & gleaning a knowledge of his noble qualities, as seen in the cold mirror of letter writing, feel his loss as keenly; what must that loss be to these who for so many long years revelled in the sunlight of his smiles, intrusted by his counsel & cherished by his *love*? I feel that I have lost a *dear, dear* friend & an *ardent admirer*. & I shall ever cherish his memory.[35]

Concluding his letter to Julius, Neilson noted that he had wished that he might have had the opportunity to meet his friend "face to face in this world, but that like many other fond anticipations is now dashed to earth, but I trust that in the great hereafter . . . from which orthodoxy cannot exclude kindred spirits, that we will yet meet, when time is over."[36]

Renfro's old friend and defender F. B. Baillio also expressed his loss and wrote one last defense of the Parson in *The Alvarado Bulletin*.

> How very sorry I was to hear of the death of Henry C. Renfro. For 18 years I knew him and feel that a good man has gone to seek his reward and be judged by a merciful God according to the unerring standard of truth and justice and not according to the estimates of men. I ever thought him honest and sincere in his convictions and never yet heard his honor or integrity called in question. As to his peculiar faith and doctrine, they were his and he alone is responsible to his God.

"Peace be to his ashes," wrote the Grand View correspondent for the *Bulletin*, "Calm and quiet may they rest among those of his loved ones gone before. May his soul ever bask in the smiles of a reconciled and purified God. May he rest in peace."[37]

A final eulogy to Renfro was offered by the Masonic Lodge, which published a "Tribute of Respect" in *The Alvarado Bulletin* of April 17.

> In the demise of Bro. Renfro, society, the commonwealth, his family and this fraternity, have suffered an irreparable loss, and that if we could, in any way, compensate for the blow by enlarging upon his character and life, we would most gladly do so. Conspicuous among his many good traits, all of which were worthy of emulation, we desire to call the attention of the living to his honesty of purpose. His desire was to be true to himself and to his fellows, his mental activity led him to investigation and this in turn to a higher plane of thought than many of his contemporaries. When convinced of a truth, he would assert it at the risk of reputation and position. If this desire to induce others to see the truth as he saw it, brought reproach, it was doubtless no more than he had anticipated, for he was too well acquainted with the history of the past, not to know that all advanced thinkers had met obstacles at every step.[38]

Shortly after his death, Mary Renfro, with Annette and Julius, selected the inscription for her husband's gravestone from the poem by

Robert Burns titled, "On a Friend." The following words, taken from that ode, were inscribed on the monument:

> An honest man lies here at rest,
> As e'er God with his image blest.
> The friend of man, the friend of truth,
> The friend of age, the friend of youth.
> Few hearts like his with virtue warmed.
> Few hearts with knowledge so informed.
> If there's another world, he lives in bliss.
> If there is none, he made the best of this.[39]

Chapter 10

Epilogue

Nothing is more inevitable than change. Sometimes it occurs slowly; other times change occurs quickly and has a lightning-like effect on persons and events. In the days and weeks after Henry Renfro died at McBride's boarding house in Fort Worth, a chain of events was set in motion almost immediately that had severe effects on family and friends and lingering consequences a century later. The extended Renfro family already was in disarray because of the recent tragedies. Mary's grief was enormous upon the loss of her husband as well as her son in such a short time. Kittie Renfro was devastated by the demise of Burlie, one who seemed to have enormous promise for the future. Annette, already distracted by earlier bouts with the Baker family, could no longer count on the leveling influence of her father to keep her relationship with Julius on an even keel. The prospects of soon-to-be-born children Pearl and Jim Baker also were part of the equation, and their futures were to be heavily influenced by the death of their grandfather. All of these factors were to bear heavily on the future of the family, and most of the time the effects were negative rather than positive. Without Renfro's remarkable ability to provide cohesion when life became complicated and seemingly unbearable, the world of the Parson's family was to suffer drastic and sometimes tragic change.

One of the first trials that Mary Renfro was to endure after the deaths of her husband and son was a petition by Burlie's wife, Kittie, for a settlement and division of the part of the Renfro estate that would have gone to her husband. Since the relationship between Mary and Kittie was never a strong one, the request, made so quickly after the grief and tragedy of burying the two men, made the relationship between the two even more tenuous. On April 29, 1885, the law firm of Crane & Ramsey of Cleburne, noted to be the best attorneys in the county, drew up a legal document for Mary which outlined in detail exactly what part of the Renfro land she considered to be her homestead property. After approval by the court of the designation, Mary's attorneys entered into negotiation with Kittie for a settlement. The negotiations were to no avail, however, and a lawsuit was filed by Kittie against Mary, Annette, and Julius. The litigation was decided in Kittie's favor, as was an appeal filed in November 1885. Afterward, Mary paid Kittie what was later described as "a large amount of money" in addition to relinquishing any claims to the farm that Burlie and Kittie had been deeded by the Renfros. Several years later, Annette learned what eventually happened to her sister-in-law in a letter from Mintie Roberts, her old roommate from College Hill days. "Two years ago while visiting in North Tex," wrote Mintie, "I met Kittie Dysart[,] it is now, on the train, between Howe and McKinney. She and her new husband were going to visit his Father. I hear that they have about squandered what property he had and mortgaged her farm Burlie left. They live at Claude, out west."[1]

Another claimant to a part of the Parson's estate was Waco University, in the person of Rufus C. Burleson. One month after Henry Renfro's death, Burleson wrote a receipt to Mary Renfro for $150 in full payment of a note to the Alumni Association which "has been misplaced." According to the university president, Renfro had requested that the money be for Burleson's "personal benefit." On the same receipt, Burleson acknowledged payment by Mary Renfro of another note for $200 "in full of the amount due on the two hundred dollar note given by said H. C. Renfro[.] this is a full and clear receipt against said note which I promise to send at once to Mrs. M. R. Renfro."[2]

At the time of her father's death, Annette once again was expecting a baby. Henry had known of the forthcoming event, and had been, like his daughter and her husband Julius, jubilant at the prospects of having a grandchild in the family once again. The effects of the loss of little Ida Mintie had lingered too long, and the Parson had looked forward with great anticipation to the occasion. What neither Henry Renfro nor Annette Baker knew was that Annette would give birth to twins, a boy and a girl. They arrived on August 19, 1885, a little more than five months after Henry's fatal bout with pneumonia. There was little question but that the little boy would be named Henry Burleson Baker after his grandfather and his uncle, but the decision concerning the name of the little girl was more difficult because of the loss, only a year earlier, of Ida Mintie.

As there was no great hurry to give their new daughter a name, Julius wrote to his father-in-law's good friend, Thomas H. Neilson, and asked for his suggestions in the matter. In his reply, the Philadelphian applauded Julius and Annette on the birth. "I congratulate you & yr wife, on the advent of yr twins," he wrote, "Am glad one is to bear the name of his grandpa, & I can wish him no greater boon than that he may follow in his footsteps. I thank you for your compliment you have paid me to suggest a name for the little girl. If you desire to call her after one of the noblest, best, & most generous women in the world, you can name her Mary Neilson, after my mother. I do not care for *fancy* names, & I don't think there is a prettier name . . . than Mary." And Mary it became, Mary Pearl Baker.[3]

Henry and Pearl (as she usually was called) were an adorable pair, and they attracted attention wherever they were shown in public. Inevitably, one was carried by Julius, the other by Mary Renfro, and Annette would "come prancing behind in her best finery looking as pretty as you please." The children were a tonic to Annette, and they seemed to alleviate much of the pain that she had suffered in the loss of her father and her brother. Still, Annette complained about her health, and she often believed that she should be under a doctor's care. From February through September 1886, she was visited at home by Dr. James Pickett on ten different occasions.[4]

By early August, however, Annette's spirits soared sufficiently that she agreed, at the last moment, to accompany her mother on a visit to Arkansas to visit her Aunt Chellie Ann and the Coody family. Although Julius was pleased with Annette's decision, he did not look forward to a long period of time alone on the farm. He was devoted to his wife and children, despite the best efforts of some in the Baker family to drive a wedge in the relationship. However, he bid Annette, babies Henry and Pearl, and Mary Renfro goodby and sent them on their way. Already becoming lonely as the train pulled out from the depot in Fort Worth, he worried about how Annette and the twins would make the trip. When he received the first letter from his wife on August 12, however, his fears abated, and he wasted no time in penning a reply. "I was greatly relieved this evening when I rec'd your letter stating you went through without accident. My whole dread was that something serious might happen to you on the trip. I am so proud you was [sic] not troubled any changing [railroad] cars." Julius was full of questions, principally about the twins. "I knew our sweet babes would be showed a great deal of attention on the train. What does the folks in Ark. say about them? Was your visit unexpected to Aunt [Chellie] and the rest of them? Did ma get worn out on the trip? Were the babes fretful?"[5]

It was obvious that Julius missed his family and that he was becoming accustomed to the life of a married man. "I miss you all very much," he said, "the babes mostly at the table when Pearl will turn around to see the chickens or the cats. I think I can realize all the comforts of a married life now. If I was left alone in the world without a wife to meet me when I am through my days work and say a kind word to me, or sweet babes to embrace, I know I would be unhappy." In another letter written a week later, Julius emphasized how much he missed Annette and the twins. "There is no use for me to express how glad I would be to see you and the babes though I can do very well till you are satisfied with your stay."[6]

Julius was somewhat worried about one of the babies, however. Writing to Annette, he expressed the hope that the little boy, Henry, would "not have any more chills," then speculated that perhaps "teething is the cause." Both Julius and Annette sensed that something was not right with "Burlie," as the little boy was called, and sometimes strangers noted that he did not look as healthy as sister Pearl. Suspicions were confirmed as the baby boy grew weaker and weaker after the return from Arkansas, growing progressively thinner and sicker. Dr. Pickett made a house call to care for Burlie two days after Christmas 1886 and again on January 2, 1887. There was nothing that could be done for the little boy's chronic diarrhea, however, and the namesake of Henry Renfro passed away on January 3 at the age of one and one-half years. The emotional impact that was felt in the family with yet another death, the fourth in less than two years, was devastating.[7]

When he received word of the tragic event from Julius, Thomas Neilson sent his condolences without delay. "Yr favor of the 17th Inst. conveying the sad intelligence of the death of yr little boy, is recd, & I tender to you & yr wife my deepest sympathy. I also recd the photograph of the little *twins*. They are *lovely* children, & I can well understand yr & yr wife's grief at the loss sustained. I think little 'Mary Pearl' is *too cute*. The little boy *looks sick*, when his picture was taken." Neilson then suggested, at Julius's request, a fitting inscription for the gravestone of Henry Burleson Baker.[8]

The death of her son created once more in Annette a depression that she would have great difficulty in overcoming. Again, she began the habit of "taking to her bed," citing illness, and found it to be a way to escape from the world that she felt had treated her so badly. Only Pearl gave her pleasure, and Annette lavished love and attention on the little girl, often to the exclusion of both her mother and her husband. It was weeks before Annette began to improve, and during that time it was a rare occasion when Julius was able to get past the facade that his wife had built around herself. Already considerably alienated from the Baker family because of her earlier criticism of Darius over the foreclosure, Annette once again became a target of their reproach. Her tight-fisted handling of her father's estate evoked some criticism, and Mollie Baker Jack, her sister-in-law, was among those who voiced disapproval. Mollie had never wanted her brother to marry Annette in the first place, as she had considered her to be flippant. A year before their marriage she wrote to her brother Julius with a cautious warning, "Good luck for Annette and yourselfe [sic], only don't you marry her. I hate girls who try to beguile the boys."[9]

A Spiritualist, Mollie Jack wrote her mother soon after the Parson's death that she had been involved in a seance in which Henry Renfro was contacted. "Well, Ma, we have tried our Spiritualism since I came home and got one long message from H. C. Renfro, a regular lecture. We have it all[;] if you wish to read it I will send it to you if you will promise to take good care of it and send it home." Then, Mollie wrote that Renfro "told us to go to Annette and tell her to not hold her money [but] to do good with it—if she worshipped money she would not rise to a good hight [sic] in the spirit world. He seemed eager to talk for [to] us so we could persuade Annette to study & grow noble & rise[.] He said he was greatly to blame in not sowing different seed in regard to teching [teaching] them how to use the money he left them. God grant that she will grow as noble as her glory fied [sic] father wishes." It is of interest that the first part of this letter later was torn out, probably to get rid of even more disparaging information about Annette.[10]

Despite the harangue against his wife by his family, Julius managed to stand by Annette, and in May 1887, his love remained strong. He affectionately called her "Pet," not realizing that there was yet another emotion troubling her, unrelated to the deaths in the family and her real or imagined illnesses. On a hot, humid summer day in 1887, however, at another time when Annette had "taken to bed" complaining of sickness, Julius sat by her side, fanning her, and the conversation turned to their relationship. Unexpectedly, Annette turned to Julius and told him, matter of factly, that she would always love Buck Satterfield. The impact was shattering to Julius. He never had guessed the truth and had attributed all of Annette's unhappiness, brooding, and illness to the specter of death that had haunted the family. Julius was devastated. He still loved Annette, but after the confession he never felt quite the same as before. Yet, as in the case of Sam Houston's problems with his bride Eliza Allen, Julius vowed to keep Annette's disclosure a secret for the rest of his life.[11]

Although Annette's confession to Julius about her feelings for Buck Satterfield was to remain untold, other rumors were started by two jealous relatives of Annette, Mattie and Mollie Harris, daughters of James Henry Harris, Annette's cousin. The rumors that they concocted had no basis in fact, but the Baker family was easily misled and their distrust soon led Julius to have doubts, also. The false charges, along with his certain knowledge that Annette continued to love her old beau, caused Julius to wonder whether the innuendo about his wife was true.[12]

Julius became extremely unhappy and would have left his wife without notice but for the problem of leaving little Mary Pearl. However, he determined that he had to do something. Although Annette did not at that time realize the impact of her confession, Julius's ego was shattered at the knowledge that his wife loved someone else, and he did not believe that it would be possible for him to remain with her on the same basis as before. When he could no longer stand the prospect of living with someone he loved passionately but who loved someone else, he left. Quietly, without telling anyone of his plans, he rode off on his horse one morning, never to return as Annette's husband. Years later, Annette was to confide that Julius never indicated his displeasure and that his departure was a complete surprise.[13]

The decision to leave was made even more difficult by the fact that, once again, Annette was expecting a baby. But as important as that was, Julius knew that the child would be well cared for. Annette had sufficient money and that would never be a problem. The most difficult part of Julius's decision was leaving Mary Pearl behind. The little girl was the most precious thing in the world to him, and he felt that it would be almost impossible for him to continue to live without having her with him. Julius brooded about the matter for days, wondering how he could gain custody of the blue-eyed baby. Seeing no other recourse, Julius decided that he would simply go to the farm, lift Pearl onto his horse, and ride away with her. A bold plan, but one that he felt would work.[14]

Within days, he resolved to make the move. Knowing when Pearl probably played outside, Julius rode to the front of the farmhouse and picked up the little girl. As he prepared to ride away, however, Annette appeared on the porch with a pistol, told her husband to return the baby to her at once, then threatened him with the warning, "If you take my baby, I'll shoot!" Julius knew Annette well, however, and he was confident that she would not fire, especially while he held Pearl with him in the saddle. As a result, he ignored his wife's warning and told her that if she fired she would hit the baby; then without saying another word, Julius turned his horse and rode away from the house that had once been his home.[15]

Annette was almost hysterical at the loss of little Mary Pearl. Not knowing what to do, she rode as quickly as she could to her mother's home, then, with copius tears, told Mary Renfro of the abduction. Mary calmed her daughter, then sought to replace emotion with logic as she assured Annette that she believed that, regardless of his charges against the Renfros, Julius's actions did not have a sound legal basis. Mary knew that Pearl would be safe in Julius's hands, but she knew, also, that it would be necessary to take strong measures to get her back. Consequently, the next day both women conferred with lawyers Crane & Ramsey of Cleburne about the options that were available. Although divorce usually was considered to be a last resort in nineteenth-century Texas, the attorneys were quick to point out that it would be the best and quickest way to make sure that Annette retained custody of Pearl as well as the child that she was expecting in early 1888. Therefore, Annette "filed suit for divorce, for custody of their children, and for property both real and personal." Crane and Ramsey then began their efforts to be sure that Annette had the best possible chance of winning the case. Since both the Renfros and the Bakers were well-known in Cleburne and Johnson County, attorney Martin M. Crane decided that an impartial jury might be most easily empaneled somewhere else. Therefore, he petitioned the court for a change of venue to the nearby town of Glen Rose, Somervell County. The petition was approved, and a date for the trial was set for Monday, September 4, 1887.[16]

Annette had no way of knowing whether or not Julius would bring up her admitted love for Buck Satterfield in the trial. The relationship between the two cousins had always been platonic, and Julius himself knew that it was. Yet, Annette knew that an unscrupulous attorney might attempt to make it appear otherwise. Therefore, she wrote to Buck about the possibility of problems and told him that it might be a good idea for him to be at Glen Rose, just in case he needed to testify in her defense. However, no word was forthcoming from him, and as the trial date edged closer, Annette had no way of knowing whether or not he would be there. When the jury selection began, there was still no word from Buck, and Annette hoped against hope that her relationship with him would not become an issue.

Annette need not have worried, as Julius had no intention of airing the secret that he guarded about his wife. Jury selection began early on Monday morning, and soon the arguments were underway. Despite the fact that the case was being heard in Glen Rose, a large number of Johnson County residents were in the courtroom, some sympathetic to the Bakers, but most friendly to Annette and the Renfros. The Somervell County residents who attended took in the debates and, as the trial proceeded, began to make their own judgments. The arguments by the lawyers occupied all of Monday and Tuesday, and part of Wednesday. By midafternoon, however, all of the charges and countercharges were complete, and the judge explained their responsibilities to the jury members. Everyone, including Annette and Julius, expected a long wait in hearing the decision, but the jurors made up their minds quickly. After only seven minutes, just long enough to write their answer, they returned to the courtroom and rendered a decision in favor of Annette. "When the verdict was read," one newspaper account related, "the crowd, which was a large one, at once stamped their feet, manifesting their joy at the verdict, and their sympathy for Mrs. Baker." Annette and her mother were delighted, but the gloom in the Baker camp was extreme.[17]

On September 30, Buck Satterfield wrote a letter to Annette in which he asked, perhaps innocently, "How are you getting along with your law suits and when will be your time in Glen Rose?" Yet, even this letter was not mailed until nearly six weeks after the beginning of the trial. On October 10, Buck wrote again after hearing from Annette and learning of the outcome of the trial. "I am very sorry indeed," he wrote, "that I failed to be there . . . especially if I would have been [of] any service to you in any way. Annette, I don't want you to think that this is just an excuse that I am fixing up and that I did not want to loose [sic] the time and be at the Expense to go for I certainly would take pleasure in going regardless of time and expenses had I known it in time[,] and I went out on the road with the full intention of going there whenever you notified me." Of course, Buck was married at the time of the trial, and regardless of his feelings for Annette, it would have been a very clumsy situation for him had it been necessary for him to testify in a divorce trial for his old girlfriend. There is no denying that he had strong feelings for his cousin, but there was real question as to whether or not he received Annette's request in time for him to appear in Glen Rose had he wished to do so.[18]

On February 18, 1888, Annette gave birth to a healthy baby boy. He was the image of his father, and his appearance was what his sister Pearl later described as "a Baker, out and out." Annette named him James Renfro Baker, probably after her father's brother, James. Although Julius was notified at the birth of his new son, the atmosphere was such that it was very difficult for him to visit Annette and the new offspring. Despite the situation, Julius would come to love the little boy very much and, as years went by, to get to know him. This was to be later, however, as the legal squabbles between Julius, Annette, and their families were not yet settled.

The judicial decree of September 6, 1887, was favorable to Annette and gave her what she asked. She received a divorce from Julius; she received custody of Pearl (and ultimately, James), and she won the right to the real and personal property that the two owned before the breakup in their marriage. Yet, Julius, with the prodding of his brothers, did not accept the findings of the court in regard to the ownership of the farm which had been given to the couple by Parson Renfro. In a complicating legal maneuver before the divorce trial, Julius had transferred title of the farm to his brother John, and John subsequently claimed the property as his homestead. As a result, Annette and her mother were unable to complete the settlement. After months of unproductive haggling with the Bakers through their lawyers, Annette and Mary filed suit against Julius, John, Darius, and Jesse Baker, asking a judgment against all of them in the amount of $1,351.40, the value of the land. The trial was set for April 13, 1889, in Glen Rose; however, a preliminary court appearance was set in Cleburne for January 1889.[19]

It appeared that another major legal struggle was in the works, and Annette and Mary, with their attorneys, began to assess every possible option that could be utilized in order to be sure that they were successful once again. One of the strategies included calling witnesses who could testify as to the circumstances in the case, particularly in regard to Henry Renfro's intentions regarding the land when it was given to the newlyweds. One of those on the list was Annette's old beau, Buck Satterfield. Annette wrote Buck in early December 1888, told him of the suit, and asked if it would be possible for him to be in Cleburne for testimony, if needed. Once again, Buck was somewhat reluctant to get involved, but agreed to do whatever was necessary. "I will come up to your trial at Cleburne," he wrote, "but if I am there they will naturally expect me to be at Glenrose. You can just write me and tell me what you think of it and if you say so I can be at Cleburne, but if I can be of no service it would be best not to go until the trial at Glenrose."[20]

Evidently, Annette wrote to Buck that his attendance at the preliminary hearing in Cleburne would not be necessary, and Satterfield answered her letter in mid-January, inquiring as to the date of the lawsuit. "Oh yes," he wrote, "you never told me in your letter when your trial would come up at Glenrose. Be sure to tell me in your next letter so I can make my arrangements to go for I am going to be there. If I live." Buck then ended his letter with an inquiry as to the results of the Cleburne hearing.[21]

In her next correspondence, Annette complained to Buck that she was ill and that the events of the past two years had been a terrible strain on her. Sympathetically, Buck answered with the advice that "if you sit down and grieve over the past you will never find any enjoyment in it, but the best way I think is to go any where that you care, enjoy yourself and try to forget as much of the past as you can. By doing so I hope you will get so you will never think of what has happened[;] but of course you can't until your Law suits are ended which I hope will be soon and you come out victorious." Buck then acknowledged Annette's information that the trial in Glen Rose would be about April 15. "Yes," he said, "I will be ready to go when you let me know." [22]

It was not long before a court date for the Glen Rose trial was set for April 13, and Annette wrote to Buck informing him of the change. The railroad man was agreeable, but in a reply to Annette he let her know that he was still worried about the possible gossip about his trip. He wrote that he and his wife had company, and that he "could not write while the young ladies were here," and that he hoped that "none of those people are aware of my going to Glenrose." For the first time, however, Buck then began to make definite arrangements for his appearance. "I will try to be there on Sunday if I can. Can't you drop me a note and tell me where you will be so we can talk the matter over some before the case comes up, but then I suppose it is a small town [and you will] not be very hard to find. . . . Well," he concluded, "I hope you will come out victorious." [23]

As promised, Buck arrived in Glen Rose on Sunday, April 12, and immediately met with Annette to discuss what the next day's proceedings might offer. Then, on Monday morning, Buck testified as a witness for Annette and her mother, providing very convincing testimony as to what he believed the intentions of his relative Henry Renfro to be when he deeded the 108-acre farm to Annette and Julius Baker. Eager to disengage himself, however, Buck quickly said his goodbys, boarded the next train, and headed for Waco and home and wife. Combined with the skills of Crane and Ramsey, the testimony of Buck and others prevailed, and on the same day that the trial began, Annette Baker and Mary Renfro received a judgment against Julius, Darius, John, and Jesse Baker in the amount of $1,351.40, the value of the farm deeded to Annette and Julius by her father, the Parson. John Baker later sought and received an injunction prohibiting Annette and Mary from selling the land until an appeal could be made. However, he also lost the appeal. [24]

Despite Buck's rapid departure from Glen Rose, James Henry Harris, Annette's cousin, immediately began talk about Satterfield's meeting with Annette before the trial. The chatter mushroomed, as gossip usually does, and it was not long before many of those in attendance at the trial, including those in the Baker camp, picked up the false tales that were being told. Soon, the news traveled beyond Somervell County, and by April 19, Buck himself had heard the stories that were being spread. Writing to his cousin about it, Buck noted that he was "very sorry James Henry took it to heart so about you and I talking a few minutes together though I lay it more on his ignorance than anything else. I thought it was policy to act in a way to keep the other side from getting up anything to talk about, but I find our side was the first to commence the talk. I would [have] liked to have had a chance to talk more with you for I think I am capable of giving you some good advice." In closing, Buck noted that he was pleased with the verdict in the case, and he hoped that would be the end of it. "I guess the Bakers will surely take a tumble sometime for there is no use in their trying to gain any kind of a law suit against you as everybody is so bitterly against them." [25]

In the months after Annette and her mother returned to the farm in Johnson County after the trial, the rumors about Annette and Buck grew more and more titillating. Yet, it was neither James Henry Harris, his sisters, nor the Bakers that were spreading the tales; it was Buck's family—the Roddys and the Satterfields. Perhaps it was their way of getting even because of old disputes between S. C. Roddy and Henry Renfro. Although Annette knew that Buck had no control over what his family did, she lashed out at her cousin in a letter written in November 1889. In his reply, Satterfield noted that "from the tone of it [Annette's chastisement], I was lucky to ever receive another letter from you. I am very sorry that some of my relations have let their tongues run away with them, but I thought you had heard enough of that kind of talk to not believe any of it, at least not become offended at it. . . . I don't appreciate some of their talk, and for that reason I don't visit among them anymore than I do for there are some people you know will tell things the way they imagine it to be and not the way they know it to be." [26]

Buck then asked Annette to "write me once more and tell me what was said and who said it and in fact give full particulars. I promise on my word of honor that I will never say anything to them or any one else about it. I just want to know who are my friends and who are my enemies." Buck ended his note with a request that "if you think my relatives will not tongue lash too much, write me again and give me a history of it and I will never say a word about it and will destroy your letter as soon as I read it so there will be no danger of it ever getting out." [27]

There is no record of whether or not Annette gave the requested information to her cousin Buck, but she did her best to quash the rumors and get back to the business of living once again. Nevertheless, Annette continued her correspondence with her old friend and cousin for thirty-eight more years before Buck was killed in a tragic railroad accident. In his last letter to her, however, Buck recalled the past and wished that there was some way to do things differently. "There is nothing I enjoy better," wrote Satterfield, "than to meet with the old timers and talk about old times. Oh, my but what would hapen [sic] if it was posible [sic] for us to all be set back just as we were 45 or 50 years ago and know then what we know now. We have all made mistakes that would certainly not be made if we could only travel that road again." [28]

Mary Renfro, like Annette, was glad that the legal wars were over, and she did her best to return to a normal life once more. This was made more difficult, however, because of the fact that Mary Renfro had been severely crippled in the fall of 1888 after being gored by a cow. Mary was not used to being incapacitated, and she did not savor the attention of others as did Annette. The difficulty she had in walking, combined with the excruciating pain that it caused, made a vast difference in Mary Renfro's ability to enjoy herself in the manner to which she was accustomed. The accident caused her to have to use a crutch the rest of her life. [29]

Despite her physical problems, however, Mary Renfro continued life with zest. Four years after the end of the Baker lawsuits, Mary decided to leave the farm, partially because of the trouble that she experienced in getting around, but also because she wanted to build a new home in Burleson—one that would be, without question, the finest in town. She contracted with a Mr. Pribble to build the structure at a cost of about $2,000. According to family tradition, Pribble was a perfectionist, and he refused to accept a piece of lumber that had a knot in it. A Victorian showplace, the new home sported a large second-story cupola from which the entire town of Burleson could be seen. Like all of the better houses of its time, the house utilized several lightning rods and was covered with elaborate "gingerbread" trim which Pribble himself cut on a foot-powered jigsaw.[30]

At about the same time that the new house was constructed, Annette decided to marry once again, this time to a mild-mannered and highly intelligent man named James Clark. Like the Renfros, Clark was originally from Georgia, and he quickly found a respected place in the family. Wary because of lawsuits and conflicts in the past, however, Annette insisted that the property owned by James and herself remain separate, an arrangement with which Clark had no problem. Although he was not at all wealthy, Clark owned and continued to buy property on his own after the marriage. Soon dubbed with the name "Pa" by all the family, James Clark became almost as a father to Annette's children, and later, to her grandchildren.

Julius Baker, Pearl and Jim's real father, did not remain in Johnson County long after the divorce from Annette. With his brother Darius, he moved to the northwest Texas town of Clarendon, where he continued to be a farmer. He kept in touch with his children and, like the rest of the Baker family, soon realized the folly of the problems that he had with Annette. Many years later, he told his daughter Pearl that he would be happy if he could hold Annette in his arms just one more time. This was not to be, however, and after the death of Darius, Julius joined in a marriage of convenience with Julia Baker, Darius's wife—a union that was heartily approved by all.[31]

After they recognized that Annette had not been the problem in the divorce proceedings of 1887, many of the Baker family visited Annette and Pearl on a regular basis and were extremely friendly to them. In 1915, even John Baker, Julius's brother and the principal in one of the land suits of 1889, visited Annette and Pearl, as did two young ladies named Tommie and Anna. In writing to Pearl about them, Julius noted that he knew that "they were treated nice—I should feel bad, indeed, to know they were treated otherwise." Three years later, in 1918, John Baker wrote a long untitled poem about the "days of '87 [1887]," when the bitter divorce trial separated the family. In it, Baker expressed remorse about the divisions and penned his hopes for reunions in the hereafter:

> Settled, I trust it all will be,
>   If not before, then after death,

When in Heaven, loved ones we see
Where happiness is true and not a myth.

And be it not, as on Earth, amiss,
When we reach the hights [sic] of glory
Bestowing on those we love, a caress, a tender little kiss
And truthfully eternal life can tell, its mighty story.[32]

Referring to the problems of the past, Julius said that he was sure that the girls who had visited Annette and Pearl knew "nothing of the details of our trouble, and for my part will never know. I would like to bury that part of the past deep down in my own heart—so deep that it could not be resurrected for the gaze of anyone. But—like Banco's Ghost it will not down, at least, for any considerable time." Julius then wrote to Pearl his opinion of the farce that had caused the trouble in the first place. "From the beginning that play was staged and the players picked their part—played their part as well as they were able and the world knows the result. For my part I would make it a sealed book."[33]

If Julius had had his way, he would have eliminated that era of the past in the same way that he believed that he had in the matter of the secret about Annette's love for Buck Satterfield. In his lifetime, he never divulged Annette's confidence to him except to his daughter Pearl, whom he also swore to secrecy. Nearly thirty years after his separation from Annette, Julius wrote to Pearl about their pact. "In reference to the secret—I think you are perfectly correct. It will never do for anything of the kind to be known other than *us*. I am not concerned about myself; of what people may say of me, for I think I am immune to long-tongues; but you and your's must be protected. You are perfectly aware of how things like this turns out sometimes—in a world of trouble and no end of scandal."[34]

Mollie Baker Jack, Julius's sister, was one of the Baker family who realized, many years later, that she had been taken in by the farce, and she was extremely remorseful at the consequences. Writing to Annette after the death of Julius in 1936, Mollie recognized that the problem had been caused by persons in the family who wanted to generate dissension:

It has been a long time to wait to say how sorry I am for you that your Julius is gone. I know how sad all the world has been for you all your life since the great trouble. I know how that great trial was more than most women could have borne and loved on. Oh why did those who caused the trouble not have been men and women? How you have been mis-judged—looking back I wonder how Mattie & Mollie Harris could have done such an awful thing, but they did & your father's daughter bears the mark, until now. Why oh why were you to suffer & the children as well?[35]

In another letter written a year later, Mollie emotionally expressed her feelings about her brother's wife. "You and I have gone through many heartaches since I saw you, & oh darling they were so unnec-essary. If we could call it all back with our experience we could make such a heaven where we have made such a hell. Life or what we call the soul epic does walk as thru so many shadows—such piles of yel-low wind swept leaves & then the rain falls and they decay—& low [lo] they are remembered no more." Ending the note, Mollie ex-pressed her love to Annette. "I hope Darling this Christ-mas letter will make you understand me & mine love you & yours—better & better as the river rolls away. So receive my love my dear dear love—& sometime when the burden gets too heavy write to me[,] your only loving sister."[36]

From time to time, Annette heard other voices from the past, re-ceiving letters from those whose lives had influenced hers as well as that of her father, the Parson. In 1901, in response to a request from Annette for a release on land, Thomas Neilson penned that he had moved to New York, stating that he had "lost a fortune after yr fa-ther's death & have had a struggle ever since. I never had the pleasure of *meeting* yr father in the flesh." Concluding his letter, Neilson told Annette that he had "corresponded with him [Renfro] up to his death & until advised he had passed away. Hope we will *meet* in the 'Better World.'"[37]

Another of the Parson's friends, James D. Shaw, continued to have an interesting yet controversial life. *The Independent Pulpit* flourished, and by 1887 it had a circulation of 1,700 copies per month. Shaw boasted to prospective advertisers that the paper was mailed to every state in the United States as well as several foreign countries. Yet, financial problems with the Religious and Benevolent Association grew as time went by, forcing Shaw to cease the lectures in Liberal Hall and to consolidate the *Pulpit* print shop into the hall in order to save money. The efforts were of no avail, however, as a tragic fire swept Liberal Hall on October 5, 1889. Shaw was able to continue publication of *The Independent Pulpit*, but the tragedy was the beginning of the end of Shaw's efforts to spread the gospel of liberalism in Texas.[38]

J. D. Shaw did not, however, cease to be a powerful leader, and his advice and endorsement were sought by many who sought political power and influence. He was selected to serve on a committee that prepared a public eulogy for deceased governor and Indian fighter Lawrence Sullivan Ross, and he chaired a mass meeting for the occasion. Active in city politics, Shaw enthusiastically promoted the commissioner form of government for Waco.[39]

Shaw's personal life was not a happy one. His first wife and child died in 1881, and although he married once again in 1884, his second wife died in 1901 soon after the death of his son, John Shaw. Another son, Tyus (nicknamed Tye), assumed the role of publisher of *The Independent Pulpit*. He changed the name of the publication to *The Search Light*, but the liberal publication had lost its dynamism and was soon closed. It is of interest that in 1909, Shaw was invited to participate in the sixtieth anniversary celebration of the First Methodist Church in Waco. He willingly assented, and during the ceremonies he sat on the front pew, near the pulpit at which he once held sway.[40]

From the standpoint of liberal thought, however, one of Shaw's last hurrahs came in 1898 when, on April 2, he made the graveside address for William Cowper Brann, the editor of another Waco news magazine which achieved national circulation, *The Iconoclast*. Brann, like Shaw, was both loved and hated by many Wacoans, and he was killed on a downtown street by a gunshot wound in the back by a man named Tom Davis. During the graveside address at Oakwood Cemetery, Shaw extolled Brann as a man who "not only could soar intellectually," but also was able "to entertain the civilized world with burning words, with thoughts that were winged and went like lightning." In conclusion, Shaw noted that Brann was "a man of heart and of honor, and a man of the warmest and most generous love." A few months later, Shaw wrote a short but stirring biography of the editor of *The Iconoclast* for a book of the compiled writings of Brann. After Shaw's death in December 1926, in Glendale, California, he was buried near his old friend in Oakwood Cemetery.[41]

Interestingly, one of the regular targets of W. C. Brann in his *Icono-*

clast was the Baptist Church and Rufus C. Burleson. Brann targeted what he considered to be abuses of the church, failings of Burleson and others, and Baylor University in general. These attacks, without question, made many enemies for the publisher, and they may well have driven Brann's assassin, Tom Davis, to his violent actions. Burleson's stature was too well established, however, for Brann to inflict permanent damage, and the university president continued his role as the leader of Baptist education in Texas.[42]

Although the paths of Rufus Burleson and Annette Renfro Baker did not often cross after the death of the Parson, she did hear from Burleson as late as May 1898, when he wrote to her asking her support for one of his former graduates, Mozelle Edmondson, for the job of principal of Burleson High School. "May I ask you," wrote the venerable educator, "as a friend of mine and as the daughter of my oldest and dearest friend in Texas to aid in securing her the position."[43]

Although it is not known whether Annette used her influence in helping to secure the administrative job for the young lady, Burleson's request was one of the last known contacts between the Renfro and Burleson families. The Renfros had heard little from Rufus Burleson since the deaths of Henry and Burleson Renfro, and neither Mary Renfro nor Annette had made an effort to stay in touch with him. Mary had never been an enthusiastic correspondent, and her willingness to write letters diminished as she grew older. Her old injury caused her to become more and more infirm as the years went by, and by 1897, she was in such severe pain that her doctor prescribed potent pain relievers so that she could continue to get around. Despite her physical problems, however, she continued to be mentally active. She and Annette spent hundreds of hours making quilts, some for use and some for show, and she enjoyed the company of friends and family. She and her sister Chellie Ann continued to correspond until Mary quietly died in June 1897. Chellie lived five more years, passing away in March 1902.[44]

Rufus Burleson died in Waco on May 14, 1901. His funeral was held the following day, and it was one of the most extensive and well-attended in the history of the city. Among the speakers for the occasion were W. H. Parks, Henry Renfro's classmate at Baylor at Independence, and D. R. Wallace, a faculty member when Renfro was at Baylor and his friend as the surgeon of the old 15th Texas Regiment of the Confederacy. Soon after her husband's death, Georgia J. Burleson compiled and published a volume entitled *The Life and Writings of Dr. Rufus C. Burleson*. Despite the long friendship and association of Burleson and the Parson, the 887-page book made no mention of Henry Renfro. It is not known whether Annette was aware of the book or the omission of her father's name. It is likely, however, that because of the enmity between the Parson and the Baptist Church, she would not have expected her father to be included in what essentially was a Baptist publication. Yet, it is of interest to note that the disappointment of the Renfro, Baker, and Clark families with the Baptist Church never healed completely with the passage of time, and Annette never again entered one of the congregation's buildings except for funerals for her friends.[45]

Margaret Annette Renfro Baker Clark died in 1943 in Fort Worth, only blocks from the site of the McBride boardinghouse where her beloved father, the Parson, had passed away fifty-eight years before. Her funeral was held in the parlor of the Victorian house on Clark Street in Burleson, and she was buried in the little cemetery by the side of the road between Burleson and Alvarado, the pathway that she happily had traveled many times in the past. It was fitting that the two objects most precious to Annette were placed with her. On her hand was a little ring, inside of which were the engraved initials of Annette and Julius Baker; on her breast was a gold-trimmed pin containing a photograph of her father, the one that the Parson had requested be given to his beloved Burlie should he die in battle during the Great War.[46]

The legacy of Henry Renfro was remembered by his daughter Annette all of her life. She thought of him often and related her memories to her children, her grandchildren, and even her great-grandchildren. She rarely criticized those who had denounced her father; rather, her attitude was that those who did not agree with him were poor nonthinking souls who were more to be pitied than vilified. She never again was a member of the Baptist Church, although she had many friends in it, and she did not attach lasting blame to that congregation for any real or imagined wrongs to her or her father. Until the end of her life, Annette always remembered her father's wishes, expressed to her in the final verses of a poem written on her thirteenth birthday, to neither lament his passing nor continue her rancor toward his tormenters:

You must not be unkind to them
   Whose aim has been to blot my name
Time has no gold, earth has no gem
   That cruelty may not defame
Annettie, dear, when I am gone
   And all the world is dark to thee
Then do not grieve though left alone
   That I am from this bondage free.[47]

The years during which Henry Renfro was a minister were a period of enormous change within the American religious community. The writings and philosophy of men such as Thomas Paine, the author of *Common Sense* and *The Age of Reason* who excited Americans to pursue independence from England, were read by thousands. Work by philosophers such as Baruch Spinoza, Immanuel Kant, and David Hume cast doubt on established religious practices and were eagerly studied by large numbers of Americans, particularly those who had better than average educations. In 1859, within a year after Renfro left his ministry at the Independence Baptist Church, Darwin's *On the Origin of Species* was published. Although not immediately available or understood by churchmen, particularly those in rural areas, this research concerning evolution was to have a phenomenal impact on the concepts of the Bible relating to the creation of the world. Ten years later, in 1869, English biologist Thomas Henry Huxley invented the word "agnostic," which thousands of persons would apply to their doubts or skepticism about religion. During the same period, men such as Robert Ingersoll, an attorney from Illinois, were on the lecture circuit throughout the United States, preaching a new "religion" of agnosticism. Although the defection from the ministerial ranks to this new liberalism, particularly among Baptists, is not thought to be high, the fact that formerly devoted ecclesiastics such as Renfro joined those ranks signaled a stunning change in the status quo.

Within the Baptist Church in Texas and the South, changes also were occurring in the last half of the nineteenth century. Differing philosophies about slavery caused a schism between Northern and Southern churches that are not completely healed nearly 150 years later. Some historians believe that this rift was one of the principal causes of the Civil War. This period also saw, on the one hand, the development of educational institutions and dynamic missionary efforts, and on the other hand, evolution of Baptist subgroups, usually called Primitives, which were stubbornly anti-missionary, anti-intellectual, and extremely class-conscious. According to historian David Harrell, these groups were generally "strongly predestinarian" and "an obstinate resistance movement among the poor whites against the condescending leadership of their betters." Also developing during this period among Southern Baptist churches was a movement called Landmarkism. This, according to Harrell, was "a renewed effort to save Baptist churches from liberalism." By 1885, the year of Henry Renfro's death, Southern religion began to experience "serious strains" as Baptist leadership began to attach itself "firmly to middle-class aspirations of the New South," a movement which precipitated many mainline Baptists to move to the Landmark movement as well as Primitive and even Pentecostal divisions such as the Free-Will Baptist Church. With the knowledge of these changes, it is not hard to understand the divisions and strains that were evident within the Baptist movement. Henry Renfro reflected many of the changes in the church during this period. He became a part of the liberal wing that the Landmark Baptists were pledged to eliminate. His exclusion reflected the prevailing mood of the usually rural congregation which would not allow any threat to the established social order. Because of his education and his increasingly liberal views, Renfro and others like him fostered the formation of both an anti-intellectual movement and the Primitives. Yet, the acceptance of Renfro by many others in and out of the church reflected a willingness to allow a liberal wing of the church that still, today, engages in debate with the conservatives of the Baptist movement.[48]

The last half of the nineteenth century was one not only of change in the philosophy of religion, but also in a large number of other areas. The Industrial Revolution that began in England but became a North American phenomenon also precipitated modifications in everything from working conditions to lifestyle to social mores, even in the South.

This multiplicity of change was reflected in the family of Henry Renfro. Deviation from established Baptist doctrine, something that Henry's father and grandfathers would have considered unthinkable, was taken in course by Renfro's wife and children. Annette's divorce from Julius, another facet of family life that reflected tremendous modification in lifestyle, was previously an almost unthinkable action to the genteel Southern lady. Annette proceeded to do as she liked, however, and society and her family adjusted. Education, in earlier years a privilege for only a few families, became for the Renfros a necessary and worthwhile activity. The financial success of the Renfro family also reflected the upward mobility of many families on the Texas frontier—a phenomenon that was a magnet to thousands of Americans who followed the continuing line of the American settlement.

By 1900, fifteen years after Henry Renfro's death, Texas and the United States entered a new century—a new era of technology, of changing social mores, and of conflict that Renfro might have found difficult to imagine. Yet, it is interesting to note that vehement debates within the Baptist Church about the interpretation of the Bible remain strong even into the final decade of the twentieth century. One cannot help but speculate as to how Henry Renfro might have perceived these ongoing conflicts. It is likely, however, that the Parson would have felt at least some sense of vindication as he viewed the ongoing struggle for power and for the minds of Christians.

Notes

CHAPTER 1. MOST SANGUINE EXPECTATIONS

1. Ira Bishop, Annona, Texas, to M. O. Green, Burleson, Texas, September 30, 1939, Renfro-Clark Papers, in possession of the author; Rufus C. Burleson became the president of Baylor University at Independence in June 1851, the same year that Henry Renfro enrolled as a student. See Georgia J. Burleson, comp., *The Life and Writings of Dr. Rufus C. Burleson*, 97; Noble Lafayette Clark and Ruby Richeson Clark, Burleson, Texas, interview with author, August 11, 1975, tapes in possession of author. The Cross Timbers is a long belt of trees which extends from Central Texas into southern Oklahoma. It had much significance during the early settlement of the area, as it provided timber in an area with large expanses of prairie on each side. Henry C. Renfro, Affidavit of Settlement on Vacant Public Land, March 16, 1860, File 586, General Land Office of the State of Texas; State of Texas, Johnson County, Field Notes of W. Douglass, C. S., of H. C. Renfro Preemption, 160 acres, Robertson Scrip, Survey Number 1063, June 25, 1860, File 586, General Land Office of the State of Texas.

2. Thelma Clark Griggs, "A Profile of Mu and Remembrances of the Old Family Home," Ms., 1977, in possession of author; Noble and Ruby Clark interview with author, August 11, 1975. The 1894 structure received a historical marker through the Texas Historical Commission on March 28, 1971, when it was dedicated as the new home for the Burleson library. See "Burleson's Library Dedicated," *Fort Worth Star-Telegram*, March 29, 1971.

3. Henry C. Renfro, "The Endurance of Afflictions," in W. H. Parks, *Texas Baptist Pulpit: A Collection of Sermons from the Baptist Ministry of Texas*, 269–281. Family tradition relates that Absalom was sent to Tennessee from Virginia "in disgrace" by his father after being expelled from school for "radical ideas." See Susan Collins, great-great-great-granddaughter of Absalom Renfro, Dallas, Texas, to William C. Griggs, Canyon, Texas, October 5, 1982, in possession of author; United States, Department of Commerce, Census of 1850, Walker County, Georgia; J. G. M. Ramsey, *The Annals of Tennessee to the End of the Eighteenth Century . . .* , 431–432; James R. Gilmore, *John Sevier as a Commonwealth Builder*. This entire book is dedicated, more or less, to the conflicts between Colonel John Tipton, Levicy Tipton Renfro's grandfather, and John Sevier. The sentiments of the book's author are decidedly in favor of the latter. For information on the participation of the Renfros in the Donelson Expedition, see Ramsey, *Annals of Tennessee*, 197–203; Donald O. Manshardt, Peoria, Illinois, to Mrs. Fred E. Dunn, Soda Springs, Oklahoma, c. 1950, copy in Renfro-Clark Papers; Shannon P. Warrenfells, Chattanooga, Tennessee, to Annette Renfro Clark, Burleson, Texas, November 17, 1938, Renfro-Clark Papers. Warrenfell's wife was Edna Harris Warrenfells, the great-granddaughter of Absalom Renfro. William S. Renfro, Henry's nephew who was later called "Uncle Billy," was the son of Jefferson Tipton Renfro, Henry's older brother. The visit of Sam Houston to Maryville was probably the one which occurred in October 1831 on the occasion of Houston's mother's death. See Marquis James, *The Raven: The Biography of Sam Houston*, 161. Houston did not reach Texas until over a year later, in December 1832. James, *The Raven*, 186.

4. James Alfred Sartain, *History of Walker County, Georgia*, reprint, 251–252; United States, Department of Commerce, Census of 1850, Walker County, Georgia, Household #773; Shannon P. Warrenfells to Annette Renfro Clark, November 17, 1938, Renfro-Clark Papers; Donald O. Manshardt, a genealogist and a meticulous researcher of the Renfro family, noted that the Renfros "seemed to be among the first settlers in every new county in the Westward Expansion." See Donald O. Manshardt, Peoria, Illinois, to Thelma Clark Griggs, Lubbock, Texas, April 12, 1971, Renfro-Clark Papers.

5. Parks, *Texas Baptist Pulpit*, 269. When the author visited Peavine Church in Walker County in 1979, it was still a flourishing congregation. The original church building had been replaced, but the old cemetery, dating to the 1830's, was still intact and well cared for. It may be that Absalom and Levicy Renfro were charter members of the Peavine Baptist Church, as it began in 1836, the same year the Renfros came to the Rock Spring area, although records cannot be located. See "Peavine Baptist Church History," in brochure entitled "Peavine Baptist Church: Rock Spring, Georgia," c. 1979, in possession of the author.

6. Henry C. Renfro [Absalom Renfro's brother, Carter County, Tennessee] to Dear Brother [Absalom Renfro], Rock Spring P.O., Georgia, March 21, 1851, Renfro-Clark Papers. Absalom and Levicy Renfro were married in Carter County, Tennessee, on March 12, 1817. Abraham Tipton was surety. See State of Tennessee, Carter County, Marriage Records, vol. 1 (1796–1850); also, see Worth S. Ray, *Tennessee Cousins: A History of the Tennessee People*, 62.

7. For a complete listing of the Renfro family, see United States, Department of Commerce, Census of 1840, Walker County, Georgia.

8. Ramsey, *Annals of Tennessee*, 142, described the location of the Renfro farm. He noted that it had been owned previously by one Joshua Horton, who also had owned the property which became the home of Samuel Tipton. Pinpointing the Renfro farm even more accurately, Ramsey noted that one of Mr. Horton's sons, Richard, lived at the place "now occupied by Mr. Renfro." This statement was made prior to 1853, the date of publication of Ramsey's book. The Renfro property to which Ramsey refers was purchased on December 2, 1815, by Joseph Renfro (Absalom's father) from Joshua Jobe and Richard Miller, the executors of John Miller, deceased. The price was $1,000, and it was for 297 acres on the north side of the Watauga River, "part of Joshua Horton's grant." See State of Tennessee, Carter County, Deed Records, Record C:71, December 2, 1815. It is likely that Joshua Jobe was the grandfather of Absalom Renfro's wife, Levicy Tipton Renfro. Levicy's mother, who married Thomas Tipton, the son of Colonel John Tipton, had the maiden name of Jobe. See Ray, *Tennessee Cousins*, 67. Some of the Jobe family followed the Renfros to Johnson County, Texas, and Henry Renfro referred in one of his letters to "Cousin Samuel Jobe." See Henry C. Renfro, "Camp on the Road," to Dear Sister Margaret [Margaret R. Harris], December 24, 1864, Renfro-Clark Papers.

9. Henry C. Renfro [Absalom Renfro's brother, Carter County, Tennessee] to Dear Brother [Absalom Renfro], Rock Spring P.O., Georgia, March 21, 1851, Renfro-Clark Papers. An interesting note in the same letter notes that William Renfro, another brother of the two men, "died I believe in the extreme part of Iowa and as I have every reason to believe from the effects of liquor."

10. Benjamin Harris also received a grant for 160 acres in Cass County, Texas, which he later transferred to his brother-in-law, James Renfro. Isaac Renfro was granted 179.3 acres, later sold to one Joseph S. Blair; James Renfro was the original grantee of a 320-acre plot, as was Absalom Renfro. See records of Cass County in *Abstract of Land Titles in Texas: Comprising the Titled, Patented and Located Lands in the State*, 1: 187–201. It is of interest that Benjamin Harris was the brother of Jefferson's wife, Lucinda. This was only one of a series of marriages of Renfro family members to brothers and sisters of other

related families. It is of interest that a community called Hickory Hill is still recalled by residents of Avinger, Cass County, Texas.

11. Renfro family tradition relates that Henry traveled from Georgia to Texas, alone, at age eighteen. This appears to be questionable, as no correspondence or supporting material has been found. Renfro would have been eighteen in 1849. In the letter from Shannon P. Warrenfells to Annette Renfro Clark, November 17, 1938, Warrenfells attempted to date Absalom's emigration to Texas based on the age of his son Henry, who Warrenfells said was eighteen at the time. However, it is known that Absalom Renfro was still in Georgia in 1849, the year that Henry would have turned eighteen. See Henry C. Renfro [Absalom Renfro's brother, Carter County, Tennessee] to Dear Brother [Absalom Renfro], Rock Spring P.O., Georgia, March 21, 1851, Renfro-Clark Papers. In a letter written in 1859, Henry Renfro admitted that he "once loved that woman [Miss Gerl] with all the devotion of my nature." See Henry C. Renfro, [Johnson County, Texas], to Mary R. Ray, "At Home" [Johnson County, Texas], August 4, 1859, Renfro-Clark Papers. Efforts to determine the identity of Miss Gerl and her family have been to no avail. The family is not listed in either the 1850 or 1860 census of Cass County. An attempt was made by the author in November 1992 to locate any recollection of the Gerl family in Cass County, but none was found.

12. An excellent account of the founding of Baylor University is Lois Smith Murray, *Baylor at Independence,* 15–73; also see Burleson, comp., *The Life and Writings of Dr. Rufus C. Burleson,* 99–109; Shannon P. Warrenfells to Annette Renfro Clark, November 17, 1938, Renfro-Clark Papers; *The Story of Baylor University at Independence: 1845–1886,* brochure published by Baylor University, 1986; an interesting little book which presents a good overview of Independence and Washington County at the time that Henry Renfro was there is Gracey Booker Toland, *Austin Knew His Athens;* a letter from Rufus C. Burleson to Renfro written in 1884 noted that Renfro had repaid all aid that he had received from churches. See Rufus C. Burleson, Waco University, Texas, to Henry C. Renfro, Johnson County, Texas, January 18, 1884, Renfro-Clark Papers.

13. The *Catalogue of the Trustees, Officers, and Students of Baylor University* for 1851–1852 notes that the curriculum included three-year courses in both Greek and Latin, four years of mathematics, as well as other courses in ancient history, philosophy, natural philosophy, chemistry, geology, astronomy, logic, surveying, navigation, political economy, rhetoric, and Evidences of Christianity. See Murray, *Baylor at Independence,* 109; Jefferson Tipton Renfro and Lucinda Rilla Renfro, Walker County, Georgia, to Henry C. Renfro, [Independence, Texas], July 23, 1852, Renfro-Clark Papers.

14. Jefferson Tipton Renfro and Lucinda Rilla Renfro to Henry C. Renfro, July 23, 1852, Renfro-Clark Papers. One of the men named by Jefferson Ren-

fro as being "obnoxious to the claims of orthodoxy" was John Wesley, one of the founders of Methodism; the other was the person responsible for the founding of the Church of Christ, Alexander Campbell. This letter of Jefferson to Henry, in which he alluded to the "Faculty, Students, and Citizens of Baylor," is the basis for the supposition that Renfro enrolled in 1851.

15. Ibid. It is of interest that Jefferson never emigrated to Texas with the rest of his family, although some of his children moved from Georgia to Texas. Jefferson remained in Walker County the rest of his life. Although little is known about Jefferson and his wife Lucinda, it was reported that they celebrated their sixty-sixth wedding anniversary. See Sartain, *History of Walker County*, 315. Sartain also lists J. T. Renfro as one of the "original settlers" of Walker County. See Sartain, 46.

16. Murray, *Baylor at Independence*, 97–98; Burleson, comp., *The Life and Writings of Dr. Rufus C. Burleson*. The date of Graves's resignation varies in different accounts, probably because the date that the resignation was offered and the date that it went into effect are not the same. Murray notes the date of the offer as June 14 and the acceptance as June 16. See Murray, *Baylor at Independence*, 112. These dates are confirmed in Eugene W. Baker, *Nothing Better than This: The Biography of James Huckins, First Baptist Missionary to Texas*, 84–85.

17. Burleson, comp., *The Life and Writings of Dr. Rufus C. Burleson*, 53–112; Murray, *Baylor at Independence*, 100–102. William M. Tryon was the pastor of the First Baptist Church in Houston and also one of the founders of Baylor University. Rufus Burleson noted that the establishment of the school was "chiefly by the instrumentality of the devoted and lamented Wm. M. Tryon." An excellent biography of Tryon is Eugene W. Baker, *A Noble Example: A Pen Picture of William M. Tryon, Pioneer Texas Baptist Preacher, Co-Founder of Baylor University*.

18. For additional information about Abner Lipscomb, see Walter Prescott Webb, ed., *The Handbook of Texas*, 2: 61–62. It should be noted that Burleson visited the Baylor campus one year earlier when he served as Abner Lipscomb's proxy at the Board of Trustees meeting on June 13, 1850. See Murray, *Baylor at Independence*, 95; Burleson, comp., *The Life and Writings of Dr. Rufus C. Burleson*, 112; information about the candlelight meeting is found in Murray, *Baylor at Independence*, 98–99.

19. Burleson, comp., *The Life and Writings of Dr. Rufus C. Burleson*, 116; Murray, *Baylor at Independence*, 107–108.

20. Murray, *Baylor at Independence*, 99–109.

21. Burleson, comp., *The Life and Writings of Dr. Rufus C. Burleson*, 117.

22. Ibid., 122.

23. Murray, *Baylor at Independence*, 110. George Washington Baines was the grandfather of Lyndon Baines Johnson, the thirty-sixth president of the

United States, who served from 1963 until 1969. By 1856, Burleson was pressing for more funds for the theological department, stating in a letter to his brother that he was anxious to "see if we cannot raise some funds in the older states for our new hall for young preachers." See Rufus C. Burleson, Independence, Texas, to Dearest Richard [Richard Burleson], October 1, 1856, Burleson Papers, Texas Collection.

24. Murray, *Baylor at Independence*, 137, 393. Baylor had 250 students in the male and female departments in February of 1854, "among whom will be 7 or 8 young ministers." See Rufus C. Burleson, Independence, Texas, to Dear Brother [Richard Burleson], February 6, 1854, Burleson Papers, Texas Collection.

25. Hosea Garrett, "Revival at Chappell Hill," *Texas Baptist*, September 5, 1855, 3. The Providence Church near Chappell Hill, Washington County, had long been an important Baptist congregation. It was established in May 1842 by William M. Tryon, R. E. B. Baylor, Hosea Garrett, and Elias Rogers. See Providence Baptist Church, Minutes, May 7, 1842, archives of Southwestern Baptist Theological Seminary, Fort Worth, Texas; Baker, *A Noble Example*, 25. The Union Association held its Fourth Annual Meeting at Providence Church in October 1843, and several bedrock articles of the Baptist Church in Texas were accepted at that time. See Baker, *Nothing Better than This*, 43–44.

26. Absalom C. Renfro was always active in the affairs of the Baptist Church, even in Georgia. In Cass County, Texas, A. C. Renfro was shown as clerk of the Baptist Church of Christ. See "A Deceiver," *Texas Baptist*, May 30, 1855, 3. Absalom was elected as the chairman of a new regional Baptist association formed in August 1856 at Pleasant Hill Church in Upshur County. See "The Proposed New Association," *Texas Baptist*, September 20, 1856, 2. Henry Renfro and his sister, Margaret Harris, were without doubt each other's "favorite" of the Renfro children. They corresponded and kept up with each other all of their lives.

27. Absalom Renfro's grandfather Isaac Renfro also had been a Baptist minister. See Donald O. Manshardt, Peoria, Illinois, to Thelma Clark Griggs, March 22, 1971, Renfro-Clark Papers. Although absolute documentation of the date the Rays moved to Johnson County has not been found, it is known that they moved there from Concordia, Tennessee, about 1853; for an obituary of Amanda Harris, written by her father and mother, see Benjamin Harris and Margaret R. Harris, Letter to the Editor of *The Texas Baptist*, August 26, 1856, 4. There is a loose connection between Margaret Harris and Elisha and Susan Ray. Margaret's brother, Isaac, was married to Elizabeth A. (Bockmon) Renfro, who was a cousin of Mary Ray. See Elizabeth A. Renfro, Cass County, Texas, to "Dear Cousin Mary" [Mary Robinson Ray, Elisha Ray's sister], Concordia, Tennessee, June 12, 1853, Renfro-Clark Papers.

28. Jolene Rutledge, "Bethesda Awaiting Historical Marker," *Burleson News*, August 6, 1987, B2; Henry C. Renfro, Letter to the Editor of *The Texas Baptist*, September 2, 1856, 2. William Robinson also participated in the organization of the West Fork Association in 1855. Some accounts recognize Robinson as the first pastor of the Bethesda Church, although it appears he continued to be a circuit preacher and to make his home in Erath County. The author has concluded that the first *bona fide* minister of the Bethesda Church who was also a resident of the community was John C. Hunton. See Edward D. and Patricia J. Morelock, "A Brief History of Bethesda Community: Cemetery, Church, School," historical narrative submitted to the Texas Historical Commission as part of a historical marker application, 1987.

29. Renfro, Letter to the Editor of *The Texas Baptist*, September 2, 1856.

30. Ibid.

31. See grave marker of Benjamin Harris, Bethesda Cemetery, Johnson County, Texas.

32. Rutledge, "Bethesda Awaiting Historical Marker." By this time, Absalom and Levicy Renfro were beginning to consider seriously a permanent move to Johnson County and had no set plans to return to the Cass County farm. Consequently, it was left to Henry to do what work he could until a final decision was made.

33. Henry did not cease his infatuation with Miss Gerl until shortly before he finally married in 1859. See Henry C. Renfro, [Johnson County], Texas, to Mary Robinson Ray, "At Home" [Johnson County], August 4, 1859, Renfro-Clark Papers.

34. Henry C. Renfro, "A Mistake," *Texas Baptist*, October 11, 1856, 3. The expression "Tell it not in Gath" was common in nineteenth century religious writing. Gath was one of five cities of the Philistines. The expression is derived from 2 Samuel 1:20 and was a part of "the lament of the bow," which David ordered that the men of Judah be taught.

> Your glory, O Israel, lies slain on your
>   heights,
> How the mighty have fallen!
>
> Tell it not in Gath,
> proclaim it not in the streets of
>   Ashkelon,
> lest the daughters of the Philistines be
>   glad,
> lest the daughters of the
>   uncircumcised rejoice.

35. Henry C. Renfro, Huntsville, Texas, to Margaret R. Harris, [Johnson County, Texas], November 2, 1857, Renfro-Clark Papers. Within a year of his arrival in Johnson County, Absalom Renfro was the clerk of the Bethesda Baptist Church and an active participant in the affairs of the West Fork Association. In the September 1858 meeting of the Association, Absalom was named to the committees on temperance, general meetings, and publications. He pledged $1 "to the benefit of the Baptist State Convention." See "Minutes of the West Fork Association, Held with Lonesome Dove Baptist Church, Tarrant County, in September, 1858," *Texas Baptist*, November 11, 1858, 1. Absalom Renfro purchased a Johnson County farm from William R. Crockett on September 10, 1857, so the evidence is strong that by that date he definitely did not plan to return to Cass County. See State of Texas, Johnson County, Bill of Sale of 160 acres from William R. Crockett to Absalom C. Renfro, September 10, 1857, File 4175, General Land Office of the State of Texas.

36. Henry C. Renfro, Huntsville, Texas, to Margaret R. Harris, [Johnson County, Texas], November 2, 1857, Renfro-Clark Papers. For information on John C. Hunton, see *Minutes of the Texas Baptist State Convention, Held with the Independence Church, Washington County, Texas, in October, 1858*. In this publication, Hunton was characterized as a missionary who "Labored 45 weeks, supplied 3 churches, 4 other stations, delivered 107 sermons, 51 addresses, [and] attended 17 prayer meetings." James Henry Harris, Lucinda Harris, and Ellen Caroline Harris were Margaret's three remaining children after the death of daughter Amanda. The "young Henry C. Renfro" to whom Henry Renfro made reference was the son of his brother, James, and James's wife Elizabeth. The younger Henry was born June 25, 1857, and died on September 11, 1909. See inscription, grave of Henry C. Renfro, Bethesda Cemetery, Johnson County, Texas.

37. Henry C. Renfro to Margaret R. Harris, November 2, 1857, Renfro-Clark Papers; Murray, *Baylor at Independence*, 125–129. Murray devotes considerable space to Houston's activities in Independence when he lived there before making his home in Huntsville. Although there is no evidence one way or another, it is presumed that Henry Renfro had renewed the old Houston-Renfro friendship while both were in Washington County. This would explain his mild enthusiasm about staying with Houston in Huntsville during the convention.

38. The controversy was evident as early as 1855 when the minutes of the Baptist State Convention expressed the hope that Clark would soon "be released from serving tables," with the clear indication that the reference was to the so-called subservience of Clark to Burleson. See Murray, *Baylor at Independence*, 135. Also, see Murray, 152–154; Burleson, comp., *The Life and Writings of Dr. Rufus C. Burleson*, 213–221; Samuel B. Hesler, *A History of*

Independence Baptist Church: 1839–1969 and Related Organizations, second print-ing, 59–69. This struggle for power was not just between Clark and Burleson; it was an internal struggle among the members of the Independence Baptist Church, and it almost caused the destruction of Baylor University.

39. Hesler, *A History of Independence Baptist Church,* 59–69.

40. Thelma Clark Griggs, Lubbock, Texas, great-granddaughter of Henry C. Renfro, interview with author, December 24, 1987, tape recording in possession of author; R. C. B. [Rufus C. Burleson], "Rev. H. C. Renfro," *Guardian* 2, no. 3 (March 1885): 50.

41. Hosea Garrett, "Ordination," *Texas Baptist,* December 11, 1857, 3; D. R. Wallace, Letter to the Editor of *The Texas Baptist,* December 9, 1857, 3.

42. Wallace, Letter to the Editor of *The Texas Baptist,* December 9, 1857.

43. Ibid.

44. Ibid.

45. This notebook, now in possession of author, has the following in-scription written in it: H. C. Renfro. Presented by Sister Burleson, wife of Rev. R. C. Burleson, President of Baylor University—Dec. 14, 1857—Independence, Texas; "Pastor Renfro," in Hesler, *A History of Independence Baptist Church,* 42–44.

46. Minutes of the meeting of the Board of Trustees of Baylor University, December 17, 1857, as quoted in Murray, *Baylor at Independence,* 152.

47. The Minute Book of the Independence Baptist Church makes no note of the controversy and says simply that "Bro. H. C. Renfro was elected Pastor Dec 19th 1857, Resigned February 20, 1858." Ironically, the paragraph ends with the notation that "Brother Horace Clark was ordained to the work of the Ministry April 18, 1858." See Minute Book, Independence Baptist Church, Archives of the Independence Baptist Church, Independence, Texas.

48. Murray, *Baylor at Independence,* 175–186.

49. Ibid., 184–187.

50. Ibid., 185–187.

51. Ibid.

52. Ibid., 188–189. The Task Clay referred to by Burleson was Tacitus Thomas Clay, a plantation owner who lived in a home named "Clay Castle" one and one-half miles east of Independence, Texas, in Washington County. When Independence was incorporated in 1859, Clay was elected mayor. See Webb, ed., *The Handbook of Texas,* 1: 359; Toland, *Austin Knew His Athens,* 4.

53. Murray, *Baylor at Independence,* 189; Rufus C. Burleson, Waco Univer-sity, Texas, to William Carey Crane, [Independence, Texas], April 23, 1869, Barker Archives, Center for American History, University of Texas, Aus-tin, Texas.

54. Vincent L. Milner, *Religious Denominations of the World; Comprising a General View of the Origin, History, and Condition of the Various Sects of Christians,*

the Jews, and Mahometans, as Well as the Pagan Forms of Religion Existing in the *Different Countries of the Earth; With Sketches of the Founders of Various Religious Sects*, 45. David Edwin Harrell, Jr., "The Evolution of Plain-Folk Religion in the South," in Samuel S. Hill, ed., *Varieties of Southern Religious Experience*, 29. The anti-mission movement was largely expressed by the Primitive Baptist Association, a group that espoused Calvinist predestination which, according to historian Harrell, endorsed "loyalty to the beliefs of their fathers, . . . [and] opposition to education and soft-headed modern ideas."

55. Donald G. Mathews, *Religion in the Old South*, 18.

56. Howard Miller, "Texas," in Samuel S. Hill, *Religion in the Southern States: A Historical Study*, 329.

CHAPTER 2. THE TIME TO COME TO TEXAS

1. Ann Scott, *The Southern Lady: From Pedestal to Politics, 1830–1930*, 23.

2. The correspondence of Mary Ray is located in the Renfro-Clark papers, in possession of author.

3. Charity H. Ray, Lockhart, Texas, to Pearl Clark, Burleson, Texas, October 22, 1957, Renfro-Clark Papers. An overview of the Ray family included in this letter notes that Michael Ray, Mary Ray's father, "died Feb. 17, 1844, about 6 oclock in the evening." Anne Ray, Michael's wife, "died Sept. 18, Friday 7:00 P.M. 1835." Thelma Clark Griggs, interview with author, December 24, 1987.

4. Mary Robinson Ray to Susan Ray, May 19, [1852]. The family with whom Mary stayed in Mississippi was evidently that of her mother Ann's brother. The only clues are that the woman's name was "Aunt Mary," and her husband's name was "Uncle E," probably for Elisha. "Aunt Mary" had a brother named John Searff. See letter from "Cousin Fee," [Mississippi], to Elisha Boykin Ray, Johnson County, Texas, March 22, [1853], Renfro-Clark Papers. It is of interest that Mary said that Chellie did "not like to write," as the two carried on a regular correspondence for the next forty years.

5. William George Ray, Concordia, Tennessee, to "Bro. & Sue" [Elisha B. Ray and Susan Ray], Johnson County, Texas, February 6, 1854, Renfro-Clark Papers. Elisha Boykin Ray was one of the original 107 petitioners for the incorporation of Johnson County in 1854. See *A Memorial and Biographical History of Johnson and Hill Counties, Texas*, 78, 79. Research has not revealed the exact relationship of "Cousin David" to Elisha Ray. It is assumed, however, that he was the son of one of Susan's brothers or sisters.

6. William George Ray to "Bro. & Sue," February 6, 1854, Renfro-Clark Papers. The person George Ray calls "Jes" was probably Jess Cothran, a good friend and neighbor in Concordia.

7. *Abstract of Land Titles in Texas*, 1: 197; Elizabeth A. Renfro, Cass County, Texas, to Mary Robinson Ray, Concordia, Tennessee, June 12, 1853, Renfro-Clark Papers; Scott, *The Southern Lady*, 25, provides insight into early marriages.

8. Elizabeth A. Renfro to Mary Robinson Ray, June 12, 1853, Renfro-Clark Papers.

9. Mary Robinson Ray, [Mississippi], to Susan Ray, Johnson County, Texas, May 19th, [1853], Renfro-Clark Papers. A comparison with similar thoughts from the diary of one Sarah Morgan is of real interest and provides further insight into the thoughts of the well-bred lady of the period. See Scott, *The Southern Lady*, 23.

10. Mary Robinson Ray to Susan Ray, May 19th, [1853], Renfro-Clark Papers. The man whom Mary was seeing but did not want to marry was probably Churchill Wright, M.D., also of Tipton County. Dr. Wright attended Jefferson Medical College in Philadelphia, so he could certainly be the one Mary said was "well calculated to make me happy." Churchill Wright wrote to Mary in March 1852 asking for the "privilege of courting her." If not granted, Wright said that he felt that he would "be very unhappy in this life." See J. C. [James Churchill] Wright, Tipton County, Tennessee, to "Miss Mary" [Mary R. Ray], March 29, 1852, Renfro-Clark Papers.

11. Chellie Ann Coody, Covington, Tennessee, to "Brother & Sister" [Elisha B. Ray and Susan Ray], Johnson County, Texas, August 5, 1854, Renfro-Clark Papers; Elisha B. Ray, Johnson County, Texas, to Mary Robinson Ray, [Concordia, Tennessee], August 20, 1854, Renfro-Clark Papers. It is of interest that in 1850, the census counted a population in Texas of 212,000, of which 58,000 were slaves. See William Ransom Hogan, *The Texas Republic: A Social and Economic History*, 10.

12. Elisha B. Ray to Mary Robinson Ray, August 20, 1854, Renfro-Clark Papers. "Ana Bet" was Anna Elizabeth Ray, who was born on January 13, 1853. "Bucy" must be a nickname for Thatcher, the second of Elisha and Susan Ray's daughters.

13. Ibid.

14. Sarah A. Jackson, Concordia, Tennessee, to Mary Robinson Ray, Johnson County, Texas, March 27, 1855, Renfro-Clark Papers. Sarah Jackson was the daughter of Susan (Ray) Jackson, Mary Ray's sister.

15. Ibid.; Chellie Ann Coody, Covington, Tennessee, to Mary Robinson Ray, Johnson County, Texas, April 18, 1855, Renfro-Clark Papers; Chellie Ann Coody, [Covington, Tennessee], to Mary Robinson Ray, Johnson County, Texas, September 2, 1855, Renfro-Clark Papers; Sarah A. Jackson to Mary Robinson Ray, March 27, 1855, Renfro-Clark Papers. The "Aunt Mat" mentioned by Chellie Ann Coody is no doubt Martha Ann Ray, Mary Ray and Sarah Jackson's aunt and the sister of Mary's father, Michael. See Charity H.

Ray to Pearl Clark, October 22, 1957, Renfro-Clark Papers. This letter contains a brief genealogy of the Ray family which evidently was compiled by Lamkin Ray, a grandson of William George Ray.

16. Chellie Ann Coody to Mary Robinson Ray, September 2, 1855, Renfro-Clark Papers. The identity of "John M" has not been determined.

17. Mary Robinson Ray, Cross Timbers, Johnson County, Texas, to Chellie Ann Coody, [Searcy, Arkansas], April 30, 1856, Renfro-Clark Papers.

18. Ibid. No further identification of "Mr. Upten" has been made.

19. Henry C. Renfro, Letter to the Editor of *The Texas Baptist*, September 2, 1856, 2; Mary Robinson Ray to Chellie Ann Coody, April 30, 1856, Renfro-Clark Papers. The camp meeting is generally conceded to be an outgrowth of an outdoor revival held at Gaspar River, Kentucky, and a later gathering known by scholars as the "Great Revival" held in the summer of 1801 at Cane Ridge, Logan County, Kentucky. See Mathews, *Religion in the Old South*, 49–52; John B. Boles, "Evangelical Protestantism in the South," in Charles Wilson Reagan, ed., *Religion in the South*, 14.

20. Mary Robinson Ray, to Chellie Ann Coody, April 30, 1856, Renfro-Clark Papers. Chellie Ann Coody's real name was Charity Ann, but she was almost always called "Chellie" or "Chep" by her family. She will be referred to as Chellie in much of the text of this book. Bettie Ray was the wife of William George Ray, Mary Ray's brother.

21. Scott, *The Southern Lady*, 25, 26.

22. Jessie Douglas was listed as one of 107 voters who signed a petition for the formation of Johnson County in 1854. See *A Memorial and Biographical History of Johnson and Hill Counties*, 78–79. Douglas received a grant of 320 acres of land prior to 1857. Located south of the property of Elisha B. Ray, Mary's brother, it was patented on July 23, 1857, by one John Armstrong. See *Abstract of Land Titles in Texas*, 1: 803.

23. R. M. Tandy [one of the owners of the Tandy and Gilmore store], ledger page of the account of "Miss Mary A. [R.] Ray," August 28, 1856, Renfro-Clark Papers. For information on Tandy, see Viola Block, *History of Johnson County and Surrounding Areas*, 36.

24. Henry C. Renfro, Johnson County, Texas, to Mary Robinson Ray, Johnson County, Texas, August 4, 1859, Renfro-Clark Papers.

25. Gárrett, "Ordination," *Texas Baptist*, December 11, 1857, 3.

26. Henry C. Renfro, Hickory Hill, Cass County, Texas, to Margaret R. Harris, Johnson County, Texas, April 24, 1858, Renfro-Clark Papers.

27. Chellie Ann Coody, Covington, Tennessee, to Mary Robinson Ray, Johnson County, April 18, 1855, Renfro-Clark Papers; Sarah A. Jackson, Concordia, Tennessee, to Mary Robinson Ray, Johnson County, Texas, December 24, 1855, Renfro-Clark Papers; Chellie Ann Coody, Sharran, [Tennessee], to Mary Robinson Ray, Johnson County, Texas, June 15, 1857,

Renfro-Clark Papers. No record has been found as to whether or not Mary Ray sold any of her slaves. However, correspondence between Mary and Henry Renfro during the Civil War has reference only to Sofe [Sopha].

28. Henry C. Renfro, to Mary Robinson Ray, August 4, 1859, Renfro-Clark Papers; Mary Robinson Ray, Johnson County, Texas, to "Sister and Brother [Chellie Ann Coody and W. R. Coody], [Searcy, Arkansas], June 19, 1859, Renfro-Clark Papers. Bettie Ray married a Mr. Thompson after her return to Tennessee, but it was not long before she, too, passed away. Elisha Ray then went to Tennessee and brought the children back to Texas.

29. Henry C. Renfro to Margaret R. Harris, April 24, 1858, Renfro-Clark Papers. Evidently the fact that Henry's father already had purchased a tract of land in Johnson County was not sufficient evidence that Absalom planned to stay. See State of Texas, Johnson County, Bill of Sale of 160 acres from William R. Crockett to Absalom C. Renfro, September 10, 1857, File 4175, General Land Office of the State of Texas.

30. Henry C. Renfro, [Johnson County, Texas], to "My Dear M——" [Mary Robinson Ray], [Johnson County, Texas], n.d., Renfro-Clark Papers.

31. Henry C. Renfro to Mary Robinson Ray, August 4, 1859, Renfro-Clark Papers.

32. Ibid. The evident love between Henry and Mary contrasts with a statement by Rebecca Latimer Felton, *Country Life in Georgia in the Days of My Youth*, 62–63, in which she declared that "If there was a prospect of plantation or slaves as a dowry there was a rush into matrimony." See Scott, *A Southern Lady*, 26.

33. Mary Robinson Ray, [Johnson County, Texas], to Chellie Ann Coody, [Searcy, Arkansas], June 19, 1859, Renfro-Clark Papers.

34. Chellie Ann Coody, Searcy, Arkansas, to Mary Robinson Ray, [Johnson County, Texas], September 1, 1859, Renfro-Clark Papers.

35. Henry C. Renfro to Mary Robinson Ray, August 4, 1859, Renfro-Clark Papers.

36. Ibid.

37. Henry C. Renfro to Miss Mollie, n.d., Renfro-Clark Papers.

38. Mary Robinson Ray, [Johnson County, Texas], to Henry C. Renfro, [Johnson County, Texas], August 10, 1859, Renfro-Clark Papers.

39. Ibid.

40. Henry C. Renfro to "Miss Mollie" [Mary R. Ray], "At Home," n.d., Renfro-Clark Papers.

41. State of Texas, General Land Office, Map of Johnson County, Texas, 1943; State of Texas, Johnson County, Affidavit of Settlement of H. C. Renfro, March 15, 1860, in File 586, General Land Office of the State of Texas; State of Texas, Johnson County, Field Notes of W. Douglass, C. S., of H. C. Renfro Preemption, 160 acres, Robertson Scrip, Survey Number 1063, June 25, 1860,

in File 586, General Land Office of the State of Texas; State of Texas, Johnson County, Certificate of Occupancy of H. C. Renfro, March 16, 1860, in File 586, General Land Office of the State of Texas.

42. *Abstract of Land Titles in Texas*, 1: 810; also, see Map of Johnson County, Texas.

43. *Minutes of the Thirteenth Annual Session of the Baptist State Convention of Texas Held with Independence Church, Washington County, Commencing Oct. 27th, and Closing Nov. 1st, 1860.* The above minutes, along with others originally printed separately, are bound together in the *Texas Baptist Annual: 1854–1872,* in the Texas Collection at Baylor University. Colportage is defined, in this context, as evangelism or spreading the word of the church by preaching or by distribution of literature.

44. It is of interest that one record shows the marriage of Henry Renfro and Mary Ray much earlier, on May 24, 1859. This date is not credible, however, as keeping a marriage secret on the Texas frontier would have been virtually impossible. See Weldon I. Hudson, comp., *Johnson County, Texas, Marriage Records: 1854–1883*, 5.

45. State of Texas, Johnson County, Field Notes of W. Douglass, C. S., of H. C. Renfro Preemption, 160 acres, Robertson Scrip, Survey Number 1063, June 25, 1860, in File 586, General Land Office of the State of Texas.

CHAPTER 3. THE MOURNFUL PEALS OF THE MUFFLED DRUM

1. One of the best studies of the Missouri Compromise is Glover Moore, *The Missouri Controversy: 1819–1821.*

2. Holman Hamilton, *Prologue to Conflict: The Crisis and Compromise of 1850.*

3. Eric Foner, *Free Soil, Free Labor, Free Men: The Ideology of the Republican Party before the Civil War*, 125–126.

4. James A. Rawley, *Race and Politics: "Bleeding Kansas" and the Coming of the Civil War*, 81–94.

5. Ibid., 125–134.

6. Ibid., 187–193; Don Fehrenbacher, *The Dred Scott Case, Its Significance in American Law and Politics;* Benjamin C. Howard, *Report on the Decision of the Supreme Court of the United States, and the Opinions of the Judges Thereof, in the Case of Dred Scott versus John. F. A. Sandford, December Term, 1856.*

7. In the referendum on secession which was presented to free Texans on January 23, 1861, 76 percent of the voters favored secession. See Ernest W. Winkler, ed., *Journal of the Secession Convention of Texas: 1861*, 252–261; Theodore Clark Smith, *Parties and Slavery, The American Nation, A History,* vol. 18, 302.

8. Noble L. Clark [great-grandson of Henry Renfro] and Ruby Richeson Clark, interview with author, August 11, 1975.

9. Ibid.

10. Winkler, ed., *Journal of the Secession Convention of Texas: 1861*, 252–261.

11. Excellent first-person accounts of the first Battle of Manassas, or Bull Run, from both Union and Confederate perspectives are found in Robert Underwood Johnson and Clarence Clough Buel, eds., *Battles and Leaders of the Civil War*, 1: 167–261.

12. Henry C. Renfro, Unnamed Poem, n.d., Renfro-Clark Papers.

13. United States, National Archives, Records of Company Muster Roll, Company C, Griffin's Regiment Texas Infantry, copy in possession of author; the date Renfro left home is noted in H. C. Renfro, [Galveston], to [Mary R. Renfro], July 5, 1862, Renfro-Clark Papers; for the information about Isaac Renfro being in the same military unit as Henry, see Henry C. Renfro, Galveston, to "My Dear Wife" [Mary R. Renfro], [Johnson County], March 2, 1863, Renfro-Clark Papers; the information on Summerfield's unit is in Henry C. Renfro, Galveston, to "Dear Mother and Father" [Absalom and Levicy Renfro], [Johnson County, Texas], February 1, 1863, Renfro-Clark Papers; "Isaac A. Jackson," in Joshua Historical Committee, *Joshua: As It Was and Is: 1853–1976*, 108. Jackson was the husband of Fannie Evaline Renfro Jackson, Henry Renfro's sister; Colonel William Henry Griffin, a West Point graduate of the class of 1835, was the commander of Griffin's Regiment Texas Infantry. See Marcus J. Wright, comp., and Harold B. Simpson, ed., *Texas in the War: 1861–1865*, 98. Colonel Allison Nelson of Bosque County, Texas, organized the 10th Texas Volunteer Infantry Regiment in the summer of 1861. See Wright and Simpson, 89.

14. Joseph W. Speight was the president of the Board of Trustees of Waco Classical School and a close friend of Rufus C. Burleson. On February 4, 1861, he wrote to Burleson on behalf of the Board of Trustees that he had been "unanimously elected President of the Faculty of said institution," along with associates Richard Burleson (Rufus's brother), O. H. Leland, G. W. Willrich, and Dr. D. R. Wallace. In early 1862, Speight organized the 1st Texas Infantry Battalion, composed primarily of men from McLennan County. The name of the regiment was changed, probably in April, to the Fifteenth Texas Infantry. Burleson's enlistment as chaplain came on April 16. Former Baylor faculty member Dr. David R. Wallace joined the unit as surgeon of the Fifteenth Texas in February 1862, two months before Burleson joined the regiment. See Murray, *Baylor at Independence*, 209; Doris Dowdell Moore, *The Biography of Doctor D. R. Wallace*, 20–21; Wright, comp., and Simpson, ed., *Texas in the War: 1861–1865*, 107; Alwyn Barr, *Polignac's Texas Brigade*, 11. Burleson, comp., *The Life and Writings of Dr. Rufus C. Burleson*, 421; H. C. Renfro, [Houston, Texas], to [Mary R. Renfro], July 5, 1862, Renfro-Clark Papers.

15. Colonel J. W. Speight, Camp Speight, Texas, to Major W. H. Griffin, [Houston], May 23, 1862, Confederate States of America, Records, Griffin's Texas Volunteer Infantry, National Archives of the United States, copy in possession of author.

16. Ibid.; an alternate name of the camp near Millican, Brazos County, Texas, was Camp Crocket. See Barr, *Polignac's Texas Brigade*, 12. Rufus C. Burleson joined Speight's Regiment on April 18, 1862, although his official commission as the chaplain of the 15th Texas was written on January 10, 1863. See James A. Sedder, Secretary of War of the Confederate States of America, Richmond, Virginia, Commission as Chaplain in the 15th Texas, to Rev. R. C. Burleson, January 10, 1863, in Burleson, comp., *The Life and Writings of Dr. Rufus C. Burleson*, 427.

17. W. H. Griffin, Major, Commanding Regiment, Griffin's Texas Volunteer Infantry, Confederate States of America, Houston, Texas, General Order, May 23, 1862, Records of Griffin's Texas Volunteer Infantry, National Archives, copy in possession of author.

18. Colonel J. W. Speight to Major W. H. Griffin, May 23, 1862, Confederate States of America, Records, Griffin's Texas Volunteer Infantry.

19. William H. Griffin, Major, Texas Volunteer Infantry, Griffin's Regiment, [Houston, Texas], to Captain George R. Nelson, A. D. C. & A. A. A. G., Department of Texas, May 24, 1862, in Confederate States of America, Records, Griffin's Texas Volunteer Infantry, National Archives of the United States, copy in possession of the author. Although Henry Renfro was forced to return to Houston, it appears that no charges were placed against him. Renfro himself does not mention any, and the National Archives records relating to Renfro in Griffin's Texas Volunteer Infantry reveal none. It is likely that the provisions for his return to Griffin's regiment called for no retribution.

20. [Mary R. Renfro], [Johnson County, Texas], to "My Dearest Henry" [Henry C. Renfro], [Houston, Texas], June 18, 1862, Renfro-Clark Papers.

21. Ibid.

22. Ibid.

23. M. R. Harris, [Johnson County, Texas], to "My Dear Brother Henry" [Henry C. Renfro], Houston, Texas, June 24, 1862, Renfro-Clark Papers.

24. Ibid.

25. Ibid.

26. Ibid.; H. C. Renfro, [Galveston], to [Mary R. Renfro], July 5, 1862, Renfro-Clark Papers.

27. H. C. Renfro, Dallas, Texas, to "My Dear Mollie" [Mary R. Renfro], [Johnson County, Texas], November 11, 1862, Renfro-Clark Papers. It is interesting that despite Burleson's letter to Renfro stating that he (Burleson)

would soon resign the chaplaincy of Speight's Regiment, it was nearly one year before he actually did so. See Burleson, comp., *The Life and Writings of Dr. Rufus C. Burleson*, 427.

28. H. C. Renfro to "My Dear Mollie," November 11, 1862, Renfro-Clark Papers.

29. H. C. Renfro, Houston, Texas, to "My dear Mollie" [Mary R. Renfro], [Johnson County, Texas], December 25, 1862, Renfro-Clark Papers.

30. H. C. Renfro, Eagle Grove, Texas, to "My dear Mollie" [Mary R. Renfro], [Johnson County, Texas], December 31, 1862, Renfro-Clark Papers.

31. Alwyn Barr, "Texas Coastal Defense, 1861–1865," *Southwestern Historical Quarterly* 65 (July 1961): 14–18. For another eyewitness account of the battle by a Texan who likely was also aboard the *Neptune*, see Jonnie Lockhart Wallis, *Sixty Years on the Brazos: The Life and Letters of Dr. John Washington Lockhart, 1824–1900*, reprint, 72–76.

32. Barr, "Texas Coastal Defense," 18; H. C. R. [Henry C. Renfro], [Galveston], to "Dear Mollie" [Mary R. Renfro], December 31, 1862, postscript written from Eagle Grove, [January 1, 1863], Renfro-Clark Papers.

33. Henry C. Renfro, Galveston, to Mary R. Renfro and little James B. Renfro, [Johnson County, Texas], January 13, 1863, Renfro-Clark Papers.

34. Ibid.

35. Ibid.

36. Henry C. Renfro, Galveston, to My Dear Mollie, [Johnson County, Texas], March 10, 1863, Renfro-Clark Papers.

37. Ibid.

38. Ibid.

39. Henry C. Renfro, Dallas, to "My dear Mollie" [Mary R. Renfro], [Johnson County, Texas], November 11, 1862; Henry C. Renfro, Galveston, to "My dear Wife" [Mary R. Renfro], March 2, 1863, Renfro-Clark Papers. Hezekiah Russell deeded his 160 acres of land to H. C. Renfro on April 19, 1873, for four dollars an acre. See Hezekiah Russell, Deed to Henry C. Renfro, April 19, 1873, in possession of the author. The Russell place bordered Renfro's land on the northeast. No reason is found for Mary's negotiation with "Brother New" on the property, as Russell was obviously still alive and able to deed the property over ten years later.

40. Henry C. Renfro, to "My dear Mollie," November 11, 1862, Renfro-Clark Papers.

41. Ibid.; Henry C. Renfro to Mary R. Renfro and James Burleson Renfro, January 13, 1863, Renfro-Clark Papers.

42. H. C. Renfro, Galveston, to "My dear Mollie" [Mary R. Renfro], [Johnson County, Texas], January 26, 1863, Renfro-Clark Papers.

43. Ibid.

44. Henry C. Renfro, Galveston, to "Dear Mother and Father" [Absalom and Levicy Renfro], [Johnson County, Texas], February 1, 1863, Renfro-Clark Papers.

45. Ibid.

46. Ibid.

47. Ibid. The Battle of Arkansas Post, or Fort Hindman, occurred on January 11, 1863. At that time, Colonel Roger Q. Mills had succeeded Allison Nelson as regimental commander. Nelson died on October 7, 1862. The Union commander, Major General John A. McClernand, reported that 4,791 prisoners were taken in the battle. See Thomas L. Snead, "The Conquest of Arkansas," in Johnson and Buel, eds., *Battles and Leaders of the Civil War*, 3: 441–461, for an in-depth report of the Confederate losses. The place where the Arkansas Post prisoners were interred was Camp Chase, Ohio; Henry C. Renfro, [Galveston, Texas], to [Mary R. Renfro], [February 5, 1863], Renfro-Clark Papers.

48. Henry C. Renfro to [Mary R. Renfro], [February 5, 1863], Renfro-Clark Papers.

49. Ibid. The person referred to as "Chep" was Chellie Ann Coody, Mary Ray Renfro's cousin, who moved to Johnson County, Texas, from Arkansas during the war. The reference to James and Elisha going to camps referred to their impending enlistment in the Confederate Army.

50. Ibid.

51. H. C. Renfro, Galveston, Texas, to "My dear Wife" [Mary R. Renfro], [Johnson County, Texas], February 12, 1863, Renfro-Clark Papers.

52. H. C. Renfro, Galveston, to "My dear Wife and Burlie Boy" [Mary R. Renfro and James Burleson Renfro], [Johnson County, Texas], February 15, 1863, Renfro-Clark Papers; H. C. Renfro, [Galveston, Texas], to [Mary R. Renfro], [Johnson County, Texas], February 20, 1863, Renfro-Clark Papers.

53. Henry C. Renfro, Galveston, to Captain E. P. Turner, Adjutant General for Colonel George Wythe Baylor, Arizona Brigade, March 1, 1863, copy in possession of author. George Wythe Baylor was said to be the brother of R. E. B. Baylor, the person for whom Baylor University was named. See Murray, *Baylor at Independence*, 16. However, other references are unclear. Joe W. Hale, "Robert Emmett Bledsoe Baylor," in Webb, ed., *The Handbook of Texas*, 1: 124, notes that R. E. B. Baylor was born in Kentucky in 1793, while John L. Waller, "George Wythe Baylor," in Webb, ed., *The Handbook of Texas*, 1: 123–124, notes that George Wythe Baylor was born at Fort Gibson, Indian Territory, in 1832. Both men, however, had relatives in Fayette County, Texas, and both lived there in the 1840's.

54. H. C. Renfro, Galveston, Texas, to "My Dear Mollie" [Mary R. Renfro], [Johnson County, Texas], March 12, 1863, Renfro-Clark Papers. In this letter, Renfro notes that the effort to become a chaplain in Baylor's Regiment was

aided by a gratuitous effort by one W. J. Joyce of Pyron's Regiment. There is no indication as to how Joyce could help except for the remote fact that Pyron's Regiment was formerly commanded by John Robert Baylor, a brother of George Wythe Baylor. Joyce could have known John R. Baylor and through him tried to exert influence in favor of Renfro. See letter. Although rumors placed Speight's Brigade in Vicksburg, they were at that time at Camp Kiamichi, Indian Territory, north of Clarksville, Texas. In December 1862, Speight's Brigade had received orders to march to Vicksburg, a city that was assumed to be an objective of Federal forces marching from Tennessee. The order was countermanded, however, and Speight's Brigade was instead ordered to reinforce Hindman's army retreating from a lost battle at Prairie Grove, Arkansas. A good overview of the engagement may be found in Johnson and Buel, eds., *Battles and Leaders of the Civil War*, 3: 448–452. In late April, Speight's command left for Louisiana. See Barr, *Polignac's Texas Brigade*, 13, 18.

55. H. C. Renfro, Galveston, to Mary R. Renfro and James B. Renfro, [Johnson County, Texas], March 2, 1863, Renfro-Clark Papers.

56. Ibid.

57. Ibid.

58. Henry C. Renfro, Galveston, Texas, to "My Dear Mollie" [Mary R. Renfro], [Johnson County, Texas], March 10, 1863, Renfro-Clark Papers.

59. Ibid.

60. Absalom C. Renfro, [Johnson County, Texas], notes written in the Renfro family Bible. The page of that Bible which contains Absalom's notes is in the Renfro-Clark Papers.

61. H. C. R. [Henry C. Renfro], [Galveston, Texas], Poem, June 27, 1863, Renfro-Clark Papers.

62. H. C. Renfro, to Mary R. Renfro and James B. Renfro, March 2, 1863, Renfro-Clark Papers.

63. E. F. Gray, Lieutenant Colonel Third Texas Infantry, Galveston, Texas, to Lieutenant R. M. Franklin, Acting Assistant Adjutant General, Second Brigade, Second Division, Galveston, Texas, August 4, 1863, in "Mutiny at Galveston, Texas," in United States War Department, *War of the Rebellion: A Compilation of the Official Records of the Union and Confederate Armies*, 38: 241.

64. Ibid., 242.

65. Ibid., 243. Phillip Noland Luckett was the commander of the 3rd Texas Confederate Infantry, which arrived at Galveston on July 12, 1863, from Brownsville. See Eldon Stephen Branda, ed., *The Handbook of Texas: A Supplement, Volume III*, 544. Henry M. Elmore was the commander of the 20th Texas Infantry Regiment, which participated in the Battle of Galveston. Its primary function was the performance of guard duty along the Texas coast. See Wright, comp., and Simpson, ed., *Texas in the War: 1861–1865*, 22, 164.

Joseph J. Cook commanded the 3rd Texas Artillery Battalion as it manned the big guns at Galveston in the early part of the war. Later, the battalion was transferred to the 1st Texas Artillery Regiment. See Wright and Simpson, 130. Gould's Texas Regiment was a part of the brigade commanded by Brigadier General Hamilton Bee, which also included Debray's Regiment. See Wright and Simpson, 3.

CHAPTER 4. TO HELP HIM SING DIXIE

1. Interestingly, a notation on Renfro's letter to George Wythe Baylor asking for appointment to the Arizona Brigade shows that the Parson also was appointed to that post. See Henry C. Renfro, Galveston, Texas, to Captain E. P. Turner, Adjutant General for Colonel George Wythe Baylor, Arizona Brigade, March 1, 1863. The 15th Texas Infantry Regiment was organized in 1862 with the expansion of Colonel Joseph Speight's old 1st Texas Infantry Regiment. Speight retained command of the unit, and in the summer of 1863 it was located at and around the Atchafalaya River in Louisiana. See Barr, *Polignac's Texas Brigade,* 20.

2. Sidney J. Romero, "The Confederate Chaplain," *Civil War History* 1 (1955): 127–140.

3. Ibid.

4. Rufus Burleson resigned as chaplain of the 15th Texas on August 28, 1864. See Burleson, comp., *The Life and Writings of Dr. Rufus C. Burleson,* 429. Because of the close friendship between Henry Renfro and Rufus Burleson, it was only natural that Burleson named Renfro as his successor when he decided to step down.

5. H. C. Renfro, [Galveston, Texas], to "My Dear Mollie" [Mary R. Renfro], [Johnson County, Texas], n.d., Renfro-Clark Papers. During the war, the Houston and Texas Central Railroad went only as far as Millican, Brazos County, a few miles south of present-day College Station, Texas. From Houston, the railroad went east as far as Baton Rouge, Louisiana.

6. Barr, *Polignac's Texas Brigade,* 24. Barr noted that the roster of the 15th Texas Infantry was in the Texas History Collection of Baylor University, and he listed it in his bibliography. Kent Keeth, the director of the Texas Collection, made an extensive search for the document but noted that it seemed to be missing or badly misplaced, as it was not in any of the places that it normally would have been found.

7. Barr, *Polignac's Texas Brigade,* 25–27; report of Thomas Green, October 2, 1863, *Official Records,* series 1, vol. 26, pt. 1, 329–332. A detailed account of the Battle of Stirling's Plantation or Bayou Fordoche is found in Cooper K. Ragan, ed., "The Diary of Captain George W. O'Brien,

1863," *Southwestern Historical Quarterly* 67 (October 1963): 235–246.

8. Ragan, ed., "The Diary of Captain George W. O'Brien, 1863," 235–246; cBarr, *Polignac's Texas Brigade*, 27–28.

9. Ragan, ed., "The Diary of Captain George W. O'Brien, 1863," *Southwestern Historical Quarterly* 67 (January 1964): 417; Barr, *Polignac's Texas Brigade*, 28, 29.

10. Barr, *Polignac's Texas Brigade*, 29. The "failure . . . to set an example for the men on the part of the regimental officers," could have been a veiled reference to some resentment of Colonel Speight's regular trips back to Texas because of "illness." Even after Speight had officially resigned his commission on April 15, 1864, rumors about him persisted in Texas. In a letter from the wife of 15th Texas surgeon David R. Wallace to Mrs. Rufus C. Burleson, Mrs. Wallace inquired, "Is Col. Speight still at home? There are rumors afloat here about Col. Speight's behavior on the battle field which I think would be very unpleasant to him were he to know such things were being said." See Merle Mears Duncan, ed., "An 1864 Letter to Mrs. Rufus C. Burleson," *Southwestern Historical Quarterly*, 44 (January 1961): 371.

11. Ragan, ed., "The Diary of Captain George W. O'Brien, 1863," 423.

12. Ibid.; Barr, *Polignac's Texas Brigade*, 29.

13. Barr, *Polignac's Texas Brigade*, 29; Ragan, ed., "The Diary of Captain George W. O'Brien, 1863," 423–424.

14. Barr, *Polignac's Texas Brigade*, 30.

15. Ibid., 30–31; James E. Harrison to Dear Ballinger [William Pitt Ballinger], November 9, 1863, Ballinger Collection, Barker Archives, Center for American History, University of Texas, Austin, Texas.

16. James E. Harrison to Dear Ballinger, November 9, 1863, Ballinger Collection.

17. Ibid.; Barr, *Polignac's Texas Brigade*, 32.

18. Barr, *Polignac's Texas Brigade*, 32.

19. Ibid.; Henry C. Renfro, Camp on the Road [Louisiana], to Dear Sister Margaret [Margaret R. Harris], [Johnson County, Texas], December 24, 1863, Renfro-Clark Papers.

20. Henry C. Renfro to Dear Sister Margaret [Margaret R. Harris], December 24, 1863, Renfro-Clark Papers. Walker's Division was commanded at that time by General Richard Taylor. The Confederate Army under General E. Kirby Smith had two major departments. The District of West Louisiana consisted of four divisions including Walker's and that of Brigadier General Alfred Mouton. In addition, it included another cavalry division under Major General John A. Wharton and Brigadier General Thomas Green, as well as two unattached Louisiana cavalry regiments. The second department was the detachment of Sterling Price's army under the command of Brigadier General Thomas J. Churchill. See "The Opposing Forces in the Red River Campaign"

in Johnson and Buel, eds., *Battles and Leaders of the Civil War*, 4: 368. Simmesport, Louisiana, is located near the head of the Atchafalaya River; James H. Torbett of Buchanan, Texas, was appointed by the first term of the county court to be a special commissioner to make titles for town lots. See Block, *History of Johnson County*, 6. Dan McAnear later lived in Caddo Grove, Johnson County, and was referred to as "Professor McAnear." It is not known where he taught, if that was his profession. See "Personal Mention," *Alvarado Bulletin*, January 18, 1884, 3. Renfro noted that the 15th Texas left Walker's Division at Simmesport. This referred to the 18th Texas, which joined them at Moundville on October 29 before the Battle of Bayou Bourbeau. See Barr, *Polignac's Texas Brigade*, 30.

21. Henry C. Renfro, to Dear Sister Margaret, December 24, 1863, Renfro-Clark Papers.

22. Ibid.

23. Ibid.

24. Barr, *Polignac's Texas Brigade*, 35.

25. Ibid.

26. Ibid., 36.

27. Ibid., 37.

28. Ibid., 25.

29. E. Kirby Smith, "The Defense of the Red River," in Johnson and Buel, eds., *Battles and Leaders of the Civil War*, 4: 369–374.

30. Banks's naval convoy sailed from New Orleans on October 26, 1863, accompanied by four Federal warships. By December, a Union armada had captured several Confederate outposts along the Texas coast. See Smith, "The Defense of the Red River," in Johnson and Buel, eds., *Battles and Leaders of the Civil War*, 4: 369–374; Richard B. Irwin, "The Red River Campaign," in Johnson and Buel, eds., *Battles and Leaders of the Civil War*, 4: 345–362.

31. Irwin, "The Red River Campaign," in Johnson and Buel, eds., *Battles and Leaders of the Civil War*, 4: 345–362.

32. Ibid.; Alwyn Barr, "Polignac's Brigade," in Branda, ed., *The Handbook of Texas: A Supplement*, 742–743.

33. Mary's sister-in-law, Susan Ray, died on March 9, 1864, and therefore was not one of those in attendance with Mary.

34. Barr, *Polignac's Texas Brigade*, 48.

35. Barr, "Polignac's Brigade," in Branda, ed., *The Handbook of Texas: A Supplement*, 742–743.

36. Richard E. Berlinger and others, *Why the South Lost the Civil War*, 424–426; James W. Silver, *Confederate Morale and Church Propaganda*, 61.

37. Silver, *Confederate Morale and Church Propaganda*, 25.

38. Ibid., 427

39. Ibid., 426.

CHAPTER 5. ENVY LOVES A SHINING LIGHT

1. *Minutes of the First Annual Session of the Alvarado Baptist Association, Held with Hillsboro Church, Hill County, Texas, September, 1865*, 1; *A Memorial and Biographical History of Johnson and Hill Counties, Texas*, 189; Noble Lafayette Clark and Ruby Richeson Clark, interview with author, August 11, 1975.

2. *Minutes of the Convention Which Organized the Alvarado Association, 1864*, 1; *Minutes of the First Annual Session of the Alvarado Baptist Association*, 1.

3. *Minutes of the Second Annual Meeting of the Alvarado Association, of the State of Texas, Held at Shady Grove, Johnson County, Commencing 15th September A. D. 1866*.

4. *Minutes of the Third Annual Session of the Alvarado Baptist Association of Texas*.

5. *Minutes of the Fourth Annual Session of the Alvarado Baptist Association of Texas, Held with the Church at Alvarado, September 18th, 1868*. In the parlance of the Baptist Church, a "messenger" is a person delegated by one organization to attend another organization's meetings.

6. Demit of Henry C. Renfro issued by the Grandview, Texas, Masonic Lodge, December 7, 1867, Renfro-Clark Papers. The Masonic Lodge in Texas traces its beginnings to 1835 when a group of Masons met in Brazoria County and petitioned the Grand Lodge of Louisiana to establish a lodge in Brazoria, Texas. The J. H. Holland Lodge opened in Houston in October 1837. Other lodges were established in Nacogdoches and San Augustine, and in December 1837, Sam Houston presided over a meeting in the Senate Chamber of the Texas Capitol which organized the Grand Lodge of Texas. One of the principal purposes of Freemasonry was the advancement of education, and fourteen Masonic schools were established in Texas before 1854. Over one hundred Masonic schools were opened between 1850 and 1873. See "Freemasonry in Texas" in Webb, ed., *The Handbook of Texas*, 1: 645; *A Memorial and Biographical History of Johnson and Hill Counties, Texas*, 182; William M. Lang, Master, Texas State Grange, Marlin, Texas, printed notice of quarterly dues, to Henry C. Renfro, Master, Liberty Hill Grange, No 564, 1875, Renfro-Clark Papers. The Grange was a new organization in Texas when Renfro headed Number 564, having been established two years earlier, in 1873, in Salado. Its purposes included cooperation in business, happier home lives, more social contacts, and better educational opportunities. See Webb, ed., *The Handbook of Texas*, 1: 716–717.

7. "Laying the Corner Stone," *Cleburne Chronicle*, February 13, 1869, 2; Joe P. Ross, "Requiem of a Cleburne School," *Texana* 6, no. 4 (Winter 1968): 323. There were about ninety-five students at the dedication of the new building. The school itself, with Reverend J. R. Clarke as principal, was formed the year before, in 1868. Five years later, the enrollment had reached two

hundred. See *A Memorial and Biographical History of Johnson and Hill Counties, Texas*, 670. For the Association's minutes in which the site and the official name of the Cleburne Institute were decided, see *Minutes of the Fourth Annual Session of the Alvarado Baptist Association of Texas*. John Collier, the master of ceremonies as well as speaker for the opening of the Cleburne Institute, was a Baptist minister and the president of Alvarado College, a school formed in 1869.

8. "Laying the Corner Stone," *Cleburne Chronicle*, February 13, 1869, 2.

9. Ibid.; Henry C. Renfro, "The Importance of Education," ms., c. 1869, Renfro-Clark Papers. Joseph Addison, referred to by Renfro, was a prominent English essayist and poet who was born in 1672 and died in 1719.

10. R. C. B. [Rufus C. Burleson], "Rev. H. C. Renfro," *Guardian* 2, no. 3 (March 1885): 50; tombstone records, cemetery at Bethesda Baptist Church; Henry C. Renfro, "The Coward's Castle," *Alvarado Bulletin*, June 20, 1884.

11. Interested 1 [pseud.], Letter to the Editor, *Cleburne Chronicle*, November 6, 1869, 2.

12. Ross, "Requiem of a Cleburne School."

13. *A Memorial and Biographical History of Johnson and Hill Counties, Texas*, 181–182; Thelma Clark Griggs, great-granddaughter of Henry C. Renfro, interview with author, April 10, 1990, notes in possession of author. Alvarado College continued until about 1872, when its funding became insufficient for continued operation. By 1875, the institution was referred to as "Alvarado High School." The Alvarado Masonic Institute, located on the site of the present Alvarado High School, was located on seven acres out of the Ira Glaze survey and was deeded to the school trustees "for Masonic and school purposes." See James D. Carter, "Early Masonic Schools and Masonic Influence," *Texas Grand Lodge Magazine* [1957], 304, in Scrapbook, Renfro-Clark Papers.

14. Noble Lafayette Clark and Ruby Richeson Clark, interview with author, August 11, 1975.

15. Mary Pearl Baker Clark, unnamed ms., c. 1960, Renfro-Clark Papers.

16. Ibid.; Henry C. Renfro, "The Endurance of Afflictions," in Parks, *The Texas Baptist Pulpit*, 269–281.

17. Clark, unnamed ms., Renfro-Clark Papers.

18. Henry C. Renfro, "Elder Hines," Letter to the Editor of the *Cleburne Chronicle*, ms., c. 1873, Renfro-Clark Papers. Hines was still a presiding elder as late as 1875. See *Minutes of the Weatherford District Conference of the Methodist Episcopal Church, South, held in Caddo Grove, Johnson County, Texas, July 7–10, 1875, T. W. Hines, Presiding Elder, D. R. Carmichael, Secretary*. Hines died in 1881 and was buried at Weatherford, Texas. See Olin W. Nail, Editor-in-Chief, *Texas Methodist Centennial Yearbook*, 484.

19. Renfro, "Elder Hines," Letter to the Editor of the *Cleburne Chronicle*, ms., c. 1873, Renfro-Clark Papers.

20. Ibid.

21. Ibid.

22. Ibid.

23. Ibid.

24. Henry C. Renfro, ms. poem written on the thirteenth birthday of his daughter, Annette Renfro, July 24, 1877, Renfro-Clark Papers.

25. Johnson County, State of Texas, Deed of 160 acres of land from Hezekiah Russell to Henry C. Renfro, April 19, 1873, Renfro-Clark Papers. Also, see State of Texas, Johnson County, Deed of 160 acres from Hezekiah Russell to H. C. Renfro, April 19, 1873, Book K, p. 430, Deed Records, Johnson County, Texas.

26. Thomas H. Neilson, Philadelphia, Pennsylvania, to Henry C. Renfro, Johnson County, Texas, April 13, 1874, Renfro-Clark Papers.

27. Ibid.

28. Thomas H. Neilson, Philadelphia, to Henry C. Renfro, Johnson County, Texas, February 5, 1878, Renfro-Clark Papers; Thomas H. Neilson, Philadelphia, to Henry C. Renfro, Johnson County, Texas, n.d., Renfro-Clark Papers.

29. Henry C. Renfro, Johnson County, Texas, to Thomas H. Neilson, Philadelphia, Promissory Note payable to City National Bank, Fort Worth, Texas, March 19, 1878, Renfro-Clark Papers; "Deed from Mary A. Neilson et al to Thomas H. Neilson," June 16, 1877, Renfro-Clark Papers; State of Texas, Land Grant Number 755 to Hall Neilson, assignee of Samuel M. Williams, Austin, March 4, 1856, Renfro-Clark Papers; State of Pennsylvania, City of Philadelphia, deed and indenture of 640 acres from Thomas H. Neilson and Katherine Clemson, his wife, to Reverend Henry C. Renfro, March 19, 1878, Book R, pp. 77–79, Deed Records, Johnson County, Texas.

30. Thomas H. Neilson to Henry C. Renfro, February 5, 1878, Renfro-Clark Papers.

31. Minutes, Alvarado Baptist Church, "3rd Lord's Day in September, A.D. 1878" [September 15, 1878], ledger page 117, microfilm copy, Texas Collection, Baylor University, Waco, Texas. John Ezell was a cotton gin owner who lived in eastern Johnson County near the town of Venus. Although no record has been found of Isaac Kelly, a Mrs. I. C. Kelly was listed as a director of the Home National Bank in Cleburne in 1916. No specific reference has been found to B. B. Prestridge; he is, no doubt, a member of the Prestridge family which were early settlers in Alvarado, Johnson County. See Block, *History of Johnson County and Surrounding Areas*, 31, 110, 153, 251.

32. Minutes, Alvarado Baptist Church, November 3, 1878, ledger page 124, Texas Collection, Baylor University.

33. Ibid.

34. Henry C. Renfro, "S. C. Roddy, or Much Ado about Nothing," *Cleburne Chronicle*, n.d., clipping in Julius E. Baker ledger, in Renfro-Clark Papers. The Renfro-Roddy hard feelings had antecedents going back over a century. In 1789, Colonel John Tipton, Henry Renfro's great-grandfather, had a bitter argument with a Mr. Roddy during a meeting of the North Carolina legislature, of which both were members. The disagreement resulted in a challenge to a duel, but the difficulty was "honorably accommodated" by mutual friends. See Ramsey, *Annals of Tennessee*, 432. Like the Renfros, the Roddy family moved to Georgia from Tennessee, settling at Ringgold. See "Visits Old Home in Georgia," clipping in Renfro scrapbook, Renfro-Clark Papers.

35. Henry C. Renfro, "S. C. Roddy, or Much ado About Nothing," Renfro-Clark Papers. Although the public controversy soon ended, the animosity between the Renfro and Roddy families continued. Over eighty years after the event, Renfro's granddaughter, Mary Pearl Baker Clark, discussed the fact that there was a coolness between her family and the Roddys. Thelma Clark Griggs, interview with author, April 10, 1990. The notion that Baptist ministers should do nothing but preach was noted as early as the mid-1840's, when the minutes of the Eighth Annual Meeting of the Union Baptist Association exhorted ministers to "Give yourselves wholly to the ministry of the Word. You shall suffer no loss. Your families *shall be sustained.*" See Hogan, *The Texas Republic*, 206.

36. Statement of W. A. Saey, Church Clerk, Rehobath Baptist Church, and six members of the congregation, November 21, 1880, Renfro-Clark Papers.

37. Rufus C. Burleson, Waco, Texas, to Henry C. Renfro, Alvarado, Texas, November 20, 1875, Renfro-Clark Papers.

38. *Minutes of the Seventeenth Annual Session of the Alvarado Baptist Association Held with Eagle Hill Church, Tarrant County, Texas, Commencing September 15, 1881.*

39. "Cross Timbers News," *Weekly Bulletin* (Cleburne, Texas), September 3, 1880, 3. F. M. Law came to Texas in 1859 from South Carolina and served principally at churches at Brenham and Bryan. See *Centennial Story of Texas Baptists*, 97; Hesler, *A History of Independence Baptist Church*, 67; Z. N. Morrell, *Flowers and Fruits in the Wilderness; or, Thirty Six Years in Texas and Two Winters in Honduras*, 358–359.

40. "Programme for Missionary Mass Meeting to be held at Grand View, Johnson County, Texas, November 4th, 5th, and 6th, 1881," *Alvarado Bulletin*, September 30, 1881, 2. The early career of Rufus C. Burleson, the president of Baylor University and Waco University, is well covered in Chapter 1 of this book. R. C. Buckner, born in Madisonville, Tennessee, came to Texas in 1833 and was responsible for the founding of the Buckner Orphan's Home in Dal-

las. B. H. Carroll succeeded Rufus Burleson in 1871 as the pastor of the First Baptist Church in Waco after having been a professor of theology at Waco University. Carroll's first theological student was William Bagby, the minister who is given major credit by some church historians for the establishment of the Baptist Church in Brazil. See *Centennial Story of Texas Baptists*, 101–104; Hesler, *A History of Independence Baptist Church*, 78, 79, 100.

41. Rufus C. Burleson, Daybook, Box 4C178, File No. 148, Burleson Papers, Texas Collection, Baylor University, Waco, Texas; Burleson, comp., *The Life and Writings of Dr. Rufus C. Burleson*, 411.

CHAPTER 6. FATE PLAYS HER HAND

1. Griggs, "A Profile of Mu and Remembrances of the Old Family Home," ms., 1977; Bill of Sale [for piano], Daniel F. Beatty Company, Washington, New Jersey, to Henry C. Renfro, Oak Grove, Texas, July 2, 1880, copy in possession of author; Margaret Annette Baker, "Patience," ms., Renfro-Clark Papers; Margaret Annette Baker, "Should Females Be Equally Educated with Males?" ms., Renfro-Clark Papers.

2. "James Clark," in Clarence R. Wharton, *Texas under Many Flags*, 5: 37, 38. The original grantees of the land which became the townsite of Burleson were James W. Henderson, who was granted 898 acres, and David Anderson, who was granted 1/4 league and one labor. Henderson's grant was patented on March 7, 1860, by the heirs of H. G. Cotlett, and Anderson patented his land in his own name on August 3, 1855. See *Abstract of Land Titles in Texas*, 1: 801, 805; State of Texas, Johnson County, deed of right-of-way from H. C. Renfro to Missouri, Kansas, and Texas Railway Company, February 14, 1881, Book W, pp. 26–27, Deed Records, Johnson County, Texas. It appears that 301 acres was not transferred directly to the Missouri, Kansas, and Texas Railway, but instead to a third party, R. E. Montgomery of Pottawattamie, Iowa. See State of Texas, Johnson County, deed of two-hundred sixty-one acres and twenty acres from Henry Renfro to R. E. Montgomery, March 17, 1881, Book W, pp. 128–129, Deed Records, Johnson County, Texas. Major General Grenville Mellen Dodge, originally from Pottawattamie County, Iowa, was active in the promotion of several railroads including the Colorado & Southern, the Denver and Gulf, and the Missouri, Kansas, and Texas. Dodge was the president of the Union Pacific Railroad in 1894. See Stanley P. Hirschson, *Grenville M. Dodge, Soldier, Politician, Railroad Pioneer*.

3. Thelma Clark Griggs, interview with author, April 10, 1990.

4. Ira Bishop, Annona, Texas, to M. O. Green, Burleson, Texas, September 20, 1939, Renfro-Clark Papers.

5. Ibid.

6. Thelma C. Griggs, interview with author, April 10, 1990.

7. Block, *History of Johnson County and Surrounding Areas*, 145–146; William H. McGuffy, *McGuffy's New Fourth Eclectic Reader: Instructive Lessons for the Young*, enlarged edition. Both Burlie and Annette used this book, Burlie in 1870 and Annette in 1873, according to inscriptions. This volume is in possession of author. Although there are no family recollections of her having done so, later publications state that Annette also went to school in Cleburne, Texas. See Wharton, *Texas under Many Flags*, 5: 37–38; also, see "Mrs. M. A. Clark, Native of Johnson County, Buried Sunday Afternoon in Burleson Cemetery," *Burleson News*, June 3, 1943. The attendance of James Burleson Renfro and Annette Renfro at the Masonic Institute is confirmed in James Burleson Renfro, Alvarado, Texas, to Dora Coody, [Searcy, Arkansas], December 7, 1880, Renfro-Clark Papers, in which Burleson Renfro states that "[your] Cousin Annette and I are going to school at Alvarado to Pro. Fuller; he is a very wise man." Fuller succeeded Professor I. A. Patton, who left the school in 1878. See *A Memorial and Biographical History of Johnson and Hill Counties, Texas*, 182.

8. Darius Baker, a former resident of Arcadia, Louisiana, was a member of the Union Army, becoming a second lieutenant in Company C, 2nd Regiment, Louisiana Cavalry. Although Baker originally was from Natchez, he and his wife Martha Ann Anderson Baker were married in Hinds County, Mississippi, on April 12, 1846. Frances Dickson Abernathy, "The Building of Johnson County, and the Settlement of the Communities of the Eastern Portion of the County," vol. 1 of "A History of the Builders of Johnson County," Master's thesis, University of Texas, 1936, 128; Martha A. Baker, General Affidavit, "Pension Claim of Martha A. Baker, Widow of Darius Baker, Co. C, 1st Reg't, Scouts-Cav. Vols, No. 302,011, June 12, 1890," United States, National Archives, copy in possession of author; James Burleson Renfro to Dora Coody, December 7, 1880, Renfro-Clark Papers; Block, *History of Johnson County and Surrounding Areas*, 143.

9. Julius Baker, Alvarado, Texas, to Annette Renfro, [Masonic Institute], Alvarado, Texas, November 24, 1881; Julius Baker, Alvarado, Texas, to Annette Renfro, [Masonic Institute], Alvarado, Texas, November 29, 1881; Julius Baker, Alvarado, Texas, to Annette Renfro, [Masonic Institute], Alvarado, Texas, December 6, 1881; Julius Baker, Alvarado, to Annette Renfro, [Masonic Institute], Alvarado, December 13, 1881. All of the above-listed correspondence is in the Renfro-Clark Papers.

10. Thelma Clark Griggs, interview with author, November 26, 1990; "Advice Remembered," newspaper clipping found among loose papers in the Renfro-Clark Papers. This article discussed the relationship of I. W. Satterfield to S. C. Roddy. Both Julius's brother and father were named Darius Baker.

11. Julius Baker, Alvarado, Texas, to Annette Renfro, [Renfro farm], Feb-

ruary 10, 1882; Julius Baker, Alvarado, Texas, to Annette Renfro, [Renfro farm], April 20, 1882; Julius Baker, Alvarado, Texas, to Annette Renfro [Renfro farm], July 6, 1882; Julius Baker, Alvarado, Texas, to "Miss Annette My Darling Girl," August 6, 1882; Annette Renfro, [Renfro farm], to Julius Baker, Alvarado, August 9, 1882. All of above-listed correspondence is in the Renfro-Clark Papers.

12. Julius Baker, Alvarado, Texas, to Annette Renfro, [Renfro farm], August 25, 1882; Julius Baker, Alvarado, Texas, to Annette Renfro, [Renfro farm], September 1, 1882. All of above-listed correspondence is in the Renfro-Clark Papers.

13. Julius Baker, Alvarado, Texas, to Annette Renfro, [Renfro farm], October 4, 1882, Renfro-Clark Papers.

14. Clipping from *Alvarado Bulletin,* n.d., from Julius Baker ledger/scrapbook, Renfro-Clark Papers; *Alvarado Bulletin,* April 7, 1882, 4; *Alvarado Bulletin,* November 17, 1883, 3.

15. Thelma Clark Griggs, interview with author, November 26, 1990.

16. Julius Baker, Alvarado, Texas, to Annette Renfro, [Renfro farm], October 14, 1882, Renfro-Clark Papers; Julius Baker, Alvarado, Texas, to Annette Renfro, [Renfro farm], November 2, 1882, Renfro-Clark Papers.

17. "Hymen's Harvest," newspaper clipping from Renfro scrapbook in Julius Baker ledger, in possession of author; Annette Renfro, [Renfro farm], to Dearest One [Julius Baker], November 19, 1882, Renfro-Clark Papers.

18. "Married," *Alvarado Bulletin,* December 15, 1882, 3.

19. Thomas H. Neilson, Philadelphia, Pennsylvania, to Rev. H. C. Renfro, [Burleson, Texas], February 20, 1883, Renfro-Clark Papers.

20. *Alvarado Weekly Bulletin,* March 23, 1883, 3; John C. Weaver, M.D., "Affidavit to Date and Cause of Soldier's Death," June 12, 1890, in Baker, "Pension Claim of Martha A. Baker, Widow of Darius Baker, Co. C., 1st Reg't, Scouts-Cav. Vols, No. 302,011, June 12, 1890," Pension Records, National Archives of the United States, Washington, D.C.

21. Thelma C. Griggs, interview with author, November 26, 1990; Annette Renfro Baker to Mary R. Renfro, [Searcy, Arkansas], June 7, 1883, Renfro-Clark Papers.

22. "Marystown," *Alvarado Bulletin,* May 25, 1883, 4.

23. J. B. Renfro, Burleson, Texas, to Mrs. M. R. Renfro, [Searcy, Arkansas], May 26, 1883, Renfro-Clark Papers; Kittie Renfro, Burleson, Texas, to Mrs. M. Renfro, [Searcy, Arkansas], [May 26, 1883], Renfro-Clark Papers. John Renfro, the "John" referred to in the above letter, was the son of Isaac Renfro, Henry's brother.

24. Julius Baker, Burleson, Texas, to Mrs. M. R. Renfro, [Searcy, Arkansas], June 5, 1883, Renfro-Clark Papers; Annette Renfro Baker, Burleson, Texas, to Dear Ma, June 7, 1883, Renfro-Clark Papers.

25. Julius Baker, Burleson, Texas, to Mrs. M. R. Renfro, [Searcy, Arkansas], June 17, 1883, Renfro-Clark Papers.

26. Henry C. Renfro, Johnson County, Texas, to Mary R. Renfro, [Searcy, Arkansas], June 17, 1883, Renfro-Clark Papers. Interestingly, much of Renfro's text in this letter concerning the problems of Annette and Julius has been carefully erased.

27. Thelma Clark Griggs, interview with author, April 14, 1991, notes in possession of author.

CHAPTER 7. A HEART WARM FOND ADIEU

1. Mosheim, John Laurence, *An Ecclesiastical History, Ancient and Modern; In Which the Rise, Progress, and Variations of Church Power, are Considered in their Connexion with the State of Learning and Philosophy, and the Political History of Europe during that Period;* Milner, *Religious Denominations of the World;* Renfro's copy of *Theology: The Philosophy of Religion*, like many other works that were a part of Renfro's library, is in poor condition with no title page. The same is true of Pierre Pithou, comp., *Juvenal Delphini* (the satires of Decimus Junius Juvenalis and Aulus Persius Flaccus); Robert Burns, *Poetical Works of Robert Burns: With Critical and Biographical Notices, by Allen Cunningham, and a Glossary;* Thomas Moore, *The Poetical Works of Thomas Moore.* All of the above-cited works are from Henry Renfro's personal library, in possession of author. Information regarding Renfro's desire to inquire into the deeper meaning of life and man's relationship to God was secured from Renfro's great-granddaughter, Thelma Clark Griggs, interview with author, April 14, 1991.

2. *Minutes of the Seventeenth Annual Session of the Alvarado Baptist Association.*

3. Renfro's land ownership in Johnson County consisted of five different plots of land with a total of 1046 acres. Its assessed tax value was $8,158, and he paid taxes of $50.93. See Johnson County, Texas, Office of Collector of Taxes, Receipt Number 219 for taxes, 1882, Cleburne, Texas, March 2, 1883, in possession of Noble L. Clark, Burleson, Texas, copy in possession of author. *Minutes of the Eighteenth Annual Session of the Alvarado Baptist Association, Held with the Baptist Church at Grand View, Johnson County, Texas, Commencing September 14, 1882.* The only mention of Renfro in the minutes was in the list of ordained ministers in the Association; however, it is likely that he did attend, as his daughter Annette wrote to Julius Baker on September 4, 1882, that "he [Henry Renfro] wants to go to the association and wishes me to go also." See Annette Renfro, Burleson, Texas, to Julius Baker, Alvarado, Texas, September 4, 1882, Renfro-Clark Papers.

4. "Laying the Corner Stone," *Alvarado Bulletin*, November 17, 1882, 3;

Henry C. Renfro, "Dedication of New Court House, Johnson County, Texas," ms. in possession of author.

5. Robert G. Ingersoll was born in Dresden, New York. He was the son of a Congregational minister, and thus was raised in a religious atmosphere. He studied law and moved to Illinois, and he eventually made Peoria his home. Ingersoll became an agnostic and afterward lectured extensively concerning the pitfalls of orthodox religion. See *Complete Lectures of Col. R. G. Ingersoll.* Baruch (or Benedict) Spinoza was born to Jewish emigrant parents from Portugal in Amsterdam, Holland, in 1632. He became disaffected with Judaism and, after learning Latin, became a vociferous reader of philosophy. Although Spinoza thought religion must be subject to some state control, he believed in complete freedom of expression, both in belief and in thought. He was considered to be a Pantheist, and he believed that God was the equivalent of nature. See Andrew Seth Pringle-Pattison, "Baruch Spinoza," in *Encyclopaedia Britannica*, 11th ed., 25: 687–691. Thomas Paine was born in England in 1737. After a disappointing youth, Paine met Benjamin Franklin in London, providing the impetus for his going to North America in 1774. Two years later, he wrote *Common Sense,* a pamphlet generally considered to be one of the principal motivators for the American Revolution. Among other literary works was Paine's *Age of Reason,* a book which pronounced that "all religions are in their nature mild and benign." See Daniel Edwin Wheeler, ed., *Life and Writings of Thomas Paine.*

6. S. W. Geiser, "Dr. L. J. Russell and the Pike's Peak Gold Rush of 1858–1859," *Southwestern Historical Quarterly* 48, no. 4 (April 1945): 573; Belton (Texas) *Journal*, October 31, 1877; *A Memorial and Biographical History of McLennan, Falls, Bell, and Coryell Counties, Texas,* 558–559. Interestingly, Russell and his two brothers were the founders of what became Denver, Colorado. They built a log cabin in 1858, and a settlement grew around it. Named "Auraria," by the Russells, the name was changed to Denver in the fall of 1858.

7. "Special to the Dallas Herald from Waco," *Alvarado Bulletin*, September 22, 1882, 2; for an in-depth study of Shaw, see Blake Barrow, "Freethought in Texas: J. D. Shaw and the Independent Pulpit," Master's thesis, Baylor University, 1983.

8. Virginia Ming, "J. D. Shaw: Freethinker," in *Waco History and Heritage* 10, no. 2 (Summer 1979): 1–21; a defense of the way that the Methodist Conference handled Shaw's case is found in an article by W. L. Nelms, "The Shaw Case: A True Statement of the Facts and Law," *Alvarado Bulletin*, November 24, 1882, 2.

9. Ming, "J. D. Shaw: Freethinker."

10. Ibid.

11. Ibid.; *Alvarado Bulletin*, March 2, 1883, 2.

12. Rufus C. Burleson, Waco, Texas, to My Dear Henry [Henry C. Renfro], Johnson County, Texas, January 18, 1884, Renfro-Clark Papers.

13. Minutes, Alvarado Baptist Church, October 6, 1883, microfilm copy, Texas Collection, Baylor University, Waco, Texas.

14. H. C. Renfro, "An Open Letter," *Alvarado Bulletin,* October 19, 1883, 3.

15. Ibid.

16. Ibid.

17. Ibid.

18. Ibid.

19. Minutes, Alvarado Baptist Church, November 3, 1883 [pp. 184–186], microfilm copy, Texas Collection, Baylor University, Waco, Texas.

20. Ibid.

21. Ibid.

22. Rufus C. Burleson, to My Dear Henry [Henry C. Renfro], January 18, 1884, Renfro-Clark Papers.

23. Ibid.

24. Ibid.; Martin V. Smith was pastor at Belton, Bell County, Texas, from 1875 to 1892 after other pastorates at Chappell Hill, Brenham, and Anderson, Texas. See *Centennial Story of Texas Baptists,* 100.

25. H. C. Renfro, "Letter from H. C. Renfro," *Independent Pulpit* 2, no. 3 (May 1884): 34–35.

26. Ibid.; John 21:25, *The New Layman's Parallel Bible,* King James Version, 2762.

27. H. C. Renfro, "An Open Letter," *Alvarado Bulletin,* February 8, 1884, 2; H. C. Renfro, "Letter From H. C. Renfro," *Independent Pulpit* 2, no. 3 (May 1884), 34–35; Minutes, Alvarado Baptist Church, February 2, 1884 [pp. 187–188], microfilm copy, Texas Collection, Baylor University, Waco, Texas. It is interesting that Texas Baptists had a history of trials of their ministers for nonadherence to orthodoxy. As early as 1840, the moderator of the Union Association, Reverend T. W. Cox, was excluded "after a long and unpleasant trial," because of his "predilection for the principles advocated by Alexander Campbell," the man who later was largely responsible for the formation of the Church of Christ. See Hogan, *The Texas Republic,* 206.

28. H. C. Renfro, "An Open Letter," *Alvarado Bulletin,* February 8, 1884, 2.

29. Ibid.; Robert Burns, "Man Was Made to Mourn," in *Poetical Works of Robert Burns,* 109.

30. H. C. Renfro, "An Open Letter," *Alvarado Bulletin,* February 8, 1884, 2.

31. Ibid.

32. Ibid.

33. Ibid.

34. Ibid. The Landmark Baptist movement gained prominence in the decade of the 1850's. The movement, according to historian David Edwin Har-

rell, Jr., "was almost entirely southern and constituted a renewed effort to save Baptist churches from 'liberalism.' The movement was basically anti-mission and emphasized the independence of the local church." It was a "predominately rural and conservative fellowship." According to Harrell, Landmark doctrine was not seriously challenged in the church until the 1950's. See Harrell, "The Evolution of Plain-Folk Religion in the South," in Hill, *Varieties of Southern Religious Experience,* 29–30, 35.

35. Renfro, "An Open Letter," *Alvarado Bulletin,* February 8, 1884, 2.

36. "Excommunicated. Elder H. C. Renfro Dispossessed of Credentials," *Alvarado Bulletin,* February 8, 1884.

CHAPTER 8. THE PAPER DEBATES

1. Harry LeFever, "The Church and Poor Whites," *New South* 25 (Spring 1970): 32, as quoted in Harrell, "The Evolution of Plain-Folk Religion in the South," in Hill, ed., *Varieties of Southern Religious Experience,* 30, 44.

2. Renfro, "An Open Letter," *Alvarado Bulletin,* February 8, 1884, 2; parts of this letter also were published in *The Independent Pulpit,* the news magazine published in Waco by former minister J. D. Shaw. See [J. D. Shaw], "Too Liberal for a Baptist," *Independent Pulpit* 2, no. 2 (March 1884): 16–17.

3. Renfro, "An Open Letter," *Alvarado Bulletin,* February 8, 1884.

4. H. C. Renfro, "A Lecture," *Alvarado Bulletin,* February 15, 1884, 3.

5. Citizen [pseud.], "Yes," *Alvarado Bulletin,* February 15, 1884, 2; Uncle Jerry [pseud.], "That Verse," *Alvarado Bulletin,* February 22, 1884, 2; although the title "Uncle Jerry" is a pseudonym, it will be referred to in the balance of this publication without the quotation marks.

6. "Lecture of Mr. Renfro," *Alvarado Bulletin,* February 22, 1884, 3.

7. [J. D. Shaw], "H. C. Renfro a Heretic," *Independent Pulpit* 2, no. 1 (March 1884): 5; "Lecture of Mr. Renfro," *Alvarado Bulletin,* February 22, 1884, 3.

8. "Lecture of Mr. Renfro," *Alvarado Bulletin,* February 22, 1884, 3.

9. Ibid.

10. [Shaw], "H. C. Renfro a Heretic."

11. Uncle Johnnie [pseud.], "A Question," *Alvarado Bulletin,* February 22, 1884, 3; H. C. Renfro, "Reply to Uncle Johnnie," *Alvarado Bulletin,* March 7, 1884.

12. [F. B. Baillio], "Grand View Items," *Alvarado Bulletin,* March 2, 1884. Baillio was the correspondent for the *Bulletin* from the small town of Grand View, which was located south of Alvarado. Born in Louisiana, Baillio was a Confederate veteran and settled in Alvarado in 1867, where he worked at a variety of jobs from farm hand to school teacher. He continued farming and

served as a correspondent for the *Bulletin* from 1884 to 1887. By 1889, he had purchased the newspaper and remained its sole editor until he bought a controlling interest in the Johnson County *Review* at Cleburne, Texas. See *A Memorial and Biographical History of Hill and Johnson Counties, Texas*, 159–160. The spelling of the name of Grandview, Johnson County, Texas, varies in the text. Today, it is known as Grandview; however, in the 1880's it often was referred to as Grand View.

13. [F. B. Baillio], "Grand View Items," *Alvarado Bulletin*, March 7, 1884.

14. H. C. Renfro, "Won Laurels," *Alvarado Bulletin*, March 7, 1884.

15. Uncle Jerry, "INNOMINATA, Squib No. 17," *Alvarado Bulletin*, March 14, 1884, 2. Robert G. Ingersoll was a well-known agnostic who had a national reputation for inspiring lectures on Free Thought. See *Complete Lectures of Col. R. G. Ingersoll.*

16. [F. B. Baillio], "Grand View Items," *Alvarado Bulletin*, March 21, 1884, 2.

17. "Bulletin Briefs," *Alvarado Bulletin*, March 21, 1884, 3.

18. H. C. Renfro, "A Soft Answer Turneth Away Wrath," *Alvarado Bulletin*, March 28, 1884, 2.

19. Ibid.

20. Ibid.

21. Ibid.

22. Ibid.; Uncle Jerry, "Was Christ Essentially Holy. Squib No. 18," *Alvarado Bulletin*, April 4, 1884, 3.

23. E. K. [pseud.], "Cross Timbers," *Alvarado Bulletin*, April 4, 1884, 4.

24. [Uncle Jerry], "That Suggestion," *Alvarado Bulletin*, May 9, 1884, 2.

25. [F. B. Baillio], "Grand View," *Alvarado Bulletin*, May 16, 1884, 2.

26. Ibid.

27. Ibid.

28. Uncle Jerry, "Make Him a Pony Purse, Squib No. 24," *Alvarado Bulletin*, May 23, 1884, 2.

29. H. C. Renfro, "An Open Letter," *Alvarado Bulletin*, June 6, 1884, 1.

30. [F. B. Baillio], "Grand View," *Alvarado Bulletin*, June 20, 1884, 1.

31. [F. B. Baillio], "Grand View," *Alvarado Bulletin*, May 30, 1884, 2.

32. Ibid.

33. Renfro, "An Open Letter," *Alvarado Bulletin*, June 6, 1884, 1.

34. Ibid.

35. Ibid.

36. Ibid.

37. Ibid.

38. Ibid.

39. Ibid.

40. Ibid.

41. Uncle Jerry, "Don't Know What to Call It. Squib No. 26," *Alvarado Bulletin*, June 6, 1884, 2.

42. Uncle Jerry, "Neither 'Silence' nor 'Abuse,'" *Alvarado Bulletin*, June 13, 1884, 2.

43. Ibid.; Uncle Jerry, "INNOMINATA. Squib No. 17."

44. Uncle Jerry, "Neither 'Silence' nor 'Abuse.'"

45. [F. B. Baillio], "Grand View," *Alvarado Bulletin*, June 20, 1884, 2.

46. A Clodhopper [pseud.], "Egan," *Alvarado Bulletin*, June 20, 1884, 2.

47. Renfro, "The Coward's Castle."

48. Uncle Jerry, "Declaration of Principles. Squib No. 28," *Alvarado Bulletin*, June 27, 1884, 3.

49. H. C. Renfro, "Uncle Jerry in the Dark," ms., 1884, Renfro-Clark Papers.

50. "Personal Mention," *Alvarado Bulletin*, July 11, 1884, 3.

CHAPTER 9. WITHOUT A MURMUR OR A FROWN

1. Although Robert Burns is almost universally cited as the author of "Auld Lang Syne," Burns himself noted that it was "an old song of the olden times, and which has never been in print, nor even in manuscript, until I took it down from an old man's singing." See *The Poetical Works of Robert Burns*, 541.

2. Annette, like many other women of the time, often took to her bed when household responsibilities and impending childbirth seemed to become overwhelming. Compare with Mahala P. Roach, "Diary of Mahala P. Roach," ms., Southern History Collection, University of North Carolina. Roach noted that she had "felt rather depressed this evening, fearing a long summer of heat & sickness—even if I keep well how can I nurse baby and my sick too?" See Scott, *The Southern Lady*, 31.

3. Annette Baker, "The Loved and the Lost," ms., Renfro-Clark Papers.

4. Thomas H. Neilson, Philadelphia, to Henry C. Renfro, [Burleson, Texas], November 27, 1884, Renfro-Clark Papers.

5. Ibid.

6. "Old Man" Tom Mills was a friend of Henry Renfro's great-grandson, Noble L. Clark of Burleson. He related this story to Clark in the 1920s (Noble L. and Ruby R. Clark, interview with the author, August 11, 1975). Renfro also noted that "Honor and moral manhood are the most fragrant flowers of the soul, and will bring peace of mind when every thing else fails . . . yet I can truly sing: 'Sweet prospects, sweet birds and sweet flowers Have lost *none* of their sweetness to me.'" Henry C. Renfro, "Mr. Renfro's Anniversary as a Liberal," *Independent Pulpit* 3, no. 1 (March 1885): 5–6.

7. Renfro, "Mr. Renfro's Anniversary as a Liberal."

8. Ibid.

9. Ibid.

10. Ibid.; for information on Dr. Russell, see Chapter 7, note 6.

11. Ibid.

12. Ibid.

13. Henry C. Renfro to J. D. Shaw, Waco, Texas, February 15, 1885, as quoted in J. D. Shaw, "H. C. Renfro," *Independent Pulpit* 3, no. 2 (April 1885): 17–18.

14. Ibid.

15. Ibid.

16. Ibid. Thomas W. Hollingsworth was a founder of the Marystown community. From Alabama, Hollingsworth came to Texas in 1870 where he started a mill and secured five hundred acres of farmland. See Block, *History of Johnson County and Surrounding Areas,* 189; also, see Joshua Historical Committee, *Joshua: As It Was and Is, 1853–1976,* 44.

17. "Died," *Fort Worth Gazette,* March 3, 1885.

18. Ibid.; "Marystown," *Alvarado Bulletin,* February 27, 1885. This notation was secured despite the fact that in the microfilm copies of *The Alvarado Bulletin,* the entire month of March was missing. This clipping was from a scrapbook kept by Annette Baker in Julius's old grocery store ledger, in which she pasted clippings and other memorabilia.

19. Shaw, "H. C. Renfro."

20. Ibid.; C. McBride, Mrs. S. P. Johnson, Mrs. N. C. McMillan, "Certificate Attesting to the Circumstances of the Death of H. C. Renfro," n.d., as quoted in Ibid.

21. "Died," *Fort Worth Gazette,* March 3, 1885.

22. J. D. Shaw, Waco, Texas, to Mrs. H. C. Renfro, Burleson, Texas, March 5, 1885, Renfro-Clark Papers.

23. Untitled newspaper clipping, scrapbook relating to the Renfro family, in possession of Thelma Clark Griggs, Lubbock, Texas.

24. Burleson, "Rev. H. C. Renfro," 50.

25. Ibid.

26. Untitled newspaper clipping, scrapbook relating to the Renfro family.

27. Ibid.; Rufus C. Burleson, Waco University, Texas, to Mrs. H. C. Renfro, [Burleson, Texas], May 18, 1885, Renfro-Clark Papers. J. C. Jones was the ticket agent and telegraph operator at the railroad depot in Burleson. See Block, *History of Johnson County and Surrounding Areas,* 43.

28. Untitled newspaper clipping, scrapbook relating to the Renfro family.

29. *Texas Baptist,* March 19, 1885; Shaw, "H. C. Renfro." The reference to Thomas Paine was concerning an exchange between Rufus Burleson and J. D. Shaw which was published in *The Independent Pulpit* concerning the supposed

deathbed confession of the author of *Common Sense*. See Shaw, "Is Christianity Declining," *Independent Pulpit* 2, no. 4 (May 1884): 25–26.

30. Rufus C. Burleson, Waco University, Texas, to Mrs. Annette Renfro Baker My Darling Daughter, [Burleson, Texas], January 23, 1886, in possession of Noble L. Clark, Burleson, Texas, copy in Renfro-Clark Papers.

31. Shaw, "H. C. Renfro."

32. Ibid.

33. Ibid.

34. Julius E. Baker, Burleson, Texas, to J. D. Shaw, Waco, Texas, n.d., in Julius Baker's ledger-scrapbook, Renfro-Clark Papers.

35. Thomas H. Neilson, Philadelphia, Pennsylvania, to Julius E. Baker, Burleson, Texas, April 22, 1885, Renfro-Clark Papers. The poem quoted by Neilson is from William Shakespeare, *Julius Caeser*, act 3, scene 3, line 71.

36. Ibid.

37. [F. B.] Baillio, untitled clipping, Renfro-Clark Papers.

38. "Tribute of Respect. To the W. M., Wardens and Brethren of Alvarado Lodge, No. 314 A. F. & A. M.," *Alvarado Bulletin*, April 17, 1885, 2.

39. *Alvarado Bulletin*, April 3, 1885, 3; Burns, *Poetical Works of Robert Burns*, 341–342. The inscription also was published by J. D. Shaw. See "Purely Agnostic," *Independent Pulpit* 3, no. 3 (May 1885): 31.

CHAPTER 10. EPILOGUE

1. Mary R. Renfro, Designation of Homestead, April 30, 1885; M. M. Crane, Crane & Ramsey, Attorneys at Law, Cleburne, Texas, to J. E. Baker, [Burleson, Texas], November 12, 1885, Renfro-Clark Papers; Mintie Roberts, Dallas, Texas, to Dearest Annette, Burleson, Texas, March 29, 1893, Renfro-Clark Papers. Claude, the county seat of Armstrong County, Texas, is located southeast of Amarillo. Also, see State of Texas, Johnson County, Designation of certain tracts of land as homestead by Mary R. Renfro, April 29, 1885, Book 30, pp. 301–302, Deed Records, Johnson County, Texas; State of Texas, Johnson County, deed of various tracts in order to separate homestead properties in Johnson County, Texas, from C. A. [Kittie] Renfro to Mrs. Mary R. Renfro, Mrs. M. A. Baker, and her husband, J. E. Baker, April 29, 1885, Book 30, pp. 301–302, Deed Records, Johnson County, Texas; State of Texas, Johnson County, Deed of 160 acres from Mary R. Renfro, Mrs. M. A. Baker, and J. E. Baker to C. A. Renfro, April 29, 1885, Book 30, pp. 303–304, Deed Records, Johnson County, Texas.

2. Rufus C. Burleson, Waco University, Texas, to Mary R. Renfro, Burleson, Texas, receipt for promissory notes, May 23, 1885, in possession of

Noble L. Clark, Burleson, Texas, copy in Renfro-Clark Papers. No record has been found as to the return of either of the notes to Mary Renfro.

3. Thomas H. Neilson, Philadelphia, to Julius E. Baker, [Burleson, Texas], January 27, 1886, Renfro-Clark Papers.

4. Griggs, "A Profile of Mu [Margaret Annette Renfro Baker] and Remembrances of the Old Family Home," ms., 1977, in possession of author; James Pickett, M.D., statement of expenses to Julius E. Baker for the years 1886–1888, Renfro-Clark Papers.

5. Julius E. Baker, Burleson, Texas, to Annette Renfro Baker, [Searcy, Arkansas], August 12, 1886, Renfro-Clark Papers.

6. Ibid.; Julius E. Baker, Burleson, Texas, to Annette Renfro Baker, [Searcy, Arkansas], August 20, 1886, Renfro-Clark Papers.

7. Julius E. Baker to Annette Renfro Baker, August 20, 1886, Renfro-Clark Papers; Griggs, "A Profile of Mu and Remembrances of the Old Family Home"; James Pickett, M.D., statement for medical expenses, to Julius Baker, 1886–1888, Renfro-Clark Papers.

8. Thomas H. Neilson, Philadelphia, to Julius E. Baker, [Burleson, Texas], January 22, 1887, Renfro-Clark Papers.

9. Mollie Baker Jack, Alexander, Texas, to Mr. Jule Baker, Dear Old Bud, [Burleson, Texas], November 27, 1881, Renfro-Clark Papers.

10. Mollie Baker Jack, Alexander, Texas, to Mrs. M. A. Baker, April 23, 1886, Renfro-Clark Papers. The nineteenth-century sect of Spiritualism began in Rochester, New York, in 1848. "The great principle of Spiritualism," wrote a contemporary theologian, "is, that the spirits of the departed, who are no longer 'in the form,' can and do hold intelligent and sensible intercourse with those still living." See Milner, *Religious Denominations of the World*, 543–547.

11. Thelma Clark Griggs interview with author, November 26, 1990; Julius Baker, Renfro's Farm, to Annette Baker, Pet, May 9, 1887, Renfro-Clark Papers. Houston left his wife Eliza Allen Houston shortly after their marriage because of some problem, but never disclosed it to anyone during his life. See James, *The Raven*, 75–85.

12. Mollie Baker Jack [Julius's sister], Arlington, California, to Annette Renfro Baker Clark, May 17, 1936, Renfro-Clark Papers.

13. Thelma Clark Griggs, interview with author, November 26, 1990.

14. Ibid.

15. Ibid.

16. Ibid.; clipping, no title, from Renfro scrapbook in possession of Thelma Clark Griggs, Lubbock, Texas. Martin McNulty Crane came to Johnson County, Texas, in 1870. He decided to become an attorney and, after completing a course to that end, was admitted to the bar in 1877. He was elected prosecuting attorney for the county the next year and served in that position

until 1882. Later, he became Lieutenant Governor of Texas. See *A Memorial and Biographical History of Johnson and Hill Counties, Texas.*

17. Ibid.

18. I. W. [Buck] Satterfield, Tyler, Texas, to Dear Cousin [Annette Baker], October 10, 1888, Renfro-Clark Papers.

19. State of Texas, Johnson County, Writ of Injunction to John F. Boyd Sheriff of Johnson County, Texas[,] Mary R. Renfro & Annette Baker, May 30, 1889, Renfro-Clark Papers.

20. I. W. [Buck] Satterfield, Waco, Texas, to Dear Cousin, December 26, 1888, Renfro-Clark Papers.

21. I. W. [Buck] Satterfield, Waco, Texas, to Dear Cousin, January 17, 1889, Renfro-Clark Papers.

22. I. W. [Buck] Satterfield, Waco, Texas, to Dear Cousin, March 14, 1889, Renfro-Clark Papers.

23. I. W. [Buck] Satterfield, Waco, Texas, to Dear Cousin, March 30, 1889, Renfro-Clark Papers.

24. Somervell County, Texas, "Injunction Writ, John Baker vs. John H. Boyd, Sheriff of Johnson County, Texas, et al, May 30, 1889," Renfro-Clark Papers; also, see "Annette M. Baker [sic] No 2102 vs. Julius E. Baker et al, Bill of Costs due Clerk and Sheriff by Plaintiff," n.d., Renfro-Clark Papers; "Mary R. Renfro et al vs. Julius E. Baker, Bill of Costs due Clerk and Sheriff by Plaintiff," n.d., Renfro-Clark Papers.

25. I. W. [Buck] Satterfield, Waco, Texas, to Dear Cousin, April 19, 1889, Renfro-Clark Papers. An animosity between Annette Baker and her family against James Henry Harris continued well into the twentieth century. Thelma Clark Griggs, interview with author, December 24, 1990.

26. I. W. [Buck] Satterfield, Waco, Texas, to Dear Cousin, November 6, 1889, Renfro-Clark Papers.

27. Ibid.

28. I. W. (Buck) Satterfield to Dear Cousin, February 26, 1927, Renfro-Clark Papers.

29. Thelma Clark Griggs, interview with author, November 26, 1990. Mary continued to be under her doctor's care. See Mary R. Renfro, Burleson, Texas, to James Pickett (her doctor), promissory note, July 16, 1889, Renfro-Clark Papers.

30. Griggs, "A Profile of Mu and Remembrances of the Old Family Home."

31. Thelma Clark Griggs, interview with author, December 24, 1990.

32. Julius Baker, Clarendon, Texas, to Mrs. Pearl Baker Clark, Burleson, Texas, August 22, 1915, Renfro-Clark Papers; John Baker, untitled poem, Beeville, Texas, August 10, 1918, Renfro-Clark Papers.

33. Julius Baker, to Mrs. Pearl Baker Clark, August 22, 1915, Renfro-Clark Papers.

34. Julius Baker, Clarendon, Texas, to My Dear [Mary Pearl Baker Clark], December 23, 1915, Renfro-Clark Papers. The "secret" was not divulged until nearly fifty years later, when Mary Pearl Baker Clark told the story to her daughter, Thelma Clark Griggs.

35. Mollie Baker Jack, Arlington, California, to Annette Renfro Baker Clark, May 17, 1936, Renfro-Clark Papers. In a searing indictment of her cousin, Mollie Harris, Annette wrote Mollie Baker Jack that she had "wondered so many times how could those men & women [have] been as mean and how God permitted them to live to tell those infamous *Lies* to wreck the lives of two, who lived with undying love and made two little innocent children fatherless. . . . I blame old Mollie Harris." Your Sister Annette [Annette Renfro Baker Clark], Burleson, Texas, to Dear Sister Mollie [Mollie Baker Jack], Arlington, California, n.d. [c. 1935], Renfro-Clark Papers.

36. Mollie Baker Jack, Arlington, California, to My Darling Sister, December 3, 1937, Renfro-Clark Papers.

37. Thomas H. Neilson, New York, to Annette Renfro Clark, Burleson, Texas, October 4, 1901, Renfro-Clark Papers.

38. Ming, "J. D. Shaw: Freethinker."

39. Ibid.

40. Ibid.

41. Charles Carver, *Brann and the Iconoclast*, 183; Ming, "J. D. Shaw: Freethinker"; also, see J. D. Shaw, "William Cowper Brann" in *Brann the Iconoclast: A Collection of the Writings of W. C. Brann*, 5–8.

42. See "Antonia Texeira," and "The Texeira-Morris Case," in *Brann the Iconoclast*, 1: 187 and 320, as examples of Brann's vehement attacks on Burleson and Baylor University.

43. Rufus C. Burleson, Waco, Texas, to Mrs. Antonette [sic] Renfro Clark, May 17, 1898, Renfro-Clark Papers.

44. Ida Yarnell [Mary Renfro's niece], Searcy, Arkansas, to Mrs. Annette Clarke [sic], June 10, 1897, Renfro-Clark Papers; Funeral Notice of Mrs. C. A. Coody, Searcy, Arkansas, March 8, 1902, Renfro-Clark Papers.

45. Burleson, comp., *The Life and Writings of Rufus C. Burleson*; Thelma Clark Griggs, interview with author, December 24, 1990.

46. Thelma Clark Griggs, interview with author, December 24, 1990.

47. Henry C. Renfro, ms. poem written on the thirteenth birthday of his daughter, Margaret Annette Renfro, July 24, 1877, Renfro-Clark Papers.

48. Harrell, "The Evolution of Plain-Folk Religion in the South," in Hill, ed., *Varieties of Southern Religious Experience*, 25–51; for a broad overview of the development of Southern religion during the period, see Mathews, *Religion in the Old South*.

Bibliography

MANUSCRIPTS

Baker, Martha Ann, and others. General Affidavits in file entitled "Pension Claim of Martha A. Baker, Widow of Darius Baker, Co. C, 1st Reg't, Scouts-Cav. Vols, No. 302,011, June 12, 1890." Pension Records, National Archives of the United States. Washington, D.C.

Ballinger Collection. Barker Archives. Center for American History. University of Texas. Austin, Texas.

Burleson, Rufus C., Papers. Barker Archives. Center for American History. University of Texas. Austin, Texas.

———, Papers. Texas Collection. Baylor University. Waco, Texas.

———. Receipt for Promissory Notes. In possession of Noble L. Clark, Burleson, Texas.

Collins, Susan, Dallas, Texas, to William C. Griggs, Canyon, Texas, October 5, 1982. In possesssion of author.

Griffin, William H., Major, Commanding Regiment, Griffin's Texas Volunteer Infantry, Confederate States of America, Houston, Texas. General Order, May 23, 1862. Records of Griffin's Texas Volunteer Infantry. National Archives. Washington, D.C.

Griggs, Thelma Clark. "A Profile of Mu and Remembrances of the Old Family Home." Ms. 1977. In possession of author.

Manshardt, Donald O., Peoria, Illinois, to Mrs. Fred E. Dunn, Soda Springs, Oklahoma, c. 1950. In possession of author.

Minute Book. Alvarado Baptist Church. Microfilm Copy. Texas Collection. Baylor University. Waco, Texas.

Minute Book. Independence Baptist Church. Archives of the Independence Baptist Church. Independence, Texas.

Morelock, Edward D. and Patricia J. "A Brief History of Bethesda Community: Cemetery, Church, School." Historical narrative submitted to the Texas Historical Commission, 1987.

Providence Baptist Church, Minutes. Archives of the Southwestern Baptist Theological Seminary. Fort Worth, Texas.

Renfro, Henry C. Affidavit of Settlement on Vacant Public Land. March 16, 1860. File 586. General Land Office of the State of Texas. Austin, Texas.

————, Galveston, to Captain E. P. Turner, Adjutant General for Colonel George Wythe Baylor, Arizona Brigade, March 1, 1863. Copy in possession of author.

Renfro-Clark Papers. In possession of author.

Roach, Mahala P. "Diary of Mahala P. Roach." Ms. Southern History Collection. University of North Carolina. Chapel Hill, North Carolina.

BOOKS AND DISSERTATIONS

Abernathy, Frances Dickson. "The Building of Johnson County, and the Settlement of the Communities of the Eastern Portion of the County." Vol. 1 of "A History of the Builders of Johnson County." Master's thesis, University of Texas, 1936.

Abstract of Land Titles in Texas: Comprising the Titled, Patented and Located Lands in the State. 2 vols. Galveston, Tex.: Shaw and Blaylock, 1878.

Baker, Eugene W. *A Noble Example: A Pen Picture of William M. Tryon, Pioneer Texas Baptist Preacher, Co-Founder of Baylor University.* Waco, Tex.: Baylor University Press, 1985.

————. *Nothing Better than This: The Biography of James Huckins, First Baptist Missionary to Texas.* Waco, Tex.: Baylor University Press, 1985.

Barr, Alwyn. *Polignac's Texas Brigade.* N.p.: Texas Gulf Coast Historical Association, 1964.

Barrow, Blake. "Freethought in Texas: J. D. Shaw and the Independent Pulpit." Master's thesis, Baylor University, 1983.

Berlinger, Richard, and others. *Why the South Lost the Civil War.* Athens: University of Georgia Press, 1986.

Block, Viola. *History of Johnson County and Surrounding Areas.* Waco, Tex.: Texian Press, 1970.

Branda, Eldon Stephen, ed. *The Handbook of Texas: A Supplement, Volume III.* Austin: Texas State Historical Association, 1976.

Burleson, Georgia J., comp. *The Life and Writings of Dr. Rufus C. Burleson.* N.p.: Georgia Burleson, 1901.

Burns, Robert. *The Poetical Works of Robert Burns: With Critical and Biographical Notices, by Allen Cunningham, and a Glossary.* Philadelphia: Porter & Coates, n.d.

Carver, Charles. *Brann and the Iconoclast.* Austin: University of Texas Press, 1957.

Catalogue of the Trustees, Officers, and Students of Baylor University. Washington, Tex.: "Lone Star" Office, 1851–1852.

Centennial Story of Texas Baptists. Dallas: Baptist General Convention of Texas, 1936.

Complete Lectures of Col. R. G. Ingersoll. Chicago: M. A. Donohue, n.d.

The Encyclopaedia Britannica. 11th ed. 29 vols. New York: The Encyclopaedia Company, 1913.

Fehrenbacher, Don. *The Dred Scott Case, Its Significance in American Law and Politics.* New York: Oxford University Press, 1978.

Felton, Rebecca Latimer. *Country Life in Georgia in the Days of My Youth.* Atlanta: Index Printing Company, 1919.

Foner, Eric. *Free Soil, Free Labor, Free Men: The Ideology of the Republican Party before the Civil War.* New York: Oxford University Press, 1970.

Gilmore, James R. *John Sevier as a Commonwealth Builder.* New York: D. Appleton and Company, 1894.

Hamilton, Holman. *Prologue to Conflict: The Crisis and Compromise of 1850.* N.p.: University of Kentucky Press, 1964.

Hesler, Samuel B. *A History of Independence Baptist Church: 1839–1969 and Related Organizations,* second printing. N.p.: Executive Board of the Baptist General Convention of Texas, 1974.

Hill, Samuel S. *Religion in the Southern States: A Historical Study.* Macon, Ga.: Macon University Press, 1983.

———, ed. *Varieties of Southern Religious Experience.* Baton Rouge: Louisiana State University Press, 1984.

Hirschson, Stanley P. *Grenville M. Dodge, Soldier, Politician, Railroad Pioneer.* Bloomington: Indiana University Press, 1967.

Hogan, William Ransom. *The Texas Republic: A Social and Economic History.* Norman: University of Oklahoma Press, 1946.

Howard, Benjamin C. *Report on the Decision of the Supreme Court of the United States, and the Opinions of the Judges Thereof, in the Case of Dred Scott versus John. F. A. Sandford, December Term, 1856.* Washington, D.C.: Cornelius Wendell, 1857.

Hudson, Weldon I., comp. *Johnson County, Texas, Marriage Records: 1854–1883.* N.p.: n.p., 1982.

James, Marquis. *The Raven: The Biography of Sam Houston.* New York: Grossett & Dunlap, 1929.

Johnson, Robert Underwood, and Clarence Clough Buel, eds. *Battles and Leaders of the Civil War.* 4 vols. New York: The Century Company, 1886–1887.

Joshua Historical Committee. *Joshua: As It Was and Is: 1853–1976.* Cleburne, Tex.: Bennett Printing Company, 1977.

McGuffy, William H. *McGuffy's New Fourth Eclectic Reader: Instructive Lessons for the Young,* enlarged edition. Cincinnati: Wilson, Hinkle & Co., 1866.

Mathews, Donald G. *Religion in the Old South.* Chicago: University of Chicago Press, 1977.

A Memorial and Biographical History of Johnson and Hill Counties, Texas. Chicago: Lewis Publishing Company, 1892.

A Memorial and Biographical History of McLennan, Falls, Bell, and Coryell Counties, Texas. Chicago: Lewis Publishing Company, 1893.

Milner, Vincent L. *Religious Denominations of the World; Comprising a General View of the Origin, History, and Condition of the Various Sects of Christians, the Jews, and Mahometans, as Well as the Pagan Forms of Religion Existing in the Different Countries of the Earth; With Sketches of the Founders of Various Religious Sects.* Philadelphia: Bradley, Garretson & Co., 1872.

Minutes of the Convention Which Organized the Alvarado Association, 1864. Dallas: "Herald" Book and Job Print, 1864.

Minutes of the Eighteenth Annual Session of the Alvarado Baptist Association, Held with the Baptist Church at Grand View, Johnson County, Texas, Commencing September 14, 1882. Dallas: Texas Baptist Publishing House, 1882.

Minutes of the First Annual Session of the Alvarado Baptist Association, Held with Hillsboro Church, Hill County, Texas, September, 1865. N.p.: n.p., 1865.

Minutes of the Fourth Annual Session of the Alvarado Baptist Association of Texas, Held with the Church at Alvarado, September 18th, 1868. Cleburne, Tex.: Cleburne Chronicle, 1868.

Minutes of the Second Annual Meeting of the Alvarado Association, of the State of Texas, Held at Shady Grove, Johnson County, Commencing 15th September A. D. 1866. N.p.: n.p., 1866.

Minutes of the Seventeenth Annual Session of the Alvarado Baptist Association Held with Eagle Hill Church, Tarrant County, Texas, Commencing September 15, 1881. Cleburne, Tex.: Chronicle Job Office, 1881.

Minutes of the Texas Baptist State Convention, Held with the Independence Church, Washington County, Texas, in October, 1858. Anderson: Texas Baptist Book and Job Print, 1858.

Minutes of the Third Annual Session of the Alvarado Baptist Association of Texas. N.p.: n.p., 1867.

Minutes of the Weatherford District Conference of the Methodist Episcopal Church,
South, held in Caddo Grove, Johnson County, Texas, July 7–10, 1875, T. W.
Hines, Presiding Elder, D. R. Carmichael, Secretary. Weatherford, Tex.: Times
Book and Job Office, 1875.

Moore, Doris Dowdell. *The Biography of Doctor D. R. Wallace.* Dallas: Timber-
lawn Foundation, 1966.

Moore, Glover. *The Missouri Controversy: 1819–1821.* N.p.: The University of
Kentucky Press, 1953.

Moore, Karl Hildreth. Doctoral thesis (untitled), Southwestern Baptist Theological Seminary, February 20, 1924.

Moore, Thomas. *The Poetical Works of Thomas Moore.* New York: D. Appleton
& Company, 1879.

Morrell, Z. N. *Flowers and Fruits in the Wilderness; or, Thirty Six Years in Texas*
and Two Winters in Honduras. Boston: Gould and Lincoln, 1872.

Mosheim, John Laurence. *An Ecclesiastical History, Ancient and Modern; In*
Which the Rise, Progress, and Variations of Church Power, are Considered in
their Connexion with the State of Learning and Philosophy, and the Political His-
tory of Europe during that Period. 2 vols. Baltimore: Phoenix N. Wood & Co.,
1832.

Murray, Lois Smith. *Baylor at Independence.* Waco, Tex.: Baylor University
Press, 1972.

Nail, Olin W., Editor-in-Chief. *Texas Methodist Centennial Yearbook.* Elgin, Tex.:
Olin W. Nail, [1934].

The New Layman's Parallel Bible. King James Version. Grand Rapids, Mich.:
Zondervan Bible Publishing, 1981.

Parks, W. H. *Texas Baptist Pulpit: A Collection of Sermons from the Baptist Min-*
istry of Texas. New York: Lange, Little & Hillman, 1873.

Peavine Baptist Church. "Peavine Baptist Church: Rock Spring, Georgia."
Brochure, c. 1979.

Pitheau, Pierre, comp. *Juvenal Delphini.* N.p.: n.p., n.d.

Ramsey, J. G. M. *The Annals of Tennessee to the End of the Eighteenth Cen-*
tury. . . . Charleston, S.C.: John Russell, 1853.

Rawley, James A. *Race and Politics: "Bleeding Kansas" and the Coming of the Civil*
War. Philadelphia: J. B. Lippencott, 1969.

Ray, Worth S. *Tennessee Cousins: A History of the Tennessee People.* Baltimore:
Genealogical Publishing Company, 1968.

Sartain, James Alfred. *History of Walker County, Georgia.* Reprint. Carrollton,
Ga.: A. M. Matthews and J. S. Sartain, 1972.

Scott, Ann. *The Southern Lady: From Pedestal to Politics, 1830–1930.* Chicago:
University of Chicago Press, 1970.

Silver, James W. *Confederate Morale and Church Propaganda.* Tuscaloosa, Ala.:
Confederate Publishing Company, 1957.

Smith, Theodore Clark. *Parties and Slavery, The American Nation, A History.* vol. 18. New York: Harper & Row, 1906.

The Story of Baylor University at Independence: 1845–1886. Waco, Tex.: Baylor University, 1986.

Texas Baptist Annual: 1854–1872. A compilation of minutes of Baptist State Conventions of Texas. N.p.: n.p., 1872.

Toland, Gracey Booker. *Austin Knew His Athens.* San Antonio: Naylor Company, 1958.

United States War Department. *War of the Rebellion: A Compilation of the Official Records of the Union and Confederate Armies.* 70 vols. in 128. Washington, D.C.: Government Printing Office, 1880–1901.

Wallis, Jonnie Lockhart. *Sixty Years on the Brazos: The Life and Letters of Dr. John Washington Lockhart, 1824–1900.* Reprint. New York: Argonaut Press, 1966.

Webb, Walter Prescott, ed. *The Handbook of Texas.* 2 vols. Austin: Texas State Historical Association, 1952.

Wharton, Clarence W., ed. *Texas under Many Flags.* 5 vols. Chicago: American Historical Society, 1930.

Wheeler, Daniel Edwin, ed. *Life and Writings of Thomas Paine.* 10 vols. New York: Vincent Parke & Co., 1907.

Wilson, Charles Reagan, ed. *Religion in the South.* Jackson: University Press of Mississippi, 1980.

Winkler, Ernest W., ed. *Journal of the Secession Convention of Texas: 1861.* Austin: Texas Library and Historical Commission, 1912.

Wright, Marcus J., comp., and Harold B. Simpson, ed. *Texas in the War: 1861–1865.* Waco, Tex.: Hill Junior College Press, 1965.

NEWSPAPER AND JOURNAL ARTICLES

Baillio, F. B. "Grand View." *Alvarado Bulletin,* May 16, 1884; May 30, 1884; June 20, 1884.

———. "Grand View Items." *Alvarado Bulletin,* March 2, 1884; March 7, 1884; March 21, 1884.

Barr, Alwyn. "Polignac's Brigade." In Eldon Stephen Branda, ed., *The Handbook of Texas: A Supplement, Volume III.* Austin: Texas State Historical Association, 1976.

———. "Texas Coastal Defense, 1861–1865." *Southwestern Historical Quarterly* 65 (July 1961): 1–31.

"Bulletin Briefs." *Alvarado Bulletin,* March 21, 1884.

Burleson, Rufus C. "Rev. H. C. Renfro." *Guardian* 2, no. 3 (March 1885): 50.

"Burleson's Library Dedicated." *Fort Worth Star-Telegram*, March 29, 1971.

Citizen [pseud.]. "Yes." *Alvarado Bulletin*, February 15, 1884.

A Clodhopper [pseud.]. "Egan." *Alvarado Bulletin*, June 20, 1884.

"Cross Timbers News." *Weekly Bulletin* (Cleburne, Texas), September 3, 1880.

"A Deceiver." *Texas Baptist*, May 30, 1855.

"Died." *Fort Worth Gazette*, March 3, 1885.

Duncan, Merle Mears, ed. "An 1864 Letter to Mrs. Rufus C. Burleson." *Southwestern Historical Quarterly* 44 (January 1961): 369–372.

E. K. [pseud.]. "Cross Timbers." *Alvarado Bulletin*, April 4, 1884.

"Excommunicated. Elder H. C. Renfro Dispossessed of Credentials." *Alvarado Bulletin*, February 8, 1884.

Garrett, Hosea. "Ordination." *Texas Baptist*, December 11, 1857.

———. "Revival at Chappell Hill." *Texas Baptist*, September 5, 1855.

Geiser, S. W. "Dr. L. J. Russell and the Pike's Peak Gold Rush of 1858–1859." *Southwestern Historical Quarterly* 48, no. 4 (April 1945): 573–574.

Hale, Joe W. "Robert Emmett Bledsoe Baylor." In Walter Prescott Webb, ed., *The Handbook of Texas*. 2 vols. Austin: Texas State Historical Association, 1952.

Harrell, David Edwin, Jr. "The Evolution of Plain-Folk Religion in the South." In Samuel S. Hill, ed., *Varieties of Southern Religious Experience*. Baton Rouge: Louisiana State University Press, 1988.

Harris, Benjamin, and Margaret R. Harris. "Letter to the Editor." *Texas Baptist*, August 26, 1856.

Interested 1 [pseud.]. "Letter to the Editor." *Cleburne Chronicle*, November 6, 1869.

Irwin, Richard B. "The Red River Campaign." In Robert Underwood Johnson and Clarence Clough Buel, eds., *Battles and Leaders of the Civil War*. 4 vols. New York: The Century Company, 1886–1888.

"Julius Baker." Advertisement. *Alvarado Bulletin*, April 7, 1882.

"Laying the Corner Stone." *Alvarado Bulletin*, November 17, 1882.

"Laying the Corner Stone." *Cleburne Chronicle*, February 13, 1869.

"Lecture of Mr. Renfro." *Alvarado Bulletin*, February 22, 1884.

Lefever, Harry. "The Church and Poor Whites." *New South* 25 (Spring 1970): 32.

"Married." *Alvarado Bulletin*, December 15, 1882.

"Marystown." *Alvarado Bulletin*, May 25, 1883.

"Marystown." *Alvarado Bulletin*, February 27, 1885.

Miller, Howard. "Texas." In Samuel S. Hill, *Religion in the Southern States: A Historical Study*, 313–333. Macon, Ga.: Macon University Press, 1983.

Ming, Virginia. "J. D. Shaw: Freethinker." *Waco History and Heritage* 10, no. 2 (Summer 1979): 1–21.

"Minutes of the West Fork Association, Held with Lonesome Dove Baptist Church, Tarrant County, in September, 1858." *Texas Baptist*, November 11, 1858.

"Mrs. M. A. Clark, Native of Johnson County, Buried Sunday Afternoon in Burleson Cemetery." *Burleson News*, June 3, 1943.

Nelms, W. L. "The Shaw Case: A True Statement of the Facts and Law." *Alvarado Bulletin*, November 24, 1882.

"Personal Mention." *Alvarado Bulletin*, January 18, 1884.

"Personal Mention." *Alvarado Bulletin*, July 11, 1884.

Pringle-Pattison, Andrew Seth. "Baruch Spinoza." In *The Encyclopaedia Britannica*. 11th ed. 29 vols. New York: The Encyclopaedia Company, 1913.

"Programme for Missionary Mass Meeting to be held at Grand View, Johnson County, Texas, November 4th, 5th, and 6th, 1881." *Alvarado Bulletin*, September 30, 1881.

"The Proposed New Association." *Texas Baptist*, September 20, 1856.

Ragan, Cooper K., ed. "The Diary of Captain George W. O'Brien, 1863." Parts 1–3. *Southwestern Historical Quarterly* 67 (July, October 1963, January 1964): 28–54, 235–236, 413–433.

Renfro, Henry C. "The Coward's Castle." *Alvarado Bulletin*, June 20, 1884.

———. "The Endurance of Afflictions." In W. H. Parks, *Texas Baptist Pulpit: A Collection of Sermons from the Baptist Ministry of Texas*, 269–281. New York: Lange, Little & Hillman, 1873.

———. "A Lecture." *Alvarado Bulletin*, February 15, 1884.

———. "Letter from H. C. Renfro." *Independent Pulpit*, 2, no. 3 (May 1884): 34.

———. "Letter to the Editor." *Texas Baptist*, September 2, 1856.

———. "A Mistake." *Texas Baptist*, October 11, 1856.

———. "Mr. Renfro's Anniversary as a Liberal." *Independent Pulpit* 3, no. 1 (March 1885): 5–6.

———. "An Open Letter." *Alvarado Bulletin*, October 19, 1883.

———. "An Open Letter." *Alvarado Bulletin*, February 8, 1884.

———. "An Open Letter." *Alvarado Bulletin*, June 6, 1884.

———. "Reply to Uncle Johnnie." *Alvarado Bulletin*, March 7, 1884.

———. "A Soft Answer Turneth Away Wrath." *Alvarado Bulletin*, March 28, 1884.

———. "Won Laurels." *Alvarado Bulletin*, March 7, 1884.

Romero, Sidney J. "The Confederate Chaplain." *Civil War History* 1 (1955): 127–140.

Ross, Joe P. "Requiem of a Cleburne School." *Texana* 6, no. 4 (Winter 1968).

Rutledge, Jolene. "Bethesda Awaiting Historical Marker." *Burleson News*, August 6, 1987.

Shaw, J. D. "H. C. Renfro." *Independent Pulpit* 3, no. 2 (April 1885): 17.

———. "H. C. Renfro a Heretic." *Independent Pulpit* 2, no. 1 (March 1884): 5.

———. "Is Christianity Declining." *Independent Pulpit* 2, no. 4 (May 1884): 25.

———. "Lecture of Mr. Renfro." *Independent Pulpit*, February 22, 1884, 3.

———. "Purely Agnostic." *Independent Pulpit* 3, no. 3 (May 1885): 31.

———. "Too Liberal for a Baptist." *Independent Pulpit* 2, no. 2 (March 1884): 16–17.

———. "William Cowper Brann." In *Brann the Iconoclast: A Collection of the Writings of W. C. Brann.* 2 vols. Waco, Tex.: Harz Brothers, 1898.

Smith, E. Kirby. "The Defense of the Red River." In Robert Underwood Johnson and Clarence Clough Buel, eds., *Battles and Leaders of the Civil War,* 4: 369–374. New York: The Century Company, 1886–1888.

"Special to the Dallas Herald from Waco." *Alvarado Bulletin,* September 22, 1882.

"Tribute of Respect. To the W. M., Wardens and Bretheren of Alvarado Lodge, No. 314 A. F. & A. M." *Alvarado Bulletin,* April 17, 1885.

Uncle Jerry. "Declaration of Principles. Squib No. 28." *Alvarado Bulletin,* June 27, 1884.

———. "Don't Know What to Call It. Squib No. 26." *Alvarado Bulletin,* June 6, 1884.

———. "INNOMINATA, Squib No. 17." *Alvarado Bulletin,* March 14, 1884.

———. "Make Him a Pony Purse, Squib No. 24." *Alvarado Bulletin,* May 23, 1884.

———. "Neither 'Silence' nor 'Abuse.'" *Alvarado Bulletin,* June 13, 1884.

———. "That Suggestion." *Alvarado Bulletin,* May 9, 1884.

———. "That Verse." *Alvarado Bulletin,* February 22, 1884.

———. "Was Christ Essentially Holy. Squib No. 18." *Alvarado Bulletin,* April 4, 1884.

Uncle Johnnie [pseud.]. "A Question." *Alvarado Bulletin,* February 22, 1884.

Wallace, David R. "Letter to the Editor." *Texas Baptist,* December 9, 1857.

Waller, John L. "George Wythe Baylor." In Walter Prescott Webb, ed., *The Handbook of Texas,* 1: 123–124. Austin: Texas State Historical Association, 1952.

GOVERNMENT DOCUMENTS

Confederate States of America. Records, Griffin's Texas Volunteer Infantry. National Archives of the United States. Washington, D.C.

State of Pennsylvania. City of Philadelphia. Deed and indenture of 640 acres from Thomas H. Neilson and Katherine Clemson, his wife, to Reverend Henry C. Renfro, March 19, 1878. Book R, pp. 77–79. Deed Records, Johnson County, Texas.

State of Tennessee. Carter County. Marriage Records, vol. 1 (1796–1850).

———. ———. Deed Records, Record C:71. December 2, 1815.

State of Texas. General Land Office. Map of Johnson County, Texas. 1943.

———. Johnson County. Affidavit of Settlement of H. C. Renfro, March 15, 1860. File 586, General Land Office of the State of Texas.

———. ———. Bill of Sale of 160 acres from William R. Crockett to Absalom C. Renfro, September 10, 1857. File 4175, General Land Office of the State of Texas.

———. ———. Certificate of Occupancy of H. C. Renfro, March 16, 1860. File 586, General Land Office of the State of Texas.

———. ———. Certificate of Occupancy of H. C. Renfro, November 5, 1872. File 586, General Land Office of the State of Texas.

———. ———. Deed of 80 acres from James A. Renfro to Henry C. Renfro, December 3, 1862. Book D, p. 540. Deed Records, Johnson County, Texas.

———. ———. Deed of 160 acres from Hezekiah Russell to H. C. Renfro, April 19, 1873. Book K, p. 430. Deed Records, Johnson County, Texas.

———. ———. Deed of 160 acres from Mary R. Renfro, Mrs. M. A. Baker, and J. E. Baker to C. A. Renfro, April 29, 1885. Book 30, pp. 303–304. Deed Records, Johnson County, Texas.

———. ———. Deed of Right-of-Way from H. C. Renfro to Missouri, Kansas, and Texas Railway Company, February 14, 1881. Book W, pp. 26–27. Deed Records. Johnson County, Texas.

———. ———. Deed of two hundred sixty-one acres and twenty acres from Henry C. Renfro to R. E. Montgomery, March 17, 1881. Book W, pp. 128–129. Deed Records, Johnson County, Texas.

———. ———. Deed of various tracts in order to separate homestead properties in Johnson County, Texas, from C. A. Renfro to Mrs. Mary R. Renfro, Mrs. M. A. Baker, and her husband, J. E. Baker, April 29, 1885. Book 30, pp. 301–302. Deed Records, Johnson County, Texas.

———. ———. Designation of certain tracts of land as homestead by Mary R. Renfro, April 29, 1885. Book 30, pp. 301–302. Deed Records, Johnson County, Texas.

———. Field Notes of W. Douglass, C. S., of H. C. Renfro Preemption, 160 acres, Robertson Scrip, Survey Number 1063, June 25, 1860. File 586, General Land Office of the State of Texas.

United States. Department of Commerce. Census of 1840, Walker County, Georgia. Microfilm Publication.

———. ———. Census of 1850, Walker County, Georgia. Microfilm Publication.

————. National Archives. Records of Company Muster Roll, Company C, Griffin's Regiment Texas Infantry.

INTERVIEWS

Clark, Noble Lafayette, and Ruby Richeson Clark, Burleson, Texas. Interview with author. Lubbock, Texas, August 11, 1975.
Griggs, Thelma Clark, Lubbock, Texas. Interview with author. December 24, 1987.
————, Lubbock, Texas. Interview with author. April 10, 1990.
————, Lubbock, Texas. Interview with author. November 26, 1990.
————, Lubbock, Texas. Interview with author. December 24, 1990.
————, Lubbock, Texas. Interview with author. April 14, 1991.

Index